STUDY GUIDE

THE CREATIVE IMPULSE
An Introduction to the Arts

STUDY GUIDE
Roger Hickman and Paula L. Sabin

THE CREATIVE IMPULSE
An Introduction to the Arts

DENNIS J. SPORRE

Ball State University

Third Edition

Prentice Hall, Englewood Cliffs, NJ 07632

Acquisitions editor: **Bud Therien**
Editorial/production supervision: **Robert C. Walters**
Prepress buyer: **Herb Klein**
Manufacturing buyer: **Robert Anderson**

Printed in the United States of America

10 9 8 7 6 5 4 3 2 1

ISBN 0-13-190034-X

Prentice-Hall International (UK) Limited, *London*
Prentice-Hall of Australia Pty. Limited, *Sydney*
Prentice-Hall Canada Inc., *Toronto*
Prentice-Hall Hispanoamericana, S.A., *Mexico*
Prentice-Hall of India Private Limited, *New Delhi*
Prentice-Hall of Japan, Inc., *Tokyo*
Simon & Schuster Asia Pte. Ltd., *Singapore*
Editora Prentice-Hall do Brasil, Ltda., *Rio de Janeiro*

Table of Contents

CHAPTER 1: PREHISTORY

CONTEXTS AND CONCEPTS

Summary
Humanity began when man first grasped notions of selfhood and individuality. In an attempt to comprehend reality and to communicate with others about that reality, man devised symbols. These symbolic expressions of the human spirit answer some of our questions about earlier cultures and times, and ultimately, these artworks communicate directly with our sensibilities, even when they are transported from their time to ours.

The study of the arts produced by prehistoric man is challenging and rewarding. The sheer length of time that must be dealt with, the variety of early man, and the scarcity of remaining evidence provide great obstacles to research. Yet, the profundity of their art and the evident human spirit fascinate us. Above all, we must remember that these "primitive" societies were capable of producing sophisticated art worthy of study and admiration.

Man first appeared during the Pleistocene Period or Ice Age, which extended through four glacial periods separated by three warmer interglacial periods. Evidence of weapons shaped from stone come from as early as one million years ago, and more sophisticated tools appeared about 250,000 years ago. At this time, some feel that man already had the ability to create symbols. Slowly our ancestors moved toward the acquisition of artistic capacities. By the last Ice Age, a complex system of notation had evolved. One type of man, the Neanderthal, lived into the period after 40,000 BC. Clearly more intelligent than his ancestors, he made tools, created burial places, and was probably capable of speaking a language.

Homo sapiens, appearing in middle Europe around 27,000 BC, hunted the mammoth, built houses, wore leather clothes, and decorated themselves with jewelry. Still at this time, agriculture and herding were unknown. Two types of Homo sapiens are described in the text: Cro-Magnon, who had a powerful build and a high forehead, and Combe Capelle, who was smaller in stature. These "modern men" were intelligent, made new types of tools, and exhibited skills in art and music.

1

Important Terms

Prehistoric: belonging to the time before recorded history. (18, 34)

Pleistocene Period: name given to the geological period beginning between 500,000 and one million years ago to about 6,000 BC. Popularly known as the Ice Age, this period saw the alternation between four glacial periods and three warmer interglacial periods. Earliest man appeared during this time. (18)

Paleolithic Age: the cultural period beginning with the earliest tools to the beginning of the Mesolithic period. Also known as the Old Stone Age. (18-19)

Mesolithic Age: the cultural period between the Paleolithic and Neolithic Ages. Also known as the Middle Stone Age. (34)

Neanderthal man: an extinct subspecies of man who lived in the period after 40,000 BC. He made tools. (19)

Homo sapiens: the only extant species of man. He appeared around 27,000 BC in middle Europe. (19)

Cro-Magnon: an early type of Homo sapiens characterized by a powerful build and a high forehead. (19)

Combe Capelle: an early type of Homo sapiens with a smaller stature than Cro-Magnon. He exhibited skills in art and music. (19)

Primitive: in these contexts, a term referring to the early stages of human culture. It should not be seen as a negative description of the quality of art or civilization. (19, 22)

Give a chronology of the major developments in the world during the Ice Age. What type of animals came from this period? (18)

Who were the Neanderthals? How did they differ from apes? (18-19)

What "advances" were made by Homo sapiens? (19)

THE ARTS OF PREHISTORIC HUMANKIND

Summary

Two-Dimensional Art: The earliest Western European art, beginning approximately 25,000 to 30,000 BC, consisted of simple lines scratched in damp clay. More sophisticated drawings appear to have come in three phases: black outlines of animals with a single colored filler; the addition of a second color within the outline; and multi-colored paintings showing an impressive naturalistic style (see Fig. 1.9). Later, naturalistic depiction gave way to greater abstraction. Particularly striking are the realistic proportions and details in Fig. 1.7 and the suggestion of three-dimensionality in Fig. 1.8.

Sculpture: The first known sculpture (Fig. 1.10), dating from 30,000 to 15,000 BC, apparently predates drawings. Although parts are missing, it shows a remarkable degree of verisimilitude. Venus figures, perhaps the first works of representational art, have been found on burial sites stretching from Western France to the central Russian Plain. Common characteristics among these figurines include tapering legs, wide hips, and tapering shoulders and head. The emphasis on female sexuality suggests that these are fertility figures. The best known figure is the Woman from Willendorf (Fig. 1.13), carbon dated as early as 30,000 to 25,000 BC. This figure is remarkable in several respects; it is complete, the bulging contours of flesh give a sense of realism, the subtle repetition of line and form moves the viewer's eye toward the reproductive organs, and the facelessness gives it a quality of idealism. The Venus figurines seem to blend women's practical and symbolic roles. This same period also produced animal carvings (Fig. 1.14) and human figures (Fig. 1.15).

Dance: Evidence of dancing can be found on a number of Upper Paleolithic art objects. Fig. 1.15 shows both a masked dancer and a "dog-faced" dancer.

Synthesis: The most significant repository of prehistoric drawings are in the Cave of Lascaux (Figs. 1.16-1.21). Hundreds of drawings can be found, and the quality of the work is excellent. Although dating from a wide period, the drawings show a certain consistency and overall unity. This is particularly remarkable, since they were drawn by people who could see only small areas at a time with light from flickering oil lamps.

Important Terms

Altamira: a cave in Northern Spain with a remarkable painting of a Bison. (22)

Venus figures: hand-sized female figurines that may symbolize fertility. Among the characteristics are tapering legs, wide hips, and an emphasis on female sexuality. (23-5)

Woman from Willendorf: the best known example of the Venus figures. It has been dated as early as 30,000 BC. (25)

Cave of Lascaux: a cave near the French town of Montignac that contains the richest and most significant repository of prehistoric paintings. (27-31)

Study Questions

What are the three phases of development in prehistoric drawing? What is unusual about the bison of Fig. 1.8? (22-3)

What are Venus figures? Describe their general features and explain why the Woman from Willendorf is so remarkable. (23-5)

What is the significance of the Lascaux paintings? Describe the general shape of the cave and the drawings illustrated in the text. (27-31)

PRACTICE TEST

1. How many glacial periods occurred during the Ice Age?
   a. 2   b. 3   c. 4   d. 5

2. How long ago did man make his first stone weapon?
   a. one million years   b. 250,000   c. 40,000   d. 10,000

3. What does not characterize the Neanderthal man?
   a. he created tools   c. he lived about 40,000 BC
   b. he produced art   d. he built burial places

4. What does not characterize the Homo sapiens of the Pleistocene
   Period?
   a. he built houses   c. he wore jewelry
   b. he produced art   d. he grew his own food

5. From what time period do the earliest drawings and sculpture come?
   a. one million BC   c. between 30,000 and 15,000 BC
   b. 250,000 BC   d. between 10,000 and 6,000 BC

6. Drawings from the Mesolithic period are known for their naturalistic
   quality.   a. true   b. false

7. What does not characterize the bison from La Grèze?
   a. situated on a rock   c. suggests 3-dimensions
   b. face is turned outward d. all 4 legs are shown

8. What does not characterize the Venus figures?
   a. facial details b. large hips c. tapered legs d. emphasis on female sexuality

9. The most significant repository of drawings comes from
   a. Willendorf   b. Lascaux   c. Altamira   d. La Grèze

10. What does not describe the drawings of Lascaux?
    a. hundreds were made   b. the Main Hall is dominated by a herd of bulls
    c. the frequent appearance of geometric figures is a mystery
    d. they were the work of a single, unnamed artist

ANSWERS
1. c   2. a   3. b   4. d   5. c   6. b   7. d   8. a   9. b   10. d

CHAPTER 2: MESOPOTAMIA

CONTEXTS AND CONCEPTS

Summary
The arts of the Mesopotamians symbolized humankind's relationship with its king and gods. The cities and empires of the Fertile Crescent were our prototype civilizations. Eventually Mesopotamia would reach out to clash with and influence our more immediate cultural forebears--the Greeks.

The world's first civilization appeared in Mesopotamia around 6,000 BC. In this region between the Tigris and Euphrates rivers, a cluster of farming villages appeared. Necessity required techniques such as irrigation and drainage, and complex social and administrative structures were established. Towns were built, mutual defenses erected, and Sumer, the first truly urban settlement, emerged. Religion in Sumer shared a close relationship with the government. Each city had its own god, and these local gods were organized into a hierarchy. At the top were three male gods who demanded sacrifice and obedience. The ruler was a king-priest, and below him were a class of priests who enjoyed great power and were responsible for education and writing.

Writing was the greatest contribution to the advancement of general civilization by Sumer. Two types of signs were developed, one to represent words and the other to represent syllables. Writing materials consisted of unbaked clay tablets and a reed stylus, which made wedge-shaped marks. This method of writing is called cuneiform. Writing was used to document irrigation patterns, tax-collections, and other events. Eventually literature developed, and the oldest known story, the Gilgamesh Epic, dates from this era. Other aspects of Sumerian life are described, including the role of women, the monogamous nature of marriage, the complex system of mathematics, and advances in technology.

From 3300 to 2000 BC, the history of the region can be divided into three periods. The Archaic period was marked by numerous wars and conflicts. Around 2400 BC, Sargon I of Akkad led his people to supremacy in the region, and this marks the beginning of the Akkadian period. With the development of the composite bow and a new military maneuver, Sargon created a truly united empire with a centralized government. The third period, called neo-Sumerian, began with the defeat of the Akkadians by a mountain people. The city-state of Ur dominated the region, and the period was characterized by a flourishing economy and the building of imposing ziggurats. Eventually, Ur was conquered by the Elamites, bringing an end to Sumerian civilization.

The remaining history of Mesopotamia may be divided into four general periods. The first Babylonian empire extended from 2000 to 1000 BC. During this time, the city of Babylonia became the hub of the world, as the empire extended from Sumer to Assyria. Hammurabi, who ruled in the 18th century BC, maintained order with a judicial code known as the Code of Hammurabi. The code, based on a rigid class system, spelled out specifically the rights and place of men and women. Within two centuries after the death of Hammurabi, his dynasty ended as the Hittites from northern Syria plundered Babylon. The second period began around 1000 BC when the powerful Assyrians began to dominate the region. Their military skill enabled them to sustain nearly continuous warfare for almost 400 years. Finally they were conquered, and the neo-Babylonian period began around 600 BC. Although lasting less than a century, this period is notable for a number of accomplishments and for the rule of Nebuchadnezzar II. The final period came when the Persians unified the Middle Eastern world. Eventually the Persians would rule over an area twice as large as any previous empire, and they would threaten to overrun Europe.

Sharing a common ancestry with the Mesopotamian civilization of Sumer and Ur were the Jews who migrated into Canaan. A number of similarities exist between the divergent cultures, but the Jews were unique in their adoption of monotheism.

Important Terms

Neolithic Age: known as the New Stone Age, this followed the Mesolithic Age. It is notable for the development of farming and the beginnings of literacy. (34)

Mesopotamia: region of land about 700 miles long and 150 miles wide between the Tigris and Euphrates rivers known as the Fertile Crescent. This is the location of the first civilization around 6,000 BC. (34)

Sumer: people who developed the first true civilization. (34-6)

Gilgamesh Epic: the oldest known story in the world. It deals with the adventures of King Gilgamesh of Erech. (34, 35, 36)

Cuneiform writing: type of writing using wedge-shaped marks developed by the Sumerians. (35)

Archaic period: the period from 3300 to 2400 BC marked by numerous regional conflicts. (36-7)

Akkadian period: the period from 2400 to 2200 BC that is dominated by Sargon I and the Akkadians. (37)

Neo-Sumerian period: the period from 2200 to 2000 BC in which the region was ruled by kings from the city of Ur. (37-8)

Ziggurats: temples with great terraced towers. (37, 49-50)

Babylon: the capital city under Hammurabi. The Babylonian empire (2000 tc 1000 BC) extended approximately 70,000 square miles. (38-9)

Code of Hammurabi: laws created by Hammurabi addressing the legal questions of the time. (38)

Assyria: region of upper Mesopotamia. From this area a military power emerged that ruled an extensive kingdom between 1000 and 600 BC. (38-39)

Neo-Babylonian period: a brief phase of Mesopotamian history (less than 100 years) that produced some notable accomplishments and individuals. (39)

Persians: nomadic tribes that unified the Middle Eastern world between 539 and 331 BC. (39)

Important Names

Sargon I (24th century BC): King of Akkad who conquered the Sumerians and ruled an empire from the Mediterranean to the Persian Gulf. (37)

Hammurabi (18th century BC): Babylonian king who is known for his code of laws. (38)

Nebuchadnezzar II (6th century BC): King during the neo-Babylonian period. He destroyed Jerusalem and carried Jews into captivity. (39)

Study Questions

What was the first civilization? Describe the religion and daily life. What was their greatest contribution? (34-6)

Who were the Akkadians? Who was their great ruler? Describe the neo-Sumerian period. (37-8)

When was the first Babylonian period? Who was its greatest leader? What was his major contribution? (38)

Who conquered Babylonia? Describe the principal historical events leading up to the Persian Empire. (38-9)

THE ARTS OF MESOPOTAMIA

Summary

Two- and Three-Dimensional Art: Three periods are discussed in the text. The first, early Sumerian art, largely consists of painted pottery and stamp seals. Pottery decoration, often abstract, filled both functional and aesthetic roles. Stamp seals clearly came to be regarded as an ideal medium for artistic expression. The development of a cylindrical seal provided even greater opportunities for creativeness and individuality (Fig. 2.6). Monsters were a common subject, perhaps because of their emotional and unrealistic character. Other scenes include raging beasts (Fig. 2.7), hunting, and battle. There seems to be a continuous conflict in Sumerian art between symbolism and naturalism. Further examples of Sumerian creativeness can be found in the low relief art. In Figs. 2.8-2.9, the alabaster vase celebrating the god of fertility reveals a preoccupation with ritual and gods. The bodies are depicted in profile and the faces lack individual characteristics, but the muscular little men realistically show the strain of their loads. Another trait, the focus on a mother goddess, can be seen in Figs. 2.10 and 2.11.

The Archaic period produced the Tell Asmar Statues. Each of these figures has great dignity, though much of the depiction is stylized. Particularly striking are the eyes, which appear to be a basic convention of Sumerian art. More graceful and delicate are the works shown in Figs. 2.13-2.15, which illustrate the golden splendor of the Sumerian court. From the Akkadian period is the victory stele of King Narmam-Sin. Unlike any of the earlier works, this depicts an historical event, thereby recording a strictly human accomplishment.

Literature: Sumerian scribes began recording literature between 2700 and 2100 BC. Texts range from epics to love songs, but, since reading skills were rare, most stories remained in the oral tradition. In Babylonia, most literature was practical in nature. Many of the texts that have come to us are student copies of classic texts. Throughout Mesopotamian literature, Sumerian tradition is strong, as almost all gods and heroes, especially in Akkadian literature, are Sumerian. The Old Testament of the Bible has largely the same content as Jewish scriptures. Taken from the Old Testament, the Psalms can be divided into various types, including hymns, laments, and wisdom Psalms.

Music: Our knowledge of music from this time is limited to the nature of their musical instruments the general function of music. Based on depictions in visual arts, the principal instruments in Sumerian music were lyres, pipes, harps, and drums. The kissor, a harp-like instrument from Assyria and Babylonia, had a moveable bar which allowed the musician to change the pitch of a given string. Assyrians possessed a variety of string, wind, and percussion instruments. They were used in solo performances, ensembles, or to accompany singers. Music appears to have been most popular as secular entertainment, but religious ceremonies also employed music.

Dance: Evidence suggests that a number of sacred dances were performed in Sumer, including a procession of singers moving slowly to liturgies played on flutes. Assyrian bas-relief sculpture shows dancers in both religious and secular contexts.

Architecture: Little architecture survives from Mesopotamia because of the extraordinary length of time that separates us from the construction of these buildings and because of the incessant warfare of the area. Three examples are illustrated in the text (Figs. 2.21-2.24): the Sin Temple at Khafaje, which follows a traditional plan of Sumerian temples; the Tell Asmar Temple, which also produced the group of statuettes shown in Fig. 2.12; and, from the neo-Sumerian Period capital Ur, the colossal ziggurat built by Ur-Nammur.

Synthesis: The city Dur Sharrukin was built and abandoned within a single generation. Yet its integrity remains intact, and it tells us much about the Assyrian civilization under the rule of Sargon II. Striking is the precedence taken by secular architecture over sacred. There is a haphazard quality to the asymmetrical design of the city, but the vast scale of the buildings, the majestic lions guarding the gate, and the naturalism and depiction of space in the relief sculptures represent the highest artistic achievements of the Assyrians.

Important Terms

Low relief art: relief sculptures are works that remain attached to their background. When the relief is carved or modeled shallowly, it is called low relief or bas relief.   (40-2)

Tell Asmar Statues: statues of worshipers and deities from Sumer found in Tell Asmar, Iraq. (43)

Psalter: a book containing the Book of Psalms. (46)

Psalm: a sacred song or hymn found in the Book of Psalms from the Bible. (46-8)

Kissor: a string instrument from Assyrian and Babylonian times. (48)

Asor: an Assyrian string instrument similar to the lyre, but struck with a stick. (48)

Important Names

Sargon II (8th century BC): under his reign, the Assyrian Empire reached its peak of power. He founded the remarkable city of Dur Sharrukin. (50-3)

Study Questions

What types of artworks survive from Sumer? What is special about the cylindrical seal? What type of subjects are depicted? (40-42)

From what period do the Tell Asmar statues come? Describe their features. (43)

What type of literature comes down to us from Mesopotamia? (46-8)

Discuss the musical instruments and the function of music during this time period. (49)

Describe the surviving architectures cited in the text. Who built the city of Dur Sharrukin? Describe its structure and its artwork. (49-53)

PRACTICE TEST

1. What activity separated Sumer from earlier communities?
   a. use of tools   b. building of weapons   c. farming   d. art

2. What does not characterize Sumerian religion?
   a. a pantheon of gods   c. gods were given human attributes
   b. sacrifices were demanded   d. goddess Ishtar ruled all gods

3. What is Sumer's greatest contribution to the advancement of general civilization?   a. irrigation   b. temples   c. writing   d. laws

4. Who is the great Akkadian leader who created an empire?
   a. Sargon I   b. Hammurabi   c. Darius I   d. Nebuchadnezzar II

5. What does not characterize the Code of Hammurabi?
   a. equality of classes   c. matters of divorce
   b. deals with wages   d. clear code of punishment

6. Who ruled a vast empire in the Middle East from 539-331 BC?
   a. Assyrians   b. Babylonians   c. Akkadians   d. Persians

7. What type of art does not represent the early Sumerian era?
   a. painted pottery   b. low relief   c. mosaic   d. stamp seals

8. What is the most prominent feature of the Tell Asmar statues?
   a. hands   b. eyes   c. dress   d. breasts

9. What does not characterize the works from the Archaic period?
   a. crude structures   c. symbols of masculine fertility
   b. animal power   d. gold inlays

10. Mesopotamian literature is dominated by stories from
    a. Sumer   b. Akkadia   c. Babylonia   d. Egypt

11. What type of literature was common in the age of Sumer?
    a. love songs   b. epics   c. records   d. all of these

12. What type of work in not included in the Psalms?
    a. laments   b. liturgies   c. wisdom psalms   d. love songs

13. What do we not know about Assyrian music?
    a. general tone quality   c. type of instruments used
    b. nature of rhythm and scales   d. function of music

14. Dance was only used in secular contexts in Sumer.   a. true   b. false

15. What were Sumerian buildings made of?
    a. blocks of granite   b. bricks   c. mud   d. skin hides

16. The city of Dur Sharrukin was built by
    a. Sargon I   b. Sargon II   c. Hammurabi   d. unknown

17. What does not characterize the city of Dur Sharrukin?
    a. emphasis on sacred buildings   c. asymmetrical arrangement
    b. strong fortifications   d. colossal guarding figures

ANSWERS
1. c   2. d   3. c   4. a   5. a   6. d   7. c   8. b   9. a   10. a   11. d
12. d   13. b   14. b   15. c   16. b   17. a

15

CHAPTER 3: ANCIENT EGYPT

CONTEXTS AND CONCEPTS

Summary

The relatively isolated location of Egypt enabled a cultural history to develop that was unbroken for thousands of years. Burial cites were the focus of the arts, as Egyptians lavished wealth and provisions on the eternal dwelling places of their pharaohs. Through art and architecture they created images which both celebrated life while providing immortality to their kings.

Egyptian civilization grew up around the rich soil near the Nile River. Spanning thousands of years and extending back into prehistoric times, the history of Egypt for our purposes can be divided into three principal eras: the Old Kingdom, the Middle Kingdom, and the New Kingdom. During the Old Kingdom, Memphis served as the capital, and the economy continued to rely on an agricultural system. Ships were the only means of transportation, which suggests (since Egypt has no forests) that there must have been a healthy commerce within a large area. Pharaohs were looked upon as god-kings and built monumental pyramids to serve as their tombs. Snofru is credited with building no less than three pyramids, and his son Cheops oversaw the building of the Great Pyramid (Fig. 3.3).

After a period of political decline, the governor of Thebes successfully unified Egypt around 2130, and the Middle Kingdom began. Despite many political intrigues, this was an age of recovery and expansion. In religion, the sun-god Ra was the supreme deity. Of particular importance were professional scribes, who were essential in recording governmental functions.

Late in the 18th century BC the Hyksos conquered lower Egypt, and the next 200 years is known as the Second Intermediate Period. The New Kingdom was established when Egyptians succeeded in driving out the Hyksos, and the new era saw significant military accomplishments. During the declining years of the empire, the pharaoh Akhenaton attempted to reform religion by imposing a monotheistic worship of the god Aton. The period is marked by pessimism. Tutankhamun, known to us for the fabulous treasures in his tomb, succeeded Akhenaton and returned to earlier religious practices. But after his brief reign, Egypt continued to decline.

Many other changes in religion occurred during the time period of Ancient Egypt, but in general, gods appeared with animal shapes or with animal heads. Egyptians believed that the pharaoh was a god and the only link between them and the creator. The soul of man was known as Ka, and while all men possessed Ka, that of the Pharaoh was far greater that those of commoners.

Important Terms

Old Kingdom: period in the history of ancient Egypt from c.2778-2263 BC. (56-7)

Middle Kingdom: period in the history of ancient Egypt from c.2130-1800. (57-9)

Second Intermediate Period: span between Middle Kingdom and New Kingdom which was dominated by the Hyksos. (59)

New Kingdom: period in the history of ancient Egypt from c.1600-1100. (59-60)

Dynasty: a succession of rulers from the same family. Ancient Egypt used the chronology of dynasties as their only system of marking dates. (56)

Pharaohs: rulers of ancient Egypt. (56)

Pyramid: a massive monument in ancient Egypt which served as tombs for pharaohs. (56)

Ra: the sun god and supreme deity. (57)

Hieroglyphs: system of writing in ancient Egypt. (57)

Scribes: members of the honored profession in Egypt who made written records of events and activities. (59)

Hyksos: Asian invaders who conquered lower Egypt in the late 18th century BC. (59)

Monotheism: the belief in a single god. (59, 77)

Aton: name given to the god of Akhenaton's monotheistic religious belief. (59)

Osiris: Egyptian god whose annual death and resurrection symbolized the self-renewing quality of nature. (60)

Ka: Egyptian concept of the human spirit. (60)

Important Names

Snofru (27th-26th centuries BC): pharaoh of the Fourth Dynasty who had three pyramids built. (56)

Akhenaton (reigned 1375-58 BC): pharaoh who attempted to convert Egypt to a monotheistic religion. (59, 77-81)

Tutankhamun (14th century BC): pharaoh who succeeded Akhenaton. His tomb left a treasure of artifacts. (59-60, 70)

Study Questions

Describe the region of ancient Egypt. What were its main assets? drawbacks? (56)

When was the Old Kingdom? Who were the leading figures and what were the major developments during this era? (56-7)

What role did scribes have in the Middle Kingdom? How does this seem to reflect Egypt's position at this time? (57-9)

What reform did Akhenaton attempt to bring about? Why was he unsuccessful? Describe the general nature of Egyptian religion. (59-60)

THE ARTS OF ANCIENT EGYPT

Summary
The most productive artistic periods were those when prosperity was high, the nation was at peace, and there was the presence of a strong ruler. Arts were also encouraged when the capital was at Memphis, whose principal god was the god of art and handicrafts.

Two-Dimensional Art: Painting, primarily a decorative medium, was subordinate to sculpture. Although proportions varied from one period to another, Egyptian artists followed a formulaic approach to the human figure (see pp. 61-2). During the Old Kingdom, verisimilitude and intricacy were combined with a flat, two-dimensional figure portrayal. Fig. 3.9, with its typical scene drawn from daily life, reveals a delicate shading and a remarkably wide color spectrum. Color replaced technique in the Middle Kingdom, as painting gained greater prominence. During the New Kingdom, the tradition of two-dimensional figure depiction and of vibrant colors continued. The painted tombs of Thebes provide most of our knowledge of Egyptian painting from this period. Representations of gods are found for the first time, and paintings often portray the vivacity and humor of daily life. The tomb of Queen Nefertari-mi-en-Mat contains a number of elegant and colorful paintings (Figs. 3.12-3.13). Typical qualities include elongated arms, the lack of verisimilitude, a frontal depiction of the upper torso and shoulders without breasts, and the diaphanous quality of the gown.

Sculpture: Sculpture was the major art form of the Egyptians. As in painting, convention rather than naturalism prevailed. Old Kingdom sculpture shows a technical mastery and craftsmanship. In the sculptures of Fig. 3.16, the striking colors typify Egyptian use of painting to decorate a surface. Realistic details can be seen, including the different shades of skin color, the revealing female figure, the appearance of hair under Nofret's wig, and her delicate, feminine hand. Two personalities are portrayed: the strength, wisdom, and alertness of the king, and the sensual, pampered queen. Realism stops with the upper body, as the lower parts are crude. Other Old Kingdom sculptures are naturalistic and vital. No action is portrayed, although some male figures place one foot forward while maintaining a rigid and stable body pose. In addition to sculptures in the round, relief sculptures were common. As seen in Fig. 3.14, many of these works are of extraordinary quality. Composition in all registers is carefully thought out and employs sophisticated devices and arrangements. Forms are delicately carved, with precise rendering of human details, and there is even an apparent attempt at spatial development.

In the Middle Kingdom, artistic style moved toward simplicity. General form was emphasized at the expense of details, but not of clarity and accuracy. Royal portraiture appears to have lost some of its dignity, but the expression of calmness and stability remains. The Ka statue of Fig. 3.17 is less naturalistic than before, although the lower body shows a high degree of anatomical accuracy. Still the king seems delicate and slender when compared to earlier depictions. The sunken relief of Fig. 3.18 draws our attention to fussy details such as wigs and jewelry, while other parts of the sculpture remain plain and flat.

The tomb of Tutankhamun provides a staggering quantity of artifacts. The funerary mask (Fig. 3.1), made of solid beaten gold and inlaid with semi-precious stones and colored glass, is highly naturalistic in style. The statue of the King (Fig. 3.19) must be nearly life-size. Carved from wood, it is highly naturalistic, although it does draw upon several conventions.

Literature: From the period 4250-2000 BC comes the book *Coming Forth by Day*, which we know as *The Book of the Dead*. Placed in tombs, the book explains how the soul is to exonerate itself with numerous statements that parallel the Ten Commandments from the Old Testament.

Theatre: The artistic concept of theatre must be separated from ritual. Some have argued that this distinction was accomplished by the Egyptians. Reference is made to *Osiris Passion Play* as one such event. Like other Egyptian dramas, this play was performed in mortuary temples and is closely linked with religion.

Music: Our knowledge of Egyptian music is primarily limited to their instruments. The principal instrument seems to have been the harp (Fig. 3.20). Other string instruments include the trigonon, lyre, and tamboura. Judging by the number of strings, Egyptian music may have been based on four- or five-note scales. Wind instruments, including double pipe instruments and trumpets, as well as percussion instruments, can be documented.

Dance: Dances of a highly formal character were developed in Egypt, and the love of dancing is clearly expressed in testimonies from tombs. A stride dance seems to be indicated in some wall paintings, and these may have been employed in funeral dancing. Fertility dances were also prominent.

Architecture: Architecture of a monumental character developed in Egypt prior to the Old Kingdom. The structures depicted in Figs. 3.25-3.29 mirror the stability and strength of the pharaoh. During the Old and Middle Kingdoms, pyramids proliferated. The most notable pyramid prior to Dynasty IV is that of King Zoser (Fig. 3.29). But our focus turns to the remarkable achievements of Dynasty IV and the great building spree in Giza. In addition to the three obvious pyramids, the area comprises burial cites for almost all of the important individuals of Dynasties IV and V. The largest pyramid is the Great Pyramid of Cheops, which is approximately 750 square feet and rises to a height of 481 feet. The complex also contains the Sphinx, carved from natural rock. Illustrating architecture of the New Kingdom is the Temple at Luxor (Figs. 3.33-3.34). Particularly striking is the beauty of the columns.

Synthesis: The reign of Akhenaton marked a break in the continuity of artistic style. Stiff poses are replaced by more natural forms, and the Pharaoh is realistically depicted in scenes of domestic life rather than in war. Akhenaton moved his court to the newly constructed city of Tell el Amarna in order to establish a new religion. Although the city is dominated by the large estates of the wealthy, it seems much less sumptuous in comparison to earlier traditions. Lines and style seem relatively simple. Among the striking details are the plant ornamentation of the columns, an altered convention of body proportions in paintings, and a turn toward secular sculpture.

Important Terms

Sculpture in the round: sculpture which has a full or nearly completed three-dimensionality. (66)

Relief sculpture: sculpture which emerges from the background in a two-dimensional manner. (66)

The Coming Forth by Day: also known as *The Book of the Dead*, it described how the should was to exonerate itself.

Osiris Passion Play: also known as *Abydos Passion Play* is often referred to as the first known theatric play. (71)

Trigonon: popular Egyptian string instrument shaped like a triangle. (71)

Tamboura: Egyptian string instrument shaped like a long narrow guitar. (72)

Sphinx: the colossal figure carved from natural rock with the head of a man and the body of a lion. (75)

Study Questions

What periods were generally most productive for art? (61)

Describe the conventions of two-dimensional art. (61-3)

Compare the paintings of the New Kingdom with those of the Old Kingdom. Cite specific examples. (63-5)

What are the realistic qualities of the sculpture of Prince Rahotep and his wife Nofret? What is crude about the art work? (66)

Describe the composition and subject matter of the relief sculpture from the tomb of Ptahotep. (67)

How does sculpture from the Middle Kingdom differ from that of the Old Kingdom?   (69-70)

Describe the two artifacts shown from the tomb of Tutankhamun. What is naturalistic? What is conventional? (70)

What distinguishes theatre from religious ritual? What kind of drama took place in Egypt? (71)

Describe the musical instruments of ancient Egypt. (71-3)

Based on the available evidence, what can we say about dance in Egypt? (73)

Describe the examples of architecture from before the Old Kingdom in your text. What do they tell us about these early Egyptians? (73-4)

From what region do we find a remarkable collection of pyramids? From what time period does this come? Describe the complex. (74-5)

How does the temple at Luxor from the New Kingdom differ from earlier examples of architecture? (76)

What break in artistic style do we find in the reign of Akhenaton? (77)

Describe the city of Tell el Amarna. What are the typical features of its architecture? (77-81)

PRACTICE TEST

1. Which pharaoh is credited with building three pyramids?
   a. Snofru   b. Cheops   c. Akhenaton   d. Tutankhamun

2. What was the principal form of transportation in Egypt?
   a. horse and cart   b. bare-back horse   c. ships   d. camels

3. Who was the sun god who headed the pantheon of gods?
   a. Ka   b. Ra   c. Aton   d. Osiris

4. What does not characterize the Middle Kingdom?
   a. recovery   c. importance placed on scribes
   b. expansive   d. move towards monotheism

5. The pharaoh who adopted monotheistic beliefs was
   a. Snofru   b. Cheops   c. Akhenaton   d. Tutankhamun

6. What does not characterize Egyptian religion in general?
   a. gods were always given human forms   c. the pharaoh was a god-king
   b. priests were delegates of the pharaoh   d. there was an after life

7. Painting was highly regarded in ancient Egypt.   a. true   b. false

8. What does not characterize Egyptian painting?
   a. a formulaic approach to human figures
   b. an emphasis on portraying three-dimensional space
   c. paint was applied by a brush
   d. color was an important element

9. Most of our knowledge about New Kingdom painting comes from tombs in
   a. Memphis   b. Thebes   c. Luxor   d. Tell el Amarna

10. What does not characterize the paintings of the tomb of Nefertari?
    a. flat profiles   c. elongated arms
    b. diaphanous dress   d. voluptuous breasts

11. What was the major art form of the Egyptians?
    a. painting   b. sculpture   c. music   d. dance

12. What characterizes the dual sculpture of Prince Rahotep and his wife
    Nofret?
    a. realistic detail of legs   c. individual expressions
    b. lack of natural detail   d. all of these

13. During the Middle Kingdom, pharaohs were depicted more majestically.
    a. true b. false

14. What does not characterize the sentry statue of King Tutankhamun?
    a. naturalistic qualities   c. careful attention to detail
    b. use of conventions   d. carved out of wood

15. In Egypt, theatre was closely tied with
    a. religion   b. the pharaoh   c. the seasons   d. death

16. What was the basic musical instrument in Egypt?
    a. trumpet   b. tamboura   c. trigonon   d. harp

17. Which is the largest pyramid?
    a. Chephren   b. Mycerinus   c. Snofru   d. Cheops

18. During which Dynasty were the great pyramids mentioned in question
    no. 17 built?   a. II   b. IV   c XI   d. XXII

19. Art from the reign of Akhenaton loses its stiffness and becomes more
    natural.   a. true   b. false

20. What is not found in the new city of Tell el Amarna?
    a. palaces that are more sumptuous than in preceding eras
    b. the use of plant capitals
    c. a change of body proportions in paintings
    d. plasticity in human forms

ANSWERS
1. a   2. c   3. b   4. d   5. c   6. a   7. b   8. b   9. b   10. d   11. b
12. c   13. b   14. c   15. a   16. d   17. d   18. b   19. a   20. a

CHAPTER 4: ARCHAIC GREECE AND THE AEGEAN

CONTEXTS AND CONCEPTS

Summary

The history of Greek civilization prior to the remarkable Classical age can be divided into three periods: the Aegean civilizations, the "Dark ages," and the Archaic period. The Aegean civilizations mark the beginning of Western culture. The earliest of these, the Minoans, flourished around 3000 BC on the island of Crete. Known for their brilliant wall paintings and the elaborate palace of Knossos, the Minoans have been the subject of a number of legends, including that of King Minos and the Minotaur. Around 1400, a strong tribe of early Greeks known as Mycenaeans inhabited the south-eastern coastline of Greece and eventually became the rulers of Crete. Despite extensive trading expeditions that took them throughout the Mediterranean and massively fortified palaces, the culture mysteriously collapsed after 1200.

The "Dark ages" designates a time period between the fall of the Mycenaeans and the establishment of city-states of the 8th century BC. This period is marked by transient migrations, as entire populations moved to new cites, including outlying shores around the Aegean. The best documentation of the time is found in two epic poems by Homer, the *Iliad* and the *Odyssey*. These poems not only memorialize a cast of heros, but also provide us with a glimpse into the social organization of this age.

The Archaic period extends from 800 to 500 BC. During this time, the Ionians, Dorians, and Aculians, united by a common language and religion, flourished on the Greek islands and peninsula. Calling themselves Hellenes, these people developed a loose organization of city-states. Geographical factors helped shape the civilization; the Aegean Sea provided a highway for trade, and the Peloponnesian mountains isolated the city states. The Olympic games, begun in 776 BC, was counted as the beginning of the Greek calendar.

Religion and philosophy played an important role in ancient Greece. Based on a large number of varied myths, Greek religion centered around the human-like family of gods with Zeus as their king. Early Greek civilization maintained a profound respect for the irrational and the mysterious. Among the early philosophers, Pythagoras exerted considerable influence with his mathematical studies.

Important Terms

Minoan Civilization: considered to be the first significant Western civilization. Named after the legendary King Minos, the Minoans inhabited the island of Crete from 3000 to 1300 BC. The central city was Knossos. (84, 88, 97-8)

Mycenaean Civilization: early Greek tribesmen who inhabited the south-eastern coastline of mainland Greece from 1400-1200 BC. The central city was Mycenae. (84, 98)

Archaic Period: artistic period between 800 and 500 BC, which can be contrasted with the Classical age of Athens. (85-7, 91-6)

Hellenes Civilization: began to flourish in Greece in the 8th century BC. Primarily derived from three different tribes--the Ionians, Dorians, and Aculians--the Hellenes cultivated a common language and religion. They settled in a number of city-states. (85)

Epic poem: an extended narrative poem, such as Homer's *Iliad*. (85)

Polis: Greek word for city, it was a community aware of the interests of the community and opposed to interests of the individual. (87)

Zeus: King of the Greek gods who is portrayed as a well-intentioned but bumbling amorist. (87)

Important Names

Minos: legendary King of the Minoans, who inhabited the island of Crete from 3000 to 1300 BC. (84)

Homer (c.800 BC): Greek poet and presumed author of the *Iliad* and *Odyssey*, which deal with minor details of the Trojan War. These works were used as textbooks in ancient Greece and created the model for the epic poem. (85, 99-103)

Hesiod (fl c.800 BC): Greek poet. His *Works and Days* describes the life of peasants, and his *Theogony* details the lineage of Greek Gods. (86, 97)

Pythagoras (c.580-c.500 BC): Greek philosopher and mathematician who deduced the Pythagorean theorem and explored the relationship between math and arts. (87)

Study Questions

What are the first two significant Western civilizations? What do we know about them? How do we know this? How are the two different? similar? (84)

What are the major works of Homer? Describe these works and discuss their significance. (85, 99-103)

What are the three groups of people who made up the Hellenes culture? From which did the Athenians descend? What bonded the Hellenic city-states together? What kept them isolated? (85)

Describe some of the unique features of Greek religion. (87-8)

Who was Pythagoras? What was significant about his philosophies? (87)

THE ARTS OF ARCHAIC GREECE
AND THE AEGEAN

Summary

Two-Dimensional Art : Two types of art are described in this section, wall painting and vase painting. Wall paintings give us a glimpse into the life of the Mycenaeans. Their decorated walls often depict activities of the time, such as seen in Fig. 4.4, showing a group of dogs hunting as a pack.

Vase painting is divided into three periods: protogeometric, geometric, and archaic. Protogeometric and geometric vases share in common an emphasis on design and symmetry. The protogeometric period, which simply means before the geometric period, is characterized by simple designs, mostly circles and semi-circles (see Fig. 4.5). Geometric vases, such as Figs. 4.1 and 4.6, contain horizontal bands containing zigzags, diamonds, and sometimes human and animal figures.

Archaic pottery, which can be divided into black-figure and red-figure types, gradually began to depict their subjects more realistically. By 550 BC, a new feeling of three-dimensional space appeared. A great diversity among individual painters from this time can be observed (Figs. 4.7-4.10).

Sculpture: Archaic sculpture can be divided into two types: kouroi (singular is kouros), meaning a "young male" and korai (singular is kore), meaning a "young female." The kouroi (Figs. 4.11-4.12) are nude figures depicted in a stiff frontal pose. The emphasis is on physicality and athleticism, and certain features are treated realistically. But, the figures appear rigid, and the block of stone from which they are carved seems to have shaped the sculptor's conception. An important innovation is the freedom from any support. The extension of the left foot forward also creates a sense of motion. The greatest of the kouroi is the Kritios Boy (Fig. 4.15). With this work, the stiffness of the Archaic style is modified, and the subtlety of the human form and the shift of weight to the back foot (creating a sense of repose) opens the door to Classical sculpture.

Unlike the kouroi, korai sculptures (Figs. 4.13-4.14) are fully clothed. Archaic sculptors worked at depicting the natural flow of cloth garments while showing the female body underneath. The extension of a hand and the bright smile of personality also add new dimensions to these works.

Dance. Dance was essential to religious rituals of ancient Greece and to the beginnings of Greek theatre. The term dance referred to almost any body movement, and it was closely tied to poetry as well as music. It was possible, for example, to dance a poem.

Literature: In addition to Homer, two additional poets are described in the text. Sappho of Lesbos, the leading figure among the poets of the Ionian coast, excelled in a form known as lyric poetry. Sappho's poems deal with the theme of love, and her style, characterized by emotions, a frank tone, simple language, and sensuousness, was much admired and imitated. The poems of Hesiod are more factual. His *Works and Days* deals with the hard life of a peasant, and *Theogony* traces the mythological history of the Greek gods.

Architecture: Three examples of architecture are described in the text illustrating different time periods: Minoan, Mycenaean, and Archaic. From the Minoans comes the palace of Knossos on the island of Crete (Fig. 4.16). The palace was unfortified, and emphasized comfort and elegance. Its labyrinth design of rooms recalls the Greek myth of the Minotaur. By contrast, Mycenaean palaces were fortresses made of large stone blocks. The Lion Gate at Mycenae (Fig. 4.17) is remarkable for its careful carving, skillful execution, and the tight jointure of the stone. The Archaic period produced an early, cumbersome version of the Doric order. The best preserved temple from this time is the "Basilica" at Paestum (Fig. 4.20).

Synthesis: Nothing better synthesizes the early Greek mind and soul than the epic poems of Homer. Both the Iliad and the Odyssey deal with the battle of Troy and its aftermath. The poems were basic texts for students of ancient Greece, and they have influenced western civilization ever since.

Important Terms

Protogeometric: the period of time prior to the Geometric period. The vases were characterized by bold, simple, and symmetrical designs. (89)

Geometric: a phase of vase painting characterized by geometric designs given on horizontal planes. (89-91)

Archaic: artistic period immediately preceding Athen's Golden Age , roughly extending from 800 to 500 BC. (91-6, 98-9)

Attic pottery: pottery from the region around Athens, a major center of pottery making. (93)

Black-figure pottery: designs appear in black against a light red clay background. Found in 6th century BC. (93)

Red-figure pottery: designs appear in red clay against a glazed black background. Examples begin to appear around 530 BC. (93)

Kouroi (singular - Kouros): sculpture of a heroic youthful male athlete. (93-4, 96)

Korai (singular -Kore): sculpture of a young woman. (94-6)

Lyric poetry: poetry that is characterized by subjective treatment of personal experiences. Sappho of Lesbos was one of the greatest of lyric poets. (97)

Doric: order of Greek temple first appearing in the Archaic period. Distinguishing characteristics include a baseless, large column and a simple slab as a capital. (98-9, 129)

Important Names

Gorgon Painter (6th century): black-figure artist named for the Gorgons that decorate his works (Fig. 4.7). (91-2)

Lydos (6th century): creator of one of the largest surviving terra-cotta kraters (Fig. 4.8). (92)

Makron (5th century): red-figure artist who painted nearly all the vases by the potter Hieron. Works show great subtlety. The profile of the eye can be seen in Fig. 4.10. (92)

Douris (5th century): over 30 vases survive with his signature. Fig. 4.9 is remarkable for its rhythmic animation. (92-3, 112-3)

Homer (c.800 BC): Greek poet and presumed author of the *Iliad* and *Odyssey*, which deal with minor details of the Trojan War. These works were used as textbooks in ancient Greece and created the model for the epic poem. (105-8)

Sappho of Lesbos (fl. c.610-c.580 BC): Greek lyric poet known for her works celebrating love between women. (108)

Hesiod (fl c.800 BC): Greek poet. His *Works and Days* describes the life of peasants, and his *Theogony* details the lineage of Greek Gods. (86, 97)

Study Questions

What do the wall paintings of the Mycenaean age tell us about the time period? (88)

Describe protogeometric and geometric vases. (88-91)

Compare the effects of black- and red-figure pottery. Cite specific examples. (91-3)

Why are the kouroi not considered to be realistic? What is innovative about them and the korai? Compare the kouroi of the early Archaic period (Figs. 4.11-4.12) to the Kritios Boy (fig. 4.15). (93-6)

Who are the three major poets of this time period. Describer their diverse works. (97, 99-103)

Describe the three examples of architecture cited in the text. What do they show us about their time period? What are the principal features of the Doric order? (97-9)

PRACTICE TEST

1. What is the name of the early civilization centering in Crete?
   a. Hellenes   b. Mycenaean   c. Minoan   d. Dorian

2. What does not describe the Mycenaean civilization?
   a. palaces were not fortified
   b. traders traveled throughout the Mediterranean.
   c. wall paintings were lively and colorful
   d. they inhabited south-eastern Greece and eventually Crete

3. Which of the following is not one of the principal Hellenic people?
   a. Dorians   b. Aculians   c. Ionians   d. Minoans

4. Why is the date 776 BC important to Greek civilization?
   a. marks the defeat of the Persians.
   b. marks Greek conquest of Troy.
   c. marks first Olympic game.
   d. marks Zeus' ascent to the throne as King of the Gods.

5. What does not describe Greek religion?
   a. gods are represented in human terms.
   b. gods dwelt on Mt. Olympus.
   c. myths were organized and codified into one central book.
   d. local deities were created to protect various regions.

6. According to Pythagoras, what was fundamental to all life?
   a. art   b. mathematics   c. the gods   d. truth

7. What does not characterize the protogeometric style?
   a. symmetry   b. bold designs   c. complicated designs   d. concern for order

8. What does not characterize the geometric style?
   a. avoids human figures   b. zigzags   c. horizontal planes   d. symmetry

9. Figures in black-figure paintings are more realistic than in red-figure.
   a. true   b. false

10. What characterizes the Archaic Kouroi?
   a. depiction of the idealized athlete
   b. strong concern for flesh
   c. portrayal of a stereotype, not an individual
   d. all of these

Matching

11.___ lyric poetry   a. Homer

12.___ epic poetry   b. Hesiod

13.___ *Theogony*   c. Sappho of Lesbos

14.___ *Iliad*

15. ___ *Works and Days*

16.___ "He Seems to be a God, that Man"

ANSWERS

1. c   2. a   3. d   4. c   5. c   6. b   7. c   8. a   9. b   10. d   11. c   12. a
13. b   14. a   15. b   16. c

CHAPTER 5: GREEK CLASSICISM AND HELLENISM

CONTEXTS AND CONCEPTS

Summary

Classical Greek culture has provided influence and inspiration to Western civilization for over 2000 years. The arts and ideas of this amazing people-- from the Greek temple to the philosophies of Plato and Aristotle--present the concepts of humanism, rationalism, and idealism. It is this approach to reality, with its fundamental appeal to man's intellect as the guide and measure of all things, that is the great legacy of the Greeks.

This chapter deals with the last two periods of ancient Greece: the Classic and the Hellenistic eras. During its Golden Age in the 5th century BC, Athens supported the world's first democracy and created, under the leadership of Pericles, the environment for many remarkable artistic achievements. A protracted military engagement with Sparta, known as the Peloponnesian Wars, eventually led to the decline of Athenian political power, but the city remained a center for arts and philosophy.

Philosophy was an important discipline in Greek culture. In the 5th century, Greece saw the rise of the Sophists, philosophers who, well-versed in rhetoric and logic, sold their services to the highest bidder. Sophists were held in contempt by many, including the great teacher Socrates. Two great philosophers emerged from the 5th and early 4th centuries. Plato, a pupil of Socrates, founded the philosophical aesthetics of Western culture in a number of writings, including the Socratic dialogues. Plato believed that Ideas were reality and objects and art were imitations of that reality. He did not believe that ideas or essences were created, rather that they simply existed eternally. Aristotle, who explored a remarkably divergent number of topics, opposed Plato's view on the role of art. Rejecting Plato's contention that art must teach a moral lesson, Aristotle felt that the purpose of art was to give pleasure.

In the 4th century BC, Alexander the Great from Macedon began his rapid conquest of the known world. This event marks the beginning of the Hellenistic period, which continued to thrive long after Alexander's death. Hellenistic influences affected several non-Western cultures and eventually centered in Alexandria, Egypt. In the Hellenistic period, three philosophical schools--the Cynics, Stoics, and Epicurians--came into prominence.

Important Terms

Delian League: a group of city states that banded together in 478 BC to protect themselves against the Persians. With Athens at their lead, they liberated a number of Greek cities around the Aegean. (106)

Golden Age: a brief but magnificent era in the 5th century BC, beginning with the defeat of the Persians and closing with the Peloponnesian Wars. Also known as the Age of Pericles. (106)

Peloponnesian Wars: lengthy struggle between Athens and Sparta, eventually won by Sparta. (106)

Sophists: members of a pre-Socratic school of philosophy. Teaching the art of rhetoric and persuasion, they sold their services to the highest bidder. Their ethical standards were not highly regarded. (107)

Techne: the ability of an artist to know what the end result will be and how to execute the artwork to achieve that result. The fundamental principles were measurement and proportions. (108)

Hellenistic Period: the final phase of the Greek Empire. It begins with the rise of Alexander the Great and extends into the period of the Roman Empire. The era is characterized by a flourishing of the arts, an emphasis on scientific thought, and the blossoming of intercultural relations. (110-1)

Cynicism: philosophical school founded by Diogenes. They felt that the good life lay in satisfying one's animal needs and that a wise man would have as few needs as possible. (111)

Stoicism: philosophical school founded by Zeno. They believed that the good life lay in following reason, wisdom, and virtue. With an awareness of one's own wisdom and virtue, a man should be able to disregard misfortune. (111)

Epicureanism: philosophical school founded by Epicurus. They believed that the good life was an untroubled life. One should strive to avoid entanglements, maintain good health, tolerate pain, and accept death. (111)

Important Names

Pericles (495?-429 BC): Athenean statesman and orator who led Athens during the Golden Age. (106)

Protagoras (481?-411 BC): one of the leading sophist philosophers. His major work is *On the Gods*. (107)

Socrates (470?-399 BC): Greek philosopher and teacher of Plato. His method of teaching by questioning students is known as the Socratic method. Plato used these teaching sessions as a basis for his "dialogues." (107-8, 121-3)

Plato (427-347BC): founder of Western philosophical aesthetics. He believed that Ideas exist independently from individual minds and that they simply existed eternally. For Plato, Ideas are reality and objects and art are only imitations of that reality. (107-8, 121-3)

Aristotle (384-322 BC): Greek philosopher whose works touched on a remarkably diverse body of knowledge, including biology, politics, logic, and art. He was the teacher of Alexander. His major work is *Poetics*. (108-10)

Alexander (356-323 BC): King of Macedon who conquered Greece, the Persian Empire, and Egypt. During his brief reign, which initiated the Hellenistic period, the arts flourished. He founded the city of Alexandria, which became one of the most influential cities in the Hellenistic world. (110)

Diogenes (412?-323 BC): Greek founder of Cynic philosophy. (111)

Zeno (335?-263? BC): Greek founder of Stoic philosophy. (111)

Epicurus (341-270 BC): Greek founder of Epicureanism. (111)

Study Questions

What were the three events described in your text that transformed Athens into a dynamic civilization? (106)

Athens created what is considered to be the first democracy. How did it function? What were its strengths? weaknesses? (106)

What led to the downfall of Athens? How did this affect the arts from this center? (106-7)

Who were the Sophists? How were they viewed in their time? (107)

Describe Plato's philosophy of art and beauty. What does he consider to constitute reality? What is imitation? How did he view the arts? How do Aristotle's views on art differ from those of Plato? (107-1)

What political and economic events contributed to the flourishing of the arts during the Hellenistic period? Which were the leading families and where did they rule? Describe the intercultural relationships of this era. (110-1)

What are the three schools of philosophical thought emerging in the Hellenistic world? Who were their founders? How do they differ from each other? How are they similar? (111)

THE ARTS OF THE GREEKS

Summary

Two-Dimensional Art : For the most part, Greek arts are characterized by the dominance of intellect over emotion. The principal element separating classical painting from archaic is a new sense of idealized reality in figure depiction (Figs. 5.6-5.7). Such realism, often set against a white background, reflected technical advancements in perspective and the use of light and shadow. The essence of the classical style is an appeal to the intellect. This appeal has four basic characteristics: emphasis on form, idealization, use of convention, and simplicity. The dominant qualities of classicism were modified in the Hellenistic period, as a less formal, more naturalistic, and more emotional style evolved. Hellenistic paintings often portray mundane, and sometimes vulgar scenes.

Sculpture: Although more examples of sculpture have come down to us than of two-dimensional art, great quantities of Greek sculpture no longer exist, and many of the surviving "Greek" sculptures are really Roman copies. Sculptures from the Classic age, as exemplified in the works of Myron and Polyclitus, contain detailed depictions of the human flesh, an emphasis on controlled movement, and more natural, relaxed stances. *The Fates* (Fig. 5.11) originally decorating the east pediment of the Parthenon, shows a sophisticated treatment of cloth that is natural and yet reveals the Classical perfection of human form underneath. Late 4th-century sculpture, such as found in the works of Praxiteles and Lysippos, illustrate a change in attitude, but the works are still grounded in Classical ideals. Significant changes occur in Hellenistic sculptures. Turning to pathos, banality, trivia, and flights of individual virtuosity, the Hellenistic sculptor explored new dramatic and dynamic subjects.

Literature: The literary spirit of the Classic and Hellenistic periods is largely contained in the works of Plato, Aristotle, Pericles, and the playwrights described in the following section. Plato's major works are the *Republic*, which describes the ideal society, the *Apology*, which treats the trial of Socrates, and the *Phaedo*, which concludes the story of Socrates' trial and death.

Theatre: The theatre of Ancient Greece was a theatre of convention. Productions did not strive to create realistic images on stage. Rather, audience members, relying on their imagination, accepted poetic descriptions of scenes and events. This allowed the Greek dramatist to focus on projecting moral themes. Early plays had only one actor plus a chorus. Often the playwright was not only the author, but the director, choreographer, musical composer, and the principal actor as well.

The earliest theatre productions stemmed from competitions held during religious festivals centering around Dionysia. From these competitions came three outstanding writers of tragedy, Aeschylus, Sophocles, and Euripides. The earliest comedies come from the post-classical period. Aristophanes, the best of the comedy writers, instilled political satire and often obscenity into his works. Obscenity not only provided humor, but also underlined the moral that natural behavior produces more happiness than artificiality. In the Hellenistic period, the New Comedy, as exemplified in the works of Menander, kept some of the bawdy aspects of the Old Comedy, but turned towards more superficial subjects.

Music: Very few examples of Greek music survive. Those that do are mostly fragments from the Hellenistic period and are impossible to interpret accurately. Still, some evidence about Greek music has come to us from writings and depictions of music making on vase paintings. The music was monophonic (single melodic line without accompaniment). The two leading instruments were the lyre (string) and aulos (wind). Both were used in contests, which were popular in Greece. Although Greek music theory did not directly influence later Western theory, many Greek terms continue to be used today.

Music occupied the thoughts of many of the greatest minds of Greece. Aristotle, while encouraging the development of musical skills, warned against developing professional abilities. He also felt that music should lead to noble thought. rather than to the opposite, as surely took place during Dionysiac rituals. According to Plato, Greek music relied on conventions that were governed by rules concerning what was acceptable for any given occasion. Pythagoras explored the relationship between math and music and felt that an understanding of numbers (through music) was the key to an understanding of the entire universe.

Dance: Because of the evanescence of dance, there is little we can do but speculate as to its nature in the time of ancient Greece. We know that dance played a principal role in the same religious rituals that led to the beginnings of drama. We suspect that these dances appealed to emotional frenzy rather than to intellect. But dance associated with later theatre, as described by Plato and Aristotle, were certainly more classically oriented.

Architecture: The classical Greek temple is a post and lintel structure. Numerous symmetrically placed columns support a massive lintel called an entablature. Three orders can be distinguished; Ionic and Doric are classical, and Corinthian is Hellenistic. The Parthenon, with its Doric construction, typifies the perfection and balance of the Greek classical style. Particularly fascinating is how aesthetic balance is created with mathematical adjustments. The Temple of Athena Nike illustrates the more delicate style of the Ionic order. Corinthian order can be seen in the temple of the Olympian Zeus. Although maintaining the balance and moderation of Classical temples, it shows the increase of proportions and the slender and ornate columns associated with the Hellenistic era.

Synthesis: The rapid change in attitude between the early and late classical period is illustrated with a comparison of two tragedies: *Prometheus* by Aeschylus and *Hecuba* by Euripides. Aeschylus embraces Greek idealism in high poetry. Man is seen as having the power through reason to remedy shortcomings and to have dominion over nature. Euripides' tragedy is more realistic, and his poetry is less flowery and more forceful. Hecuba's tragic fate can be seen as a condemnation of Athenian leadership and of the Greek gods.

Important Terms

Classic Period: artistic period coinciding with Athen's Golden Age (480-323 BC). Classical style is based on an appeal to the intellect. (106-10, 112-3, 114-9, 129-32)

Hellenistic Period: final artistic of ancient Greece characterized by greater emotional appeal. (113, 119-21, 132)

Contrapposto stance: the arrangement of body parts in sculpture so that the weight-bearing leg is apart from the free leg, thereby shifting the hip/shoulder axis. (114)

Old Comedy: sophisticated comedy from the post-classical period characterized by satire, obscenity, and biting political invectives. Leading writer was Aristophanes. (111)

New Comedy: comedy from the Hellenistic period characterized by bawdy action, lack of political invectives, and superficial plots. (126)

Kothurnoi: thick-soled boots worn by actors to increase their height. (126)

Onkos: wiglike protrusion on top of a mask worn by actors. (126)

Orchestra: the circular area in a Greek theatre where the acting and dancing took place. (126-7)

Theatron: the sloping area of the Greek theatre where the audience sat. (126)

Skene: a building in a Greek theatre where actors could change costumes. (126)

Lyre: a string instrument plucked by the hand. One of the leading musical instruments of ancient Greece. (127)

Aulos: a wind instrument associated with the cult of Dionysus. One of the leading musical instruments of ancient Greece. (127)

Hydraulos: a great water organ developed during the Hellenistic period. (128)

Post and lintel: a structure of horizontal blocks of stone laid across vertical columns. (129)

Column: a cylindrical post or support which often has 3 distinct parts--base, shaft, and capital. (129)

Capital: the transition between the top of a column and the lintel. (129)

Stylobate: the foundation immediately below a row of columns. (129)

Pediment: the typically triangular roof piece characteristic of classical architecture. (129)

Entablature: the upper portion of a classical architectural order above the column capital. (129)

Frieze: the central portion of the entablature often containing decorative lines or sculpture. (129)

Doric: order of Greek temple from the Classic period. Distinguishing characteristics include a baseless, large column and a simple slab as a capital. (129)

Ionic: order of Greek temple from the Classic period. Distinguishing characteristics include a round base, slender column, and a scroll-like capital. (129)

Corinthian: order of Greek temple from the Hellenistic period. It is distinguished by its ornate leaf-like capital. (129, 132)

Important Names

Myron (5th century BC): Greek sculptor. His masterwork, *Discus Thrower*, reveals a concern for the idealized human form and for restrained subdued vitality. (115)

Polyclitus (5th century BC): Greek sculptor and architect. His *Lance Bearer* is considered to achieve the ideal proportions of a male athlete. The body weight is thrown onto one leg in the *contrapposto* stance. (114)

Phidias (5th century BC): Greek sculpture. His Riace Warrior (Fig. 5.14) is one of the most impressive sculptural finds in recent years. (117)

Praxiteles (4th century BC): Greek sculptor. His *Cnidian Aphrodite* reflects the post-classical tendency for individualism and delicacy. (118)

Lysippos (4th century (BC): Greek sculptor known for his *Apoxymenos*, which seems to set the figure in motion. (119)

Homer (c.800 BC): Greek poet and presumed author of the *Iliad* and *Odyssey*, which deal with minor details of the Trojan War. These works were used as textbooks in ancient Greece and created the model for the epic poem. (105-8)

Aeschylus (524-456 BC): first major writer of Greek tragedies, of which seven survive. He is credited with adding second actor and reducing the size of the chorus. His plays have a strong intellectual appeal. His major work is the trilogy *Oresteia*. (124, 134)

Sophocles (496?-406 BC): writer of Greek tragedies, of which seven survive. Although his works are still grounded in the classical spirit, they show less formality, more complexity, and an emphasis on humane plots and subtle characterization. He is credited with adding a third actor. His greatest work is *Oedipus the King*. (124-5)

Euripides (480?-406 BC): writer of Greek tragedies, of which 18 survive. His works, dealing with individual emotions rather than great events, are more realistic than those of Aeschylus and Sophocles. He experimented with many of the conventions of his time and explored the mechanics of scenography. Major works include *Hecuba*. (125, 134-5)

Aristophanes (c.450-c.380 BC): Greek writer of comedy in the post-classical period. Works are characterized by satire and topical, sophisticated, and often obscene humor. (125)

Menander (c.342-c.292 BC): leading writer of New Comedy in the Hellenistic period. (126)

Thespis (6th century BC): Greek poet who is credited for beginning the concept of drama through his addition of a single actor to choric dances. (126)

Study Questions

What are the four characteristics of Greek classicism? How are these elements modified in the Hellenistic period? (112-3)

Name four vase painters and describe their works. How did vase painters of the Classic period achieve a sense of depth and reality? (112-3)

Who are the first two major sculptors of the Classic age? How do their works achieve the effect of balance, movement, and realism? (114-5)

Where did figs. 5.11 and 5.12 originally appear? How do they show the sophisticated techniques of the Classic age? How does Fig. 5.13 differ from the earlier two? (117)

Name the two leading sculptors of the late 4th century. How do their works reflect the current changes in attitude? (118-9)

How do the sculptures of the Hellenistic period differ from those of the Classic? (119-21)

What is a theatre of convention? How does it differ from the theatre of illusion? What is its advantage? (123)

What are the names of the religious festivals that led to theatre productions? How many actors were used? What was the role of the playwright? (123-4)

Who were the three great writers of tragedy? What are there major works? How do their works differ? (124-5)

What are the six parts of tragedy discussed by Aristotle? (125)

What are the characteristics of Old Comedy? New Comedy? Who are the principal writers of each? (125-6)

Describe the productions of Greek theatre. What were the costumes like? theatres? What were the seats like for the audience? (126-7)

What can we tell about the general nature of music in Greece? What was its role? What were the attitudes toward music and musicians? How do we know these answers? (127-8)

Why does the text say that when we think of one Greek temple, we think of all Greek temples? What is the basic structure of a Greek temple? (129)

What are the three orders of Greek temples? How do they differ from each other? When were they in vogue? (129)

In what ways does the Parthenon reflect balance, harmony, and perfection? (130)

What contrasting effect do the Ionic columns of the temple of Athena Nike have from that of the Doric Parthenon? (131)

What is distinctive about the Corinthian columns of the temple of the Olympian Zeus? (132)

PRACTICE TEST

1. The principal leader of Athens during its Golden Age was
   a. Pericles b. Solon c. Hesiod d. Protagoras

2. After Sparta defeated Athens in the Peloponnesian Wars, which city dominated Greek culture? a. Sparta b. Athens c. Corinth d. Delphi

3. What does not describe Greek religion?
   a. gods are represented in human terms.
   b. gods dwelt on Mt. Olympus.
   c. myths were organized and codified into one central book.
   d. local deities were created to protect various regions.

4. The Sophists excelled in
   a. rhetoric   b. writing   c. math   d. music

5. Plato based his dialogues on the teaching of
   a. Socrates   b. Aristotle   c. Pythagoras   d. Protagoras

6. For Plato, Ideas represented
   a. imitation   b. inspiration   c. evil   d. reality

7. For Aristotle, the purpose of art was to
   a. teach a moral lesson   c. uphold truth
   b. give pleasure   d. calm the passions

8. Which was not a leading philosophical school in the Hellenistic period?
   a. Cynics   b. Stoics   c. Sophists   d. Epicureans

9. Where was the center of Hellenistic culture?
   a. Athens   b. Alexandria   c. Macadonia   d. Rome

10. What was the dominant current in Classic art?   a. intellect   b. emotion

11. What does not characterize Greek classicism?
    a. emphasis on form   b. complexity   c. convention   d. idealization

12. How does Hellenistic art differ from Classic?
    a. more formal   b. simpler   c. more emotional

13. According to your text, by what year did vase painting begin to achieve as
    sense of three-dimensionality?
    a. 800 BC   b. 600 BC   c. 550 BC   d. 400 BC

14. What would we not find on a Classic-era vase?
    a. white background   c. elegance
    b. emphasis on three dimensions   d. lack of conventions

15. Who created *Doryphorus (Lance Bearer)*?
    a. Myron   b. Polyclitus   c. Praxiteles   d. Lysippos

16. What does not characterize *The Fates*?
    a. sophisticated treatment of cloth   c. controlled grace
    b. portrayal of perfect human form   d. strong emotions

17. What is new about Lysippos' *Apoxyomenos*?
    a. figure is in motion   c. flesh is realistically depicted
    b. classical proportions   d. first male nude

18. What characterizes Hellenistic sculptures?
    a. pathos   b. banality   c. virtuosity   d. all of these

19. What does not characterize early Greek plays?
    a. Use of only a single actor   c. Use of a chorus
    b. Emphasis on tragedies   d. Extensive scenic display

20. Who is the first major playwright of Greece?
    a. Euripides   b. Aristophanes   c. Sophocles   d. Aeschylus

21. Who is not a writer of tragedy?
    a. Euripides   b. Aristophanes   c. Sophocles   d. Aeschylus

22. Matching

      Aeschylus   a. *Oedipus the King*

      Sophocles   b. *Acharnians*

      Euripides   c. *Agamemnon*

      Aristophanes   d. *Hecuba*
---

23. On whose plays did Aristotle model his theories on drama?
    a. Euripides   b. Aristophanes   c. Sophocles   d. Aeschylus

24. According to Aristotle, what is not an element of tragedy?
    a. music   b. spectacle   c. plot   d. diction   e. dance

25. What characterizes the costume of a Greek actor?
    a. colorful robes   b. a mask   c. thick shoes   d. all of these

26. What does not characterize a Greek theatre?
    a. actors were completely encircled by the audience
    b. audience sat in stone seats, some with backs and arms
    c. the orchestra was circular

27. What is the earliest extant theatre?
    a. Theatre of Dionysus   c. Theatre at Epidaurus
    b. Theatre of Ephesus   d. Theatre at Sparta

28. The basic wind instrument of Greece was the
    a. hydraulos   b. aulos   c. lyre

29. What is not an attitude towards music held by Aristotle?
   a. Music should lead to noble thought
   b. Citizens should avoid professionalism in music making
   c. Citizens should not play music instruments at all

30. Who explored the relationship between math and music?
   a. Plato   b. Aristotle   c. Pythagoras   d. Protagoras

31. What probably characterized the dance of the early religious festivals?
   a. intellectual control   b. solemn worship   c. wild frenzy

32. What is the name of the structure of Greek temples?
   a. post and lintel   b. Gothic   c. rib vault

33. Which of the following orders is Hellenistic?
   a. doric   b. ionic   c. corinthian

34. The doric temple that is a monument to balance and perfection is
   a. Athena Nike   b. Parthenon   c. Olympian Zeus

35. What order is employed by the temple of Athena Nike?
   a. doric   b. ionic   c. corinthian

36. Which play described in your text suggests that man has dominion over nature?   a. *Prometheus* b. *Hecuba* c. *Oedipus Rex*

37. The poetry of Euripides is more poetic and less realistic than that of Aeschylus.   a. true   b. false

ANSWERS

1. a   2. b   3. c   4. a   5. a   6. d   7. c   8. b   9. a   10. a   11. b   12. c
13. c   14. d   15. b   16. d   17. a   18. d   19. d   20. d   21. b   22. c a d b   23. c
24. b   25. d   26. c   27. a   28. b   29. c   30. c   31. c   32. a   33. c   34. b   35. b
36. a   37. b

CHAPTER 6: THE ROMANS

CONTEXTS AND CONCEPTS

Summary
The practical contributions of Roman culture, in contrast to the temples and ideas of the Greeks, provide the foundations for our society. With their genius for organization, Romans built cities with roads, viaducts, and fortifications, they created a sophisticated yet robust legal system, and they amassed a standing army that conquered the world. They embraced the achievements of Greek culture and gave the Western world the final and most historically significant flowering of Classical civilization.

Little is known about the early history of the Italian peninsula. According to a legend, Rome was founded in 753 BC by Romulus, who had been raised with his twin brother Remus by a wolf. The legend may have ties to the Etruscans, a people of uncertain origin, who came to the peninsula perhaps as early as 1000 BC. The Etruscans, who were literate and developed metallurgy, were overthrown by the Romans in 509 BC.

The Romans established a republic. A senate, consisting of patres and plebs, elected two consuls to rule the state for one-year terms. During this time, Rome began to expand its dominions, conquering Greece, Gaul, and in a protracted engagement called the Punic Wars, Carthage. Julius Caesar capitalized on his brilliant campaign against Gaul and was declared dictator for life. After he was assassinated, the republic came to an end.

The fate of Rome after the republic often relied upon the quality of the Emperor. Rome fell into good hands with Emperor Augustus, who helped launch a period of rebuilding. This was also the age of the poets Virgil and Horace and of the appearance of the architectural style that we identify today as Roman, with vaults and arches. It also brought about the destruction of the Temple at Jerusalem in AD 70.

At the height of the Roman Empire, a new era quietly began with the birth of Jesus Christ, whose life is described in the four Gospels and the epistles of the of the New Testament. In the sixth century, the modern practice of dating the birth of Christ as AD 1 was established. Because Jerusalem was the location of Christ's crucifixion and Resurrection, this city, which is also held to be a holy city in the Jewish and Islamic faiths, became the center of religious conflicts that continue today.

About 200 years later, Emperor Constantine recognized Christianity as the state religion and created a second capital in Byzantine called Constantinople. During the fifth century AD, Rome fell to the Goths marking the official close of the Roman Empire.

By nature, Romans were practical and efficient. This not only made them outstanding soldiers, but also excellent managers and administrators. The Roman code of law--perhaps Rome's most important contribution to Western civilization--is remarkable for its legal interpretations. Roman architecture solved practical problems; their roads, aqueducts, and triumphal arches serve as present-day monuments to the Roman genius.

Stoicism, with its emphasis on the good life, virtue, and acceptance of duty, was well-suited to the Roman nature. Under the guidance of Panaetius and Posidonius, Stoicism was modified towards the Roman spirit, and Rome became the principal center for Stoics. Among the leaders of this philosophical movement were Seneca, who defended the accumulation of wealth, Emperor Marcus Aurelius, who discussed Stoicism in his *Meditations*, and Epictetus, who rose from slavery to become one of the most influential philosophers of his time. In the third century AD, another philosophical school, neo-Platonism, came into prominence. The leading exponent of this school was Plotinus.

Important Terms

Etruscans: Asian-Greek invaders who came to Italy around 1000 BC. They dominated the peninsula until the Romans' successful revolution in 509 BC. (138)

Roman Republic: the time period between the overthrow of the Etruscans (509 BC) and the rise to power of Caesar Augustus (27 BC). The period derives its name from the Republican form of government in Rome. (138-9)

Senate: a body of 300 members who conducted the business of government in Rome. (138-9)

Patres: heads of patrician families. (138)

Plebs: members of the citizenry. (139)

Consuls: two men who, elected by the Roman Senate for one-year terms, were the most important officers ruling the state. (139)

Punic Wars: three wars between Rome and Carthage eventually leading to the destruction of Carthage. (139)

Roman Empire: the time period between the rise to power of Caesar Augustus (27 BC) and the fall of Rome (c. AD 476). (139-43)

Flavian: Roman imperial dynasty extending from the fall of Nero in AD 69 to AD 96. Arts were active during this period. (142)

Stoicism: philosophy based on the teachings of Zeno in Hellenistic Greece. It was adopted and modified by the Romans in three phases known as the Old Stoa, Middle Stoa, and Late Stoa. (111, 144-5)

Neo-Platonism: a name given to a number of movements that derive their inspiration from Plato's *Dialogues*. In the 3rd century AD, Plotinus was the leading exponent of such a movement. (145)

Important Names
Romulus and Remus (8th century BC): legendary twins suckled by a wolf. Romulus founded Rome in 753 BC. (138)

Hannibal (247-183 BC): general from Carthage who led a march over the Alps in order to attack Rome. (139)

Julius Caesar (100-44 BC): brilliant Roman general who was elected dictator for life. He seized power after a successful campaign in Gaul. He is credited with creating the Julian calendar of 365 days. (139)

Augustus Caesar (63 BC-AD 14): Roman Emperor who launched Rome into a significant rebuilding period. (141)

Jesus Christ (4?BC-AD 29?): regarded by Christians as the son of God. He is the founder of Christianity. (141)

Constantine I (AD 280-337): Roman Emperor who is important as the founder of a second Roman capital in Byzantium named Constantinople and for his recognition of Christianity as the state religion. (143)

Chryssipus (c.280-c.206 BC): Greek philosopher who systematized Stoicism. He may have been with Zeno, founder of Stoicism. (144)

Diogenes of Babylon (2nd century BC): brought Stoicism to Rome. (144) Not to be confused with the Diogenes who founded cynicism. (111)

Panaetius (fl. c.180-109 BC): the founder of Roman Stoicism. (144)

Posidonius (c.135-c.51 BC): Greek Stoic philosopher, student of Panaetius and teacher of Cicero. He played an essential role in the spread of Roman Stoicism. (144)

Seneca (4?BC-AD 65): Roman philosopher, writer, and politician. A leading Stoic, he defended the right to accumulate wealth. (145)

Marcus Aurelius (121-AD 180): Roman Emperor and Stoic philosopher. Major work is *Meditations*. (145)

Epictetus (c.AD 55-c.135): Greek philosopher. Originally a slave, he became one of the most important spokesman for Roman Stoicism. Major works include *Discourses and Manual*. (145)

Plotinus (c.205-AD 270): Egyptian-born philosopher who was the leading exponent of neo-Platonism. With Plotinus, the symbolic nature of art receives its first comprehensive formulation. (145)

Study Questions

Who dominated the Italian peninsula prior to the rise of the Romans? What do we know about their culture? What influences did they exert on the Romans? (138)

Compare the governments of Athens and Rome. Who could serve on the Roman Senate? How were the consuls selected? (106, 138-9)

Describe the career of Julius Caesar. What major contribution did he make to Western culture? (139)

From what sources do we know about the life of Jesus? When did the birth of Jesus become established as AD 1? Why was the locating of the crucifixion and Resurrection in the city of Jerusalem especially significant? (142)

What are the principal events in the history of Rome after the turn of the Christian age? When did Christianity become recognized as the state religion? What city became the "second capital" of the Roman Empire? (143)

What are the basic qualities of the Romans? How do they differ from the Greeks? (143)

What role did Stoicism play in Roman empire? Who were the leading exponents? How did Roman Stoicism differ from Greek? (111, 144-5)

Why do we feel that Roman law may be Rome's greatest contribution to Western civilization? (143)

In what ways do the views of Plotinus derive from those of Plato? (107-8, 145)

THE ARTS OF THE ROMANS

Summary

Two-Dimensional Art: The limited number of Roman paintings that have survived are primarily frescoes from Pompeii. Since much of the early artwork of Rome was done by imported Greek artists, Roman paintings reflect, with some modifications, Greek characteristics. Although the paintings *Hercules and Telephos* and *Lady Playing the Cithara* (Figs. 6.10 and 6.11) treat different subjects, both reflect the naturalism of figure depiction that was typical of the Hellenistic style. Some Roman paintings (Fig. 6.12) combine landscape representation with painted architectural detail. According to a theory of theatrical scenery, wall painters began to imitate theatrical décors. There are three principal types: a tragic décor with columns and statues, a comic décor with private dwellings with balconies, and a satyric décor with trees, mountains, and rustic country settings.

Sculpture: Roman sculpture derives much of its essence from the Greeks. Many of the surviving sculptures (Fig. 6.14) are simply copies of Greek originals. Yet many Roman works show distinctively Roman qualities. The *Portrait of an Unknown Roman* (Fig. 6.15) reflects a rugged, individual character that owes more to the Etruscan heritage than Hellenistic influences.

During the Empire, sculpture turned back towards the Greek classical conception of the idealized body. Often these figures were Romanized by the addition of a realistic portrait head of a contemporary Roman citizen or of distinctively Roman dress (Fig. 6.16). Such portrayals of Roman Emperors enhanced their God-like image. Public reverence for the leaders can also be seen in sculptures such as Trajan's Column (Figs. 6.17 and 6.18), which in effect tells the story of Trajan's defense of Rome. Although such adulation for Rome's leaders waned in the early centuries AD, the power of Emperor Constantine can be felt in his monumental sculpture (Fig. 6.19).

When the practice of cremation fell out of favor in the second century AD, richly adorned marble sarcophagi became fashionable. Unlike similar works from Athens and Asia Minor, Roman sarcophagi were carved on three sides, with the fourth side against a wall. As in Fig. 6.20, mythological scenes were common.

Literature: Roman contributions to literature were considerable. Early works were written in Greek and copied Greek models. But beginning in the first century BC, a series of outstanding writers of poetry and prose lifted Latin to a lofty position. Virgil's epic poem *Aeneid* brought an instant mythology to the Romans. Livy wrote histories of Rome in a grand, sweeping style. Other important figures were the poets Horace, Martial, and Juvenal and the prose writers Petronius, Apuleius, and Lucan. Also written during this time was the New Testament of the Bible.

Theatre: Three important dramatic forms were prevalent at various times in Roman history: phlyakes farces, Roman comedy, and mime. The earthy phlyakes apparently were performed on raised stages. Vase paintings suggest that they were bawdy and lewd. Roman comedy was greatly influenced by the New Comedy of Menander. Plautus, one of Rome's most important playwrights, directly adapted Greek works into Roman settings. His treatment of characters as types, and not individuals, influenced dramas in later ages. A second influential playwright, Terence, was more literary and better educated than Plautus. The mime came into prominence during the Empire. Dealing with low life, it appealed to all classes of Romans. While such works distracted the masses from their problems, they also gave a forum in which the general public could address grievances to the bureaucracy.

Despite strong objections from the Senate, theatres flourished during the Roman Empire. The Roman theatre differed from its Greek counterpart in its use of a curtain and a roof over the stage. The stage was reduced to a semi-circle, and the action of the play took place on a raised stage. A Roman actor had low social status, and he wore contemporary clothes rather than the elaborate costumes of the Greeks.

Music: As with the other arts, Roman music is largely indebted to Greece, particularly in its music theory and in its instruments, such as the hydraulus. But the Romans also developed a number of new musical instruments--brass instruments--and the function of music was quite different than that advocated by Aristotle. Rather than shunning professionalism, Romans encouraged the attainment of virtuosity, and individual skills on an instrument were applauded. Music also played a major role in mass entertainments called "Bread and Circuses". The hydraulus at the Colosseum provided background music as Christians were fed to the lions. Surprisingly, all mention of secular music disappears in the fifth century AD.

Dance: Rome's most significant contribution to dance was the pantomime. The original purpose of pantomime was probably serious. Themes were often tragic, probably based on Greek and Roman tragedies. Some pantomimes were sexual in orientation, and it is probably because of the lewdness that pantomimes were eventually forced to leave the major cities.

Architecture: Little architecture survives from the Roman Republic. Remaining examples suggest a strong Hellenistic influence with Corinthian orders and graceful lines. Two differences can be noted: Roman temples are smaller, and they employ columns that are partly embedded in a wall. As a result of the latter, there is only one entrance to a temple, as can be seen in the Temple of Fortuna Virilis (fig. 6.26). In the Augustan age, Roman architecture was refashioned according to Greek style.

A distinctive Roman style emerged in the first through fourth centuries AD. The most significant characteristic is the use of the arch in arcades and tunnel and groin vaults.The Colosseum (Figs. 6.27 and 6.28), with its circular sweep of arches, engaged columns, and open amphitheatre, exemplifies a fully independent Roman style. Roman triumphal arches, such as the Arch of Titus (Fig. 6.29), also serve as impressive monuments to the Roman's ingenuity.

One of the most remarkable achievements of the Roman Era is the Pantheon (Figs. 6.30-6.32). The entrance is a Hellenistic porch with graceful Corinthian columns. But once inside, one is overwhelmed by the spaciousness of a round temple. What captivates our attention is the sense of open space that is created within this massive structure, an accomplishment that is still admired today.

Synthesis: The granting of absolute power to Augustus in 27 BC launched a great period of peace in which the arts flourished. Sculpture and architecture give ample evidence of the greatness of this period. Such works reflect the monumentality, the practicality, and originality of the Roman Empire.

Important Terms

Fresco: a method of painting in which pigment is mixed with wet wall plaster and applied as part of the wall surface. (146)

Phlyakes farce: first important dramatic form in Roman history. Performances tended to be bawdy and lewd. (156)

Scaenae frons: facade facing audience on stage in Roman theatres. (157).

Proscenium: a Greek word meaning "before the skene". The plaster arch or "picture frame" stage of traditional theaters. (157)

Cavea: the auditorium in the Roman theatre. (158)

Hydraulus: a water organ that was popular in Rome. Originally from Greece, it is said that it could be heard a mile away. (159)

Bread and Circuses: state provided entertainment for the mass of unemployed and dissatisfied. Music played a prominent role. (159)

Pantomime: a form of theatrical dance where a single dancer portrayed all of the parts in silence. (159-60)

Important Names

Cicero (106-43 BC): Roman statesman and orator who is credited with developing a Latin prose style capable of expressing philosophical ideas. (154)

Virgil (70-19 BC): Roman poet. His epic poem *Aeneid* created a mythical history for Rome. (154-6)

Horace (65-8 BC): Roman poet whose works expressed basic Roman attitudes and helped to raise the literary standards of Latin. (154, 156)

Livy (59 BC-AD 17): Roman historian who retold the history of Rome in a sweeping style. (154, 156)

Martial (c.AD 40-c.103): Roman poet best known for his epigrams. (156)

Juvenal (c. AD 55-c.127): Roman poet known for his satirical epigrams. (156)

Petronius (d. AD 66): Roman writer of satirical novels. (156)

Apuleius (c.AD 124-170): Roman philosopher and author of *Golden Ass*, one of the earliest novels. (156)

Lucan (AD 39-65): Roman poet who was a favorite of Nero for a short period. Later he was forced to commit suicide after a failed conspiracy. (156)

Plautus (c254-184 BC): Roman playwright. His works are for the most part copies of Greek originals. His use of character types, not individuals, influenced both Shakespeare and Moliére. (157)

Terence (c.185-159 BC): Roman playwright. His works, which are more literary than those of Plautus, had a tremendous influence on the theatre of later ages. (157)

Study Questions

From where do most of the surviving Roman paintings come from? On what type of surface were these paintings applied? What does the choice of surface suggest to us about the Romans? Their choice of subjects? (146-49)

What were the Hellenistic influences on Roman sculpture? What were the influences of the Greek classic period? When did the later begin to appear in Rome? (150)

What distinctively Roman qualities can we identify in their sculpture? How did sculpture enhance the image of the Emperor? (150-53)

When did sarcophagi sculpture come into prominence in Rome? Where are the other two centers of such work? How do the works of each of these areas differ from each other? (153)

Who are the three leading writers of Latin mentioned in your text? What was their influence? How did their works reflect Roman attitudes? How did their works serve the purposes of the Roman emperors? (154-56)

What other writers are mentioned by your text? What were their contributions to literature? (156)

What are the three important dramatic forms of Rome? Describe each. Who are the leading playwrights of comedy? (156-7)

What social function did theatre in Rome serve? (157)

How does the Roman theatre design differ from that of Greece? In what ways does the Roman theatre resemble a modern theatre? (156-7)

What influence does Greece have on Roman music? How do Roman attitudes toward music differ from those of Aristotle? (159)

What role did music play in the social life of citizens? of the general masses? (159)

Describe the Roman pantomime. Why did it fall into disfavor? (159-60)

How does the Temple of Fortuna Virilis reflect Greek influences? Etruscan? (160)

What is the most significant characteristic of the Roman style? How is it exemplified in the Colosseum? The Arch of Titus? What other distinctively Roman features are found in these structures? (160-1)

Describe the exterior and interior of the Pantheon. Why is this structure considered to be such a remarkable achievement? (162-3)

What distinctive Roman qualities can be observed in the monuments from the Augustan age? Why did the arts flourish during this time? (164-5)

PRACTICE TEST

1. The people who dominated Italy in the 6th century are
   a. Carthaginians b. Hellenes c. Etruscans d. Romulans

2. Members of the Senate from patrician families were called
   a. patres b. plebs c. consuls d. representatives

3. Who was Rome struggling with during the Punic Wars?
   a. Sparta b. Alexandria c. Carthage d. all of these

4. One of Rome's greatest contributions to Western culture was
   a. stoicism b. Roman law c. science d. music

5. A second capital of the Empire was renamed
   a. Athens b. Alexandria c. Constantinople d. Sparta

6. Most of the surviving Roman painting comes from
   a. Rome b. Pompeii c. Athens d. vases

7. Matching

   Seneca   a. leading Stoic under the Old Stoa

   Epictetus   b. Roman who modified Stoicism to the Roman world
   ---

   Chryssipus   c. Roman Emperor who was a leading Stoic

   Panetius   d. Defended the accumulation of wealth through
   ---   Stoicism

   Marcus Aurelius   e. Slave who rose to become a great spokesman of
   ---   Stoicism

8. What does not characterize *Hercules and Telephos*?
   a. Mythical and heroic nature of subject
   b. Formally composed picture
   c. Stereotyped, unnatural figure depiction
   d. Painting applied to a wall

9. According to theories of theatrical scenery, images of trees, mountains, and country places represent
   a. tragic décor   b. comic décor   c. satyric décor

10. The head of Constantine shows
    a. naturalism   b. exaggeration   c. imitation   d. all of these

11. What characterizes Roman sarcophagi?
    a. decoration on all four sides
    b. figures carved in round against architectural detail
    c. figures carved on three sides, fourth side against a wall

12. Who was the leading member of the Neo-Platonist school?
    a. Virgil   b. Plotinus   c. Horace   d. Livy

13. Matching

        Virgil   a. *Golden Ass*

        Livy   b. *Meditations*

        Apuleius   c. *Aeneas*

        Martial   d. Roman historian

        Marcus Aurelius   e. satirical poems
    ---

14. According to your text, who developed a Latin prose style capable of expressing philosophical ideas?
    a. Virgil   b. Horace   c. Cicero   d. Livy

15. What is not an important type of Roman theatre?
    a. farces b. tragedy c. comedy d. mime

16. What does not characterize the plays by Plautus?
    a. They were copied from Greek models
    b. They were set in Roman settings
    c. They depicted individual characters
    d. They were influential on the drama of later ages

17. Of the following, what was an important addition to the theatre by Romans?
   a. a curtain   c. a roof over the stage
   b. a semi-circular stage   d. all of these

18. What new instruments were developed by the Romans?
   a. brass   b. kitheras   c. hydraulus organs   d. all of these

19. What accurately describes music in Rome?
   a. professionalism was shunned   c. used in mass entertainment
   b. there was no secular music   d. developed a new theory

20. What was the most important type of dance in Rome?
   a. religious dance   b. social dance   c. pantomime   d. folk

21. Of the following, which is a Greek influence on the Temple of Fortuna Virilis?
   a. engaged columns   c. deep porch
   b. wide cella   d. delicate Ionic columns

22. The most significant characteristic of the Roman architectural style is the
   a. arch   b. column   c. post and lintel   d. arena

23. What is reminiscent of Greek classicism in the Colosseum?
   a. arches   b. engaged columns   c. closed arena   d. aesthetics

24. The Roman triumphal arch sacrifices a rich and delicate ornamentation for a massive internal structure.   a. True   b. False

25. What impressive new architectural feature distinguishes the Pantheon?
   a. a massive, yet spacious circular temple
   b. a porch with graceful Corinthian columns
   c. a cylindrical cella
   d. numerous statues of gods

ANSWERS
   1. c   2. a   3. c   4. b   5. c   6. b   7. deabc   8. c   9. c   10. b   11. c
   12. b   13. cdaeb   14. c   15. b   16. c   17. d   18. a   19. c   20. c   21. d   22. a
   23. b   24. b   25. a

CHAPTER 7: BYZANTIUM

CONTEXTS AND CONCEPTS

Summary
The geographical location of Byzantium--situated on the main land routes from Europe to Asia next to a defensible deep water port, and within fertile cultural surroundings--gave this city tremendous potential as a major metropolis. Under Constantine, Byzantium prospered, becoming the center not only of Christian orthodoxy, but also of a unique and intense style in the visual arts and architecture. By the time Rome fell to the Goths, it had long since handed the torch of civilization to Constantinople. Byzantine intellects became the custodians for Classical thought and style, preserving and nurturing the accomplishments of the Classical world for future generations.

In AD 330 Constantine established the city of Byzantium as the second capital of the Roman Empire, renaming it Constantinople. For over a thousand years, this city served as a bridge between the East and the West. Gradually it developed a distinctively Eastern culture, but its influence on Western civilization was considerable. Initially, Constantinople was seen as an extension of Western civilization, but with the divided succession of the Roman Empire in 395, the barbarian invasions of Europe in the fifth century, and the religious conflicts between the Eastern and Roman Christian Church in the fourth and fifth centuries, Constantinople developed an independent and purely Eastern culture.

The sixth and seventh centuries saw some of Byzantium's brightest and darkest moments. The Emperor Justinian (527-565) sought to unite the two heritages and to reestablish Roman greatness. Although somewhat successful in these attempts, Justinian's greatest legacy lay in his recodification of Roman law. But after his death, Byzantium was besieged from the East, and its ties to the West were further severed. The establishment of an independent, powerful, and artistically rich civilization was begun under the Isaurian dynasty (717-867). Among the principal events of this period are the establishment of a new legal system (Ecloga), the iconoclastic controversy, and the establishment of a great intellectual center. Until the middle of the eleventh century, the Byzantine Empire underwent a period of prosperity and brilliance.

The decline of Byzantium was brought about by both internal and external problems. A series of weak emperors, a rift between the intellectual elite and the military, and a new religious controversy placed the Empire in turmoil. Threats from the Normans in the West and the Turks in the East were eventually repulsed, but the crusade of 1203, which ended in the sacking of Constantinople, delivered a fatal blow and left the city unable to turn back the Ottoman Turks in 1453.

Even through its declining years, Byzantium continued to serve as an intellectual center. Preserving the Classical traditions descending from Athens, Antioch, and Alexandria, the Eastern Empire produced a series of historians and theologians that were without equal in the Western world. These accomplishments proved to be of considerable influence on later Western thought.

Important Terms

Byzantium: Greek city located in what is now Turkey. Renaming the city Constantinople, Constantine I made it the second capital of the Roman Empire. It is now known as Istanbul. (168)

Corpus Juris Civilis: Roman law as revised by Justinian. (168)

Monasticism: a system of living as practiced in a religious monastery. (169)

Corpus Ecloga: a code of laws briefer than Justinian's complex *Corpus*. It introduced a new concept in increasing rights for women and children. (169)

Iconoclastic: a person opposed to the use of icons in the worship of God. (169)

Important Names

Justinian (483-565): Emperor of the Eastern Roman Empire. Best remembered for his attempted unification of the Empire and his recodification of Roman law. (168)

Isaurian Emperors (717-867): the first oriental rulers of the Eastern Roman Empire. (169)

Study Questions

What role did the geographical location of Byzantium play on the development of its unique culture? What ties did it have to the West? How did it manage to develop a distinctively Eastern civilization? (168-72)

What contributions were made to Byzantium by Justinian? by the Isaurian Emperors? (168-9)

What factors led to the decline of the Byzantine Empire? (169-71)

Why did Byzantium become the leading intellectual center of the region? In what areas did their scholars excel? How did their writings influence later Western scholars? (171-2)

THE ARTS OF BYZANTIUM

Summary

Two-Dimensional Art: It is difficult to make generalizations about Byzantine art, which stretched for over a thousand years and was subject to a variety of different stylistic influences. Yet we know that the content and purpose of Byzantine art were always religious, and it appears that Byzantine artists felt that art could interpret as well as represent perceived phenomena. Moreover, it is clear that the individual artist was subordinate to the work.

Some progress has been made in solving questions concerning the dating of works and stylistic tendencies. Early attempts at iconography can be traced to the 3rd and 4th centuries, and the mid-5th century witnessed the development of narrative Christian art. After a period of decline and decadence, the Justinian age broke with the past, and the distinctly Byzantine qualities of abstraction and focus on feeling rather than form began to appear. By the 11th century, a hierarchical formula in wall painting and mosaics was adopted. Placement in a composition depended upon religious, not spatial relationships. Other stylistic trends that can be observed include: a two-dimensional style in the 11th century, a dramatic intensity in the 12th century, the addition of turbulent movement, architectural backdrops, and elongated figures in the 13th century (see Fig. 7. 5), and a tendency towards small-scale crowded works of narrative content and irrational perspective in the 14th century. Among the earliest examples of Byzantine two-dimensional art are the mosaics in Figs. 7.6-7.8. These figures present a curious mixture of naturalism and abstraction. In the middle centuries, the hieratic style, with its formalized and rigid depictions of figures, became prevalent in mosaics, but by the 13th century a return to more naturalistic depictions is evident.

Three other types of Byzantine two-dimensional art are mentioned in the text: manuscript illumination, wall painting, and textile weaving. Exquisite manuscript illuminations can be dated just after the iconoclastic controversy. The works of Figs, 7.9 and 7.10 tell a story, a technique called continuous narration. In the *Vision of Ezekiel*, we can easily see its classical derivation, but the lack of rational linear perspective and the crowding of figures suggest a Medieval orientation. An example of textile weaving is given in Fig. 7.11.

Sculpture: Trends in sculpture follow those of two-dimensional art closely. Early works are influenced by classical models, including vignettes and portrait sculpture. By the end of the fourth century, works, such as Fig. 7.12, begin to reflect a number of oriental influences. Large scale sculpture disappeared after the 5th century, but small-scale reliefs continued in abundance and took a strong classical turn after the iconoclastic struggle.

Ivory carvings were popular in Byzantium.The Barberini Ivory, Fig. 7.14, reflects a number of qualities typical of its time--brilliant technique, round features, high relief, and a recognizable depiction of the emperor's head. The only known free-standing sculpture in ivory is the 10th-century Virgin and Child (Fig. 7.13), which exemplifies a number of hieratic trends. Certainly one of the most impressive efforts in ivory is the Harbaville Triptych (Fig. 7.15), from the late 10th century. Despite the softness of the figures, a number of hieratic formal traits can be identified, including the placement of the figures in a hierarchy. This work belongs to the Romanus school of ivory carvers.

Literature: Literature from the Eastern Roman Empire includes works in a number of diverse languages, but the largest body of literature is in Greek. A number of generalities can be applied to these works. Except for histories, most of the works are religious. In contrast to Western tastes, the educated Byzantines prized the cliche, elaboration, and verbiage. In terms of content, Byzantine literature tends to be somber, often dealing with calamity, death, and the precariousness of human existence.

There are three principal genres of Byzantine literature: history, hagiography, and vernacular works. In this context, history is not a chronicled record of events (which was separate in Byzantium), but a literary genre that interpreted events and their influence on each other. Hagiography comprises the largest volume of Byzantine literature. The anecdotal accounts of the lives of Saints were eventually collected and then written up according to a set outline called a schema. The vernacular works include humorous poems of complaints written by Theodore Prodromos and a number of romances dealing with chivalry, knights, witches, and dragons in the fashion of the West.

Theatre: Little has survived relating to Byzantine theatre. We know that Byzantines were fond of the theatre. Justinian married an actress. But between the fall of Rome and the late Middle Ages, theatre was virtually extinct. Our only glimpses of what may have been Byzantine dramatic productions can be seen in Roman mimes and Turkish plays.

Music: Byzantium seems to have acquired much of its musical heritage from Syria. Especially important for later Western developments are the use of antiphonal psalmody and the singing of hymns. Although no manuscripts survive, we can speculate that Byzantine hymns were more elaborate than those of the West. Based on motives, these melodies, called kanones, were improvised by individual singers. The system of echoi also was influential on later Western music theory.

Dance: We know very little of Byzantine dance. Dancing did occur at Church services, and Roman pantomimes were surely present in Byzantium. Beyond this, we can only speculate.

Architecture: The Justinian age developed a new style called Byzantine. While the principal objective of Justinian may have been to glorify Justinian, the unique synthesis of East and West brilliantly captured the relationship between God and state. After Justinian's death, new construction concentrated primarily on the Palace. Still, the few churches that were built became models for later Byzantine architecture. The cross-in-square plan seen in Fig. 7.16 is copied in later churches. Other common characteristics include an evident concern for the classical principles of precise harmony between the parts, use of elevated drums and vertical silhouettes, and an emphasis on elegance and the rising line of the design. A primary consideration in later architecture is the individuality of each structure.

Synthesis: The major monument of the Justinian movement is San Vitale in Ravenna (Figs. 7.20-7.22). The concentric octagons of the structure allow a sense of expanding interior space. The second level is reserved for women, a standard feature of Byzantine churches. The sanctuary itself is alive with mosaics. The differences between Figs. 7.23 and 7.24 show the contrast between a relaxed naturalism and the more formal and rigid style of the orient. One of the crowning achievements of the East is Hagia Sophia (Fig. 7.25-7.29). Blending Roman techniques and oriental designs, it provides us with a magnificent view of Byzantine artistry.

Important Terms

Mosaic: a picture or design made by placing small colored pieces into mortar. (173-74)

Hieratic style: literally "holy" or "sacred" style. A movement in Byzantine art in which figures were presented in a formalized and rigid manner. (174)

Continuous narration: a technique of telling a story through several panels in a given artwork. (176)

Triptych: three carved panels hinged together. (179)

Romanus: a name given to a number of carved works from the late 10th and early 11th centuries sharing several recognizable features. School is named after a plaque representing Christ crowning the emperor Romanus IV. (179)

Hagiography: biographies of saints and other religious figures. (180)

Schema: a preset formula for writing a biography of a saint allowing the author to develop biographies without much information. (180)

Scaenici: Byzantine word for theatre productions. (181)

Antiphonal psalmody: the singing of psalms in which the two parts of a single line are alternated between two choirs. (181)

Hymns: songs of praise to the Lord. (181)

Kanones: melodies constructed on short melodic motives which the singer chooses and combines together. (181)

Echoi: equivalent to Western scales or modes. The system had a significant impact on Western music. (181)

Important Names

Procopius of Caesarea (early 6th century): perhaps the best known Byzantine historian. His broad, sweeping narratives were modeled after Thucydides. (180)

Athanasius of Alexandria (c.360): author of the first biography of a religious figure--St. Anthony. (180)

Theodore Prodromos (d. 1166): court poet who wrote poems that took the form of complaints to the Emperors. (180)

Anthemius (6th century): architect of Hagia Sophia. (186)

Study Questions

Describe stylistic trends in Byzantine art. What is the Hieratic style? When was it in fashion? (173-5)

What are the principal types of two-dimensional art from Byzantium? Describe the examples in your text. (173-6)

What classical traits can be found in Byzantine sculpture? Oriental? (177)

Describe the three ivory works illustrated in your text. (177-79)

How does Byzantine literature differ from that of our Western heritage? (180)

What are the three principal types of literature in Byzantium? What are the characteristics of each? Who are the leading writers? (180)

What did Byzantine music derive from Eastern music? What was its heritage to the West? (181)

What do we know about Byzantine dance? (181)

From what sources did Justinian bring about a synthesis of previous architectural styles? How did this new style reflect the relationships between God, the state, philosophy, and art? (182-9)

Describe the basic design of early Byzantine architectures? What are common features of later churches? (182-3)

Describe San Vitale in Ravenna and Hagia Sophia. Why does the text consider these to be the major monuments of Byzantine culture? (185-9)

PRACTICE TEST

1. Which Emperor sought to reunify the East and the West?
   a. Constantine I b. Justinian c. Leo III d. Constantine V

2. Justinian's greatest legacy is his
   a. recodifying of Roman law   c. attempt to reunify East & West
   b. championship of Orthodoxy   d. avoidance of Eastern conflicts

3. The stabilization of Byzantium in the 8th and 9th centuries was
   accomplished by
   a. Justinian b. Isaurian dynasty c. Comneni dynasty d. Turks

4. An iconoclast is someone who worships icons.   a. True   b. False

5. What contributed to the decline of the Byzantine Empire?
   a. weak leaders   c. religious controversy
   b. invasions from West   d. all of these

6. What was not a Byzantine area of intellectual pursuit mentioned in your
   text?   a. theology b. history c. philosophy d. physics

7. Byzantine intellectual activities exerted influence on Western thought
   through the 15th century   a. True   b. False

8. What does not characterize Byzantine art in general?
   a. the individual artist was subordinate to his works.
   b. the content and purpose of art was secular.
   c. artworks can interpret as well as represent phenomena.
   d. dating individual works is difficult

9. Which is not a two-dimensional art form prevalent in Byzantium?
   a. vase painting   c. manuscript illumination
   b. mosaics   d. textile weaving

10. A trend towards presenting a formalized, rigid depiction of men is
    called   a. Hellenistic b. hieratic c. continuous narration d. Romanus

11. A technique of telling a story through several panels in a given artwork is called
    a. tryptich b. continuous narration c. registers d. registral narration

12. What unusual material was very popular for Byzantine sculpture?
    a. marble b. ivory c. limestone d. bronze

13. The Harbaville Triptych shows no evidence of the Hieratic style.
    a. True b. False

14. Which is not a principal form of Byzantine literature?
    a. histories b. hagiography c. novels d. vernacular poems

15. What are the Prodromic poems?
    a. Biographies of Saints   c. Explanations of past events
    b. Complaints to the Emperor   d. Western-type romances

16. The building of melodies from motives by singers in Byzantine was
    called   a. echoi b. hymns c. antiphonal psalmody d. kanones

17. What was the only important building after Justinian's death?
    a. palaces b. churches c. monasteries d. universities

18. What does not characterize the later Byzantine churches?
    a. Lack of individual expression   c. Elevated drums
    b. Classical harmony between parts   d. Rising lines

19. What is the major Justinian monument in the West?
    a. St. Clement   b. St Luke   c. San Vitale, Ravenna d. Hagia Sophia

20. Despite the beautiful synthesis of East and West seen in Hagia Sophia, its general appearance still considered decadent. a. True   b. False

ANSWERS

1. b   2. a   3. b   4. b   5. d   6. d   7. a   8. b   9. a   10. b   11. c
12. b   13. b   14. c   15. b   16. d   17. a   18. a   19. c   20. b

CHAPTER 8: THE EARLY MIDDLE AGES

CONTEXTS AND CONCEPTS

Summary
Between the fall of Rome and the reawakening of Western civilization during the Renaissance is the Middle Ages. The early part of this period, the so-called Dark Ages, was a period of fear and superstition, a time when Western man seemed to creep into a world of mental and physical isolation. Yet within this barricaded existence, arts and literacy were sustained in monasteries and convents, and works of rare quality were created.

The Christian Church was the dominant force of the Middle Ages. During its first three centuries, the Church endured persecutions from Roman Emperors and fundamental, often violent internal struggles over Christian doctrine. Yet with Emperor Constantine's conversion, Christianity had not only survived, but triumphed. The Church began to build an organization in the mold of the Imperial government. But by the 4th century, there still existed no central authority. In 325 a new church institution was created--the General Council. The first of these, The Council of Nicea, decreed that Christ and God were of one substance, an issue of fundamental importance to Christian faith. Eventually, the Bishops of Rome, because they were heirs of St. Peter and because their city was the capital, began to exert a dominant position. Pope Leo I, who held considerable administrative abilities and played a significant leadership role in negotiating with invading barbarian armies, solidified Rome's predominance.

Two men played a significant role in the shaping of early Christian thought and in the development of a Western philosophy independent from Eastern doctrines. The writings of Turtullian of Carthage, which established Latin as the language of the Church, clearly delineated the differences between East and West. His elaborate analysis of the soul concluded that the spirit and matter were two separate but real entities. The spirit, being invisible, was indestructible. Other important topics found in Tertullian's writings include a discussion of the Trinity, a formulation of a list of sins, and the conclusion that the supreme Christian virtues were humility and the spirit of other-worldliness, by which Christians could escape the perils of this life.

St. Augustine was a prolific writer, whose best known works are *Confessions* and *City of God*. Inspired by Platonic and neo-Platonic thought, Augustine argued that we should not trust the senses, which give us unreliable images of the truth. He believed that intuition is the source of knowledge and that knowledge is the inner illumination of the soul by God. Among the other important philosophical questions that he dealt with are: the simultaneous creation of the universe and time; the existence of the soul; the doctrine of original sin; and the question of Foreknowledge and Foreordination. Augustine's philosophy of art represents a radical shift from that of Plato and Aristotle. He believed that the production and consumption of art should be strictly in the confines of the Church. Augustine wrestled with the problem of the sensuous gratification of art, but felt that as long as art agreed with the tenets of faith, it was justified.

While the organization of the Christian Church and its doctrines were being formulated, Rome itself faced many uncertainties. Barbarian invaders became increasingly bolder. Despite the Romanization and conversion of many of the German tribes, the fifth century saw Rome fall prey to several conquerors, and the last Roman Emperor was deposed in 476.

The weaknesses of the Empire left the Roman Church in a difficult situation. It not only had to contend with barbarians, but also with the powerful Eastern emperors, who considered themselves to be religious leaders. A brief break between the Churches of the East and West, known as the Acacian Schism, led to the formulation of a doctrine that distinguished between the roles of secular and sacred authorities. Justinian, unconcerned about such distinctions, sought to bring Rome under Byzantine dominance. These goals might have been attained if not for Pope Gregory I, whose reforms, administrative abilities, and teachings regained for Rome its position of primacy among the Western Christian churches.

During the Dark Ages, Western Europe fell into political and religious systems that allowed little growth. Feudalism, based on a complex division of territory into political divisions, prevented the rise of any dominant secular leaders. The Church attempted to exert control in such a system through manipulating fears of the devil and offering hopes for eternal life. The Church itself divided into two parts: monks who withdrew into cloistered lives and clergymen who devoted themselves to the service of society. Since learning and philosophy were confined to the monasteries, little intellectual activity occurred in the broader world.

A new threat to the West was posed by the spread of Islam beginning in the 7th and 8th centuries. The Islamic philosophy of "conquest by the sword" spread the religion quickly and threatened to overrun the West. The threat was finally repelled by Charles Martel in 732. More than just warriors, Islamic scholars studied science, math, and literature. They kept Greek classicism alive, and Arabic numerals are a lasting Moslem contribution to the West.

In the wake of the growth of Islam, the Roman Church felt a need to ally itself with secular powers. Initially, the Franks provided such a partnership. Crowned as the Holy Roman Emperor, Charlemagne helped to rekindle a brief flourishing of arts and learning. In the 9th and 10th centuries, the focus of Europe shifted to Germany, where the Ottonians unsuccessfully attempted to control the Church. Eventually the Church gained independence through wealth and power. The triumph of Christianity led to the crusades and eventually to the revitalization of Europe's economy.

Important Terms

Middle Ages: name given to the period in Western European history between the 5th and 15th centuries. Other terms designating this era are Medieval and Dark Ages. (192)

Dark Ages: name sometimes used interchangably with Middle Ages. For some, it refers only to the early Middle Ages. (192)

Council of Nicea: the first convocation of the General Council, which met in 325. It agreed upon a doctrine in which declared that the Son was "of one substance with the Father." (194-5)

Petrine theory: arguments forwarded by the Bishops of Rome supporting their claim of supremacy over the Church. (195)

Legalism: the strong legal cast given to the Catholic Church by Tertullian. (195-6)

Trinity: the concept of God as three persons in one substance posed by Tertullian. (196)

Neo-Platonism: a philosophical and religious system based on the doctrines of Plato. (196)

Pelagian Heresy: group centering around Pelagius who denied the concept of original sin. (196)

Foreknowledge: a philosophical question of whether God has knowledge of worldly events before they happen. If so, then why does a good God allow evil to befall the innocent. (196)

Feudalism: political division of territory into small units governed by one man. The system established a hierarchy of vassal service. (197)

Vassal: person who was given land by a feudal lord in exchange for political allegiance. (197)

Serf: common person who worked the land of a local lord. (197)

Islam: religion based on the teachings of Mohammed. A believer is often referred to as a Moslem. (198)

Koran: sacred book of Islam. (184)

Carolingian: related to the Frankish dynasty extending from 751 to 987. Charlemagne was the greatest Carolingian ruler. (198)

Ottonian: a dynasty of German rulers in the 9th and 10th centuries. (199)

Important Names

Alaric I (370?-410): king of the Visgoths who sacked Rome in 410. (192)

Ataulph (d. 415): successor to Alaric I. He married the Emperor's sister and took his Visgoths to Spain where he attacked the Vandals. (192)

Atilla (406?:453): king of the Huns who invaded the Roman Empire and nearly sacked Rome. (192)

Pope Leo I (390?-461): important early leader of the Roman Catholic Church. Remembered for his administrative abilities and his dramatic negotiation with invading barbarians. (195)

Tertullian (160?-230?): theologian from Carthage who created Latin as the language of the Christian Church and who broke with the Eastern dominated doctrines of Christianity. (195-6)

St. Augustine (340-430): early Christian theologian. Major works are *Confessions* and *City of God*. (196)

Pope Gelasius I: formulated distinction between the secular and sacred powers. (197)

Pope Gregory I (540?-604): great leader of Roman Catholic Church who restored Rome's leading position in sacred matters. Major work is *Book of Pastoral Care*. (197)

Mohammed (570?-632): prophet and founder of Islam. (198)

Charles Martel (689?-741): Frankish ruler who defeated the Moslems in 732. He was the grandfather of Charlemagne. (198)

Charlemagne (742-814): Frankish king who sparked a brief renaissance of art and learning. He was crowned Holy Roman Emperor. (198)

Study Questions

Why are both terms, "The Middle Ages" and "The Dark Ages" appropriate for this time period? (192)

Describe the interaction between Rome and the Barbarians. How were the Germanic people Romanized? Who were the leaders of the invaders? When was the last Emperor deposed? (192-3)

What difficulties did the Christian Church face in its early years? Why was it successful? (193-5)

Describe the early organization of the Church. What was important about the Council of Nicea? Why did Roman bishops feel that they should have the supreme voice? (194-5)

What are Tertullian's most important contributions to the Roman Catholic Church? What effect did his legal background have on his philosophies? (195-6)

How do the philosophies of Augustine differ from those of Tertullian? Which Augustinian concepts helped shape Christian doctrines? (196)

What threat to Rome's supremacy was posed by Byzantine? What role did Pope Gregory I play in restoring Rome's preeminence? (197)

What were the basic tenants of the Islamic religion? What threat did Islam pose to the West? What contributions did they make? (198)

Compare the roles of the Carolingians and Ottonians in the development of Western Europe. (198-9)

How did St. Augustine's view of art differ from that of Plato and Aristotle? (199)

THE ARTS OF THE EARLY MIDDLE AGES

Summary

Two-Dimensional Art: Early Christian painting was essentially burial art and tended to adapt to the local style. In Rome, for example, catacomb painting was Roman in style with Christian symbols. Paintings reflected absolute belief in another existence, in which the individual believer retained his identity. Since pictorialization was more important than artistic skill, the paintings are generally primitive.

Christian art continued to develop in several stages. It began to make the rites of the Church more vivid. Later, it was used to record Christian history. Throughout, it used Christian symbolism, which could only be understood by other Christians. As the West disintegrated into chaos, painting again became private.

From this time of chaos, a new form of two-dimensional art emerged-- illustrated manuscripts. Essential to this new medium was the change from papyrus roles to a book format. Both continuous narrative and single illustrations appeared in such settings. Fig. 8.5, from the St. Augustine Bible, shows St. Luke and twelve scenes from his Gospel. Although the artistic quality is not strong, the rich colors and intricate detail are striking.

Two other trends are noted.There is a wealth of art in non-traditional areas, such as clothing, jewelry, and ship-building. Also, a strong tendency towards emotionalism appears before 1000 and continues in the works of the Ottonian Empire.

Sculpture: Sculpture in the early Middle Ages can be seen in two phases: the period prior to the 11th century, in which sculpture played a minor role, and the period beginning in the 11th century, which is called the Romanesque. Most examples from the early period are funerary; the earliest examples are of sarcophagi. In general, the works tend to be on a small-scale, detailed, and emotional (Fig. 8.8). One of the most striking examples of medieval sculpture is the Bronze Doors of Hildesheim Cathedral (Fig. 8.9). Built in 1015 under the patronage of Bishop Bernward, the door displays 16 Biblical scenes in a manner similar to manuscript illumination.

During the Romanesque, life-size relief sculptures were created for the first time since antiquity. One prominent characteristic of this period is the return to heavy, solid, monumental sculpture made from stone. Primarily applied to the exterior of Romanesque Churches, Romanesque architecture (Figs. 8.10 and 8.11) appealed directly to lay worshippers. In general style, these works still retained the emotional, crowded, and nervous qualities of early medieval works.

Literature: For the most part, there was little interest in literature during the early Middle Ages. Important books and manuscripts were copied and preserved in the monasteries, largely due to the efforts of the Benedictine monks. In Spain, because of the Muslim influences, interest in Greek writings were sparked in Toledo, Seville, and especially Cordoba. Biblical literature was the central focus of the period. In addition to the works of St. Augustine, St. Jerome, who translated the Bible into Latin, was a major literary figure.

Secular writings began to appear after 1100. The German *Nibelungenlied* was a major collection of primitive hero-stories from around 1200. In France, the works of courtly poets became popular, especially the epic "Song of Roland," which tells of the heroic defense of France during the time of Charlemagne.

Theatre: Our knowledge of early theatre is so limited that we can only speculate as to its nature on the basis on scattered bits of evidence. We do know for certain that elaborations on the Mass service during festive occasions (called tropes) eventually led to the beginning of liturgical drama.

Music: Although the early Christian Church disapproved of the secular traditions of music in pagan cultures, music itself was highly regarded, and, perhaps due to the influence of synagogue rituals, it played a significant role in Christian services. Because of the fundamental role of Pope Gregory I in the organization of Church music, the body of medieval music for liturgical use is called Gregorian Chant.Three types of chant are described in your text. The first is the recitation of psalms, of which there are two types: responsorial psalmody (chorus responds to a soloist) or antiphonal psalmody (two choirs alternate). The second is the hymn, a syllabic, strophic song of praise sung by the congregation. The third includes freer types, such as the Alleulia. The latter with its long series of notes on a single syllable (called melismas) projects a strong emotional appeal.

Secular music began to appear after the 11th century. Works by the poet-composers trouvères, troubadours, and Minnesänger were predominantly concerned with love, had monophonic textures, and followed strophic forms.

The most important development in Western music took place in the 9th and 10th centuries--the development of polyphony. With these early works based on polyphony (called organum), Western civilization took a major step in a new direction not explored by other musical cultures.

Dance: The Church had a basic mistrust of dance, because of its pagan connections. But the people had deeply rooted ties to the dance, and the Church found it impossible to eradicate it completely. Most of the dancing was not artistic. It could, on occasion, produce a frenzied outpouring of emotion that was largely spontaneous.

Architecture: Four architectural styles from the early Middle Ages are described in the text. The first, the basilica form, is based on the structure of Roman law courts. Moving the entrance to the end of the building, usually facing West, Christian architects created a long, relatively narrow nave leading to an alter. The view of the alter was often enhanced by elevation and a Roman triumphal arch (Figs. 8.12-8.16).

The second style is the Carolingian design. Inspired by Roman monuments, Charlemagne modeled his palace in Aachen after the Byzantine style of San Vitale in Ravenna.

Emerging in the 11th century was the third architectural style. Taking its name from its Roman-like arches of its doorways and windows, the Romanesque represented a radical departure from the past. The size became larger, the roofs changed from wood to stone, and rounded arches replaced the sharp angle of the post and lintel. The resultant Romanesque structures are characterized by massive, static, and lightless qualities. One elegant example of the new style is the Cathedral of St. Sernin in Toulouse, France (Figs. 8. 17-8.18).

The fourth style, the English Norman style, is broadly speaking a type of Romanesque architecture. Loosely based on Roman classical architecture, the style reached England before the Norman invasion, but flourished during the rebuilding efforts following the Conquest. Most buildings were made of stone blocks, although bricks and cut flints were used when necessary. The late Norman period is marked by the appearance of ribbed vaulting, which proved to be strong and more attractive than groined vaulting.

Synthesis: The crowning of Charlemagne as the new Roman Emperor was the beginning of an attempt to revive the Roman Empire. A major goal of this undertaking was the reuniting of the scattered fragments of the classical heritage. Naturally, classical influences were strong on the new arts of the Carolingian renaissance, including manuscript illumination, wall paintings, and sculpture. The ivory covers of the Dagulf Psalter (Fig. 8.28) in particular bear a strong resemblance to Roman work. In addition to the beautiful work on the Palatine Chapel in Aachen, the major contribution of Carolingian architects was the creation of a building forming a vast rectangle. This became a model for Medieval monasteries.

Important Terms

Nibelungenlied: German folk stories from around 1200. Mixing history, magic, and myth, these tales provided material for music dramas by the 19th-century composer Richard Wagner. (205)

The Song of Roland: epic poem describing the fatal battle of Roland against the Saracens. (205-7)

Trope: an addition or elaboration of the text or music to the Roman Catholic Mass. (208)

Responsorial psalmody: the singing of the psalms in which a soloist sings the beginning of a line from the psalms and the chorus or congregation sings the remainder of the line. (208)

Antiphonal psalmody: the singing of the psalms in which the singing of each line of the psalms is alternated between two choruses. (208)

Hymn: a song of praise based on poetic texts. (208)

Syllabic: type of singing in which each syllable of a text is sung with only a single note. (208)

Melismatic: type of singing in which a single syllable of a text is sung with many notes. (208)

Gregorian chant: name given to body of liturgical music for the Roman Catholic Church. (208-9)

Schola Cantorum: the training center in Rome for Church musicians. (209)

Trouvères: courtly poet-musicians in northern France. (209)

Troubadours: courtly poet-musicians in southern France. (209)

Minnesänger: courtly poet-musicians in Germany. (209)

Monophonic: a single-line of melody without accompaniment. (209)

Strophic: a song form in which each line of a poem is sung to the same melody. (209)

Polyphony: the combination of two or more melodic lines appearing together in a musical combination. A particularly Western tradition. (209)

Vielle (fiedel): a bowed medieval string instrument. (209)

Psaltery: a medieval instrument similar to the zither. (209)

Shawm: a medieval reed instrument similar to an oboe. (209)

Organa: also called organum, these sacred works are the earliest polyphonic musical compositions. (209)

Mensural notation: new rhythmic notion which made it possible to indicate exact durations of individual notes. (209)

Joculatores: literally many jugglers, these performers continued the traditions of dance at fairs and festivals. (210)

Basilica: the architectural design of Roman law courts adopted by Christian Churches in the early Middle Ages. (210-1)

Romanesque: style of architecture that emerged in the 11th century. It is characterized by the use of arches for doorways and windows and a massive, static, lightless quality. A return to monumental sculpture is also associated with this style. (204-5, 212)

Ribbed vaulting: an arched roof containing slender architectural supports. (213)

Important Names

Bernward of Hildesheim: important patron of arts during his years as a Bishop (993-1022). (203)

St. Benedict (c.480-c.550): one of the few great scholars of the Dark Ages. The Benedictine monks were particularly important for the copying and preservation of books and manuscripts. (205)

St. Jerome (340?-420): Church scholar who translated the Bible into Latin. (205)

Hrosvitha: German nun of the 10th century who wrote 6 plays based on the comedies of Terence. (208)

St. Ambrose (370?-397): Bishop of Milan who is said to have developed the hymn. (208)

St. Hilary of Poitiers (d. 368): Bishop who is also credited with developing the hymn. (208)

Pope Gregory I (540?-604): oversaw the collecting and codifying of the diverse musical traditions of the early Christian Church. The body of literature bearing his name, Gregorian Chant, became the fundamental music of church services in the Catholic Church. (208-9)

Boëthius (c.480-c.524): Roman theologian, statesman, and musician who linked the musical traditions of the Middle Ages back to that of Greece. (209)

Alcuin of York (735-804): Scholar, theologian, and advisor to Charlemagne. Oversaw Carolingian renaissance. (216)

Study Questions

What are the principal qualities of early Christian art? Describe typical examples of artworks that appear on walls, pages of books, clothing, others. (201-2)

How do Romanesque sculptures differ from the works from earlier centuries? How are they similar? (202-5)

How do early medieval sculptures communicate with the lay worshipped? Cite examples from your text. (202)

Why was Spain important to early medieval literature? (205)

What were the major contributions to Biblical literature in the early Middle Ages? (196, 199, 205)

What are the major secular works of literature from the early Middle Ages? Where did they come from? What topics do they deal with? (205-7).

On the basis of what evidence do we feel that some sort of theatre existed in the early Middle Ages? (208)

What is the difference between responsorial and antiphonal? syllabic and melismatic? How do these differences affect the style and function of the music? (208)

What role did Pope Gregory I play in the development of early Church music? St. Ambrose? Boëthius? (208-9)

What are the names given to the principal groups of poet-musicians in Europe? What were there songs like? What did they sing about? (209)

What is polyphony? How did it first begin? What is its significance? (209)

On what Roman structures were the early basilica Churches modeled? How were the Roman models altered by Christian architects? (210-1)

Describe the construction of Romanesque architecture. How did the limitations of its structure create its general characteristics? How do these structures reflect current religious attitudes? (212)

How is the English Norman style similar to Romanesque? What is distinctive about it? (213)

How did the Carolingian renaissance affect manuscript illumination? Wall paintings? Sculpture? Architecture? (214-21)

PRACTICE TEST

1. Who led the first sack of Rome?
   a. Alaric I b. Ataulph c. Atilla d. Theodoric

2. The year 476 is significant because
   a. the Vandals sacked Rome
   b. Germans began to rule Rome
   c. Ravenna became the new capital
   d. the last Roman Emperor was deposed

3. Why did Christianity flourish in the decaying Roman world?
   a. the immediacy of its founder
   b. simplicity of it doctrines
   c. subtlety of its doctrines
   d. all of these

4. Four major centers vied for central control of the Western Church:
   Rome, Antioch, Alexandria, and
   a. Constantinople b. Carthage c. Jerusalem d. Byzantium

5. Questions concerning the nature of the Trinity were examined by
   a. the Council of Nicea
   b. the Council of Constantinople
   c. Justinian
   d. Constantine I

6. Arguments supporting Rome's ascendency in the Church were called
   a. legalism   b. neo-Platonism   c. Petrine theory   d. Nicene Creed

7. Where did Tertullian originate?
   a. Carthage b. Alexandria c. Rome d. Constantinople

8. What does not characterize the philosophies of Augustine?
   a. knowledge is an inner illumination of the soul by God
   b. time was created after the universe
   c. the soul is a spiritual entity
   d. all men are born to sin because of Adam's fall

9. Matching

St. Augustine   a. translated Bible into Latin

Gregory I   b. *Confessions*

Tertullian   c. *Book of Pastoral Care*

St. Jerome   d. separated secular and sacred powers

Gelaius I   e. established Latin as the Church language

---

10. Arabic numerals are an enduring contribution of
    a. Islam b. Byzantine c. Franks d. Germans

11. The great king of the Carolingian dynasty was
    a. Otto I b. Charles Martel c. Charlemagne d. Otto III

12. The dynasty of German emperors in the 9th and 10th centuries is
    called   a. Ottonian b. Carolingian c. Acacian d. Tertullian

13. The earliest examples of Christian art and sculpture are linked with
    a. cathedrals b. palaces c. tombs d. great monuments

14. What does not characterize early medieval art?
    a. nervousness b. crowded composition c. lack of energy

15. Early medieval sculpture is monumental in nature.   a. true b. false

16. What does not characterize the Bronze Doors of Hildesheim?
    a. they were built under the patronage of Bishop Bernward
    b. they depict 16 Biblical scenes
    c. they are unique; no other bronze doors followed
    d. the effect is similar to that of manuscript illustration

17. What characterizes Romanesque sculpture?
    a. heavy and solid in appearance   c. made of stone
    b. monumental in nature   d. all of these

18. In what city did literary schools study the works of Greeks?
   a. Cordoba b. Rome c. Aachen d. Paris

19. What does not characterize the *Nibelungenlied*?
   a. written by an unknown poet   c. collection of courtly poems
   b. mixes history, magic, and myth   d. deals with hero Siegfried

20. An addition or elaboration of the Mass is called a
   a. trope b. ludi theatrici c. melisma d. chant

21. The singing of psalms in the early Christian Church was modeled
   after a. Greek plays b. Roman festival c. Synagogue services

22. What does not characterize a hymn?
   a. syllabic text setting   c. intended primarily for soloists
   b. strophic in form   d. expressed personal ideas

23. A musical setting in which single syllables are to many notes is called
   a. melismatic b. syllabic c. polyphonic d. antiphonal

24. Of the following, what did Pope Gregory not do
   a. he collected chants   c. he codified chants
   b. he disseminated chants   d. he composed most of the chants

25. Of the following, what was important for introducing sacred music
through most of Europe?
   a. trouvères   b. Schola Cantorum   c. Minnesänger   d. troubadours

26. Singing each stanza of a poem to the same melody is called
   a. antiphonal b. melismatic c. polyphonic d. strophic

27. The texture that combines more than one musical line is called
   a. antiphonal b. melismatic c. polyphonic d. strophic

28. Organum is
   a. an ancient Roman instrument   c. a type of notation
   b. the first examples of polyphony   d. a secular song type

29. Of the following, what best describes dance in the early Middle Ages?
   a. because of Church opposition, it did not exist
   b. dance became a serious expression of art
   c. because of its appeal dance was often used in Church
   d. dance was largely a frenzied outpouring of emotion

30. Early Christian architecture that adapted the design of Roman law
   courts is called
   a. Romanesque   b. basilica   c. Carolingian   d. Norman

31. Charlemagne's palace chapel in Aachen was modeled after
   a. San Vitale in Ravenna   c. Old St Peter's in Rome
   b. Hagia Sophia in Istanbul   d. the Pantheon

32. What does not characterize the Romanesque style?
   a. Roman-like arches   c. Emphasis on light
   b. Massive qualities   d. Static qualities

33. What new material was used in the roofs of Romanesque Churches?
   a. wood   b. stone   c. bricks   d. cut flints

34. The most important influence on Carolingian sculpture were
   a. Byzantine   b. Islamic   c. Jewish   d. Classical

ANSWERS
   1. a   2. d   3. d   4. c   5. a   6. c   7. a   8. b   9.bcead 10. a   11. c
   12. a   13. c   14. c   15. b   16. c   17. d   18. a   19. c   20. a   21. c   22. c 23. a
   24. d   25. b   26. d   27. c   28. b   29. d   30. b   31. a   32. c   33. b   34. d

CHAPTER 9: THE LATE MIDDLE AGES

CONTEXTS AND CONCEPTS

Summary

The spiritual and intellectual revival of the late Middle Ages had a profound influence on Western man's creative spirit. Gothic cathedrals that pointed to God, the growth of cities and towns, and the establishment of universities were all expressions of that new spirit. As a result, the humanities began to flourish, with major developments in art, music, and literature, and the quality of life improved dramatically.

After the turn of the millennium (AD 1000), Western Europe awoke with a great sense of relief. It was time for change. Important reforms in the Church were needed, and after much effort, accomplished. The founding of the Abbey of Cluny signaled the start of a major reform movement, as the Benedictine monastery set a model of strict discipline and high morals. In the mid-11th century, the papacy began a long struggle to transform the structure of the medieval Church. The eventual resolution of the Investiture Conflict, in which kings gave up their right to appoint members of the senior clergy, greatly enhanced the prestige and power of the medieval Church.

The wave of religious enthusiasm which swept Europe coincided with a flourish of cultural activity, a zest for learning, and a more personal view of religious devotion. Bernard of Clairvaux was particularly important for presenting Mary and the Apostles as living personalities.

The rise of religious zeal peaked with the Crusades. Pope Urban II called for an army to retake the Holy Land in 1095 and was astonished by the uncontrollable response. Inspired by leaders such as the itinerant preacher Peter the Hermit, thousands marched towards Jerusalem. Following a massacre and the taking of the Holy city, the Crusaders dissolved, and eventually, following the failure of the Second Crusade, the city fell into the hands of Saladin. The Third Crusade, under the leadership of Richard I of England and Philip II of France, succeeded in reaching an agreement with Saladin which allowed Christian pilgrims to enter Jerusalem safely.

An important social change came about with a shift from the masculine traditions of feudal life to the feminine codes of courtly love and etiquette. In the hands of women such as Eleanor of Aquitaine, the Code of Chivalry became a powerful force in court and had an impact on Christians, who began to view Mary as the compassionate Mother.

The decline of the old feudal system can be seen in the rise of the middle class. Contact with the East during the Crusades opened the door for goods and services, and soon Italian trading cities became commerce-oriented centers. With the emergence of towns and cities, guilds of artisans and merchants began to accumulate wealth and power.

A number of Universities, such as Oxford and the University of Paris, gained their charters in the 12th and 13th centuries. Essentially consisting of guilds of scholars, the University spawned a core of individuals who sought knowledge for its own sake. Aristotle was rediscovered, philosophy was reconciled with religion, and Roger Bacon began a study of the physical world.

In this intellectual climate, two outstanding figures appeared: Abelard and Aquinas. Abelard believed that philosophy had a responsibility to define Christian doctrine, and, if necessary, reject beliefs that were contrary to reason. He engaged in an important argument over the nature of reality. Abelard's position, sometimes called conceptualism, held that objects are real and not just imperfect imitations of universal ideal models. Abelard regarded Christianity as a way of life. Individual actions were judged good or bad solely on the basis of intentions. For judging whether intentions were good or bad, Abelard appealed to a natural law of morality possessed in the conscience of every man and founded on the will of God.

Thomas Aquinas adopted and modified the philosophical viewpoint of Abelard, and this revised form constitutes part of the philosophy of the Catholic Church. The philosophy of Aquinas was a synthesis of Christian theology and Aristotelian thought. He distinguished between philosophy-- whatever lay open to argument with the goal of discovering truth by reason--and theology--matters of faith and "revealed truths." Aquinas concentrated upon philosophical proofs of God's existence and felt that people must seek sensory knowledge of their world in order to achieve the final revelation of God after death.

By the 14th century God and state were considered separate spheres of authority. Despite serious threats from the plague and the Hundred Years' War, secular arts gained respectability and significance during the late Middle Ages.

Important Terms

Abbey of Cluny: founded in 910 by William of Aquitaine, this Benedictine monastery set standards for strict disciplines and high morals. (224)

Investiture Conflict: a conflict between the papacy and laity over who had the authority to appoint clergy. (224)

Code of Chivalry: rules of conduct and etiquette, particularly in affairs of love, developed by women beginning in the 12th century. (228)

Guilds: associations of merchants or artisans which began to bring wealth and power to the middle class. (228)

Magna Carta: the great English charter granting civil and political liberties. (228)

Universals: eternal truths; in Platonic philosophy these essences exist independently of any mind. (229)

Conceptionalism: Abelard's belief that objects have real individuality and are not mere imitations of a universal ideal. (228)

Aristotelian: a person who tends to be empirical or scientific in his method or thought. (229)

Important Names

Bernard of Clairvaux (1090-1153): theologian who personalized the lives of Mary and the Apostles. His leadership in the Cistercian order played an important role in growth of their houses. (225)

Peter the Hermit (1050?-1115?): French monk whose preaching helped to inspire the crusades. (227)

Saladin (1138?-93): Sultan of Egypt and Syria who captured Jerusalem in 1187. He was later defeated by the Third Crusade under Richard I of England and Philip II of France. (227)

Eleanor of Aquitaine (1122-1204): Queen of France and later wife of Henry II of England. She was the mother of Richard I and John. She played a prominent role in the development of the Code of Chivalry. (228)

Roger Bacon (1214?-94): English scientist and philosopher who based all knowledge on the physical world. (228)

Pierre Abelard (1079-1142): French philosopher and theologian who felt that philosophy had a responsibility to define Christian doctrine. (228-9)

William of Champeaux (c.1070-1121): philosopher who defended the Church doctrine which viewed the study of the physical world as a waste of time. (229)

Jean Roscellinus (1051-1122): philosopher who argued that physical things are the only reality. He was a teacher of Abelard. (229)

Albertus Magnus (1206?-80): German theologian who encouraged the study of Aristotle. He was the teacher of Thomas Aquinas. (229)

Thomas Aquinas (1227-74): philosopher and theologian who sought to reconcile Aristotelian philosophies with Christianity. (229)

Study Questions
Describe the reforms within the Christian Church after AD 1000. (224)

Describe the first three Crusades. What were their goals? What were their accomplishments? (225-7)

What impact did Bernard of Clairvaux have on medieval thinking? Eleanor of Acquitaine? Abelard? Aquinas? (225, 228-9)

In what ways do we begin to see the decline of the feudal system? (228)

—

THE ARTS OF THE LATE MIDDLE AGES

Summary

Two-Dimensional Art: Two important trends can be identified with the Gothic style in two-dimensional art, the beginnings of three-dimensionality in figure representation and attempts to give these figures mobility and life within three-dimensional space. Gothic artists did not master perspective, but their works do break away from the static, frozen style of the early Middle Ages. The Gothic style is also less crowded and frantic than earlier art works.

There are three principal mediums of two-dimensional art in the 12th-15th centuries: manuscript illumination, frescoes, and alter panels. Figs. 9.6-9.9 illustrate the Gothic style in manuscript illumination from the courts of France and England. Fig. 9.6, from the Psalter of St. Louis, is elegant and lively. The figures are elongated and delicate, and the whole is balanced and, although somewhat crowded, relaxed and controlled. Typical Parisian characteristics--the elongation of figures, the use of small heads, and the image of heavy drapery--influenced English artists, as seen in Fig. 9.7. The exaggeration of the French elongation, such as in *David Harping* (Fig. 9.8), was not uncommon in England. A final striking example showing experimentation with three-dimensional space is seen in Pucelle's *The Annunciation* (Fig. 9.9).

The Gothic style in painting had its greatest center in Italy. Three outstanding Italian painters are described in the text. In Giotto's masterpiece *Lamentation* (Fig. 9.10), individual figures are charged with emotion and intensity. Particularly striking is the three-dimensional space, in which Giotto brings the horizon to eye-level. Masterful treatment of space is also seen in Lorenzetti's triptych, the *Birth of the Virgin* (Fig. 9.12). Here the figures are lifelike, and the treatment of draping fabric is realistic. Gothic monumentality can be seen in Cimabue's *Madonna Enthroned* (Fig. 9.11). The 12' high work places the Virgin Mary in a hierarchical design.

Sculpture: Like Gothic painting, Gothic sculpture shows the changes in attitude of the period. Portraying serenity, idealism, and naturalism Gothic sculpture has a human quality based on order, symmetry, and clarity. As the period progressed, several trends can be noted. The sculpture became more naturalistic, as spiritualism was sacrificed to everyday appeal. Compositional unity also became increasingly sacrificed to emotionalism. Italian Gothic sculpture, as seen in *The Crucifixion* by Pisano (Fig. 9.16), mixed Roman and medieval qualities.

The most remarkable examples of Gothic sculpture appear on Chartres Cathedral. Since the dates of these figures extend nearly 100 years, changes in style are readily seen. The later figures (Fig. 9.14) are more lifelike, less tied to the building, follow subtle S-curves, show more natural fabric drapes, and feature specific individual expressions. The didactic role of this sculpture can be seen in Fig. 9.15.

Literature: The late Middle Ages produced two outstanding literary figures, Dante and Chaucer. Dante was the greatest poet of his age, and his *Divine Comedy* brilliantly guides the reader through Heaven, Hell, and Purgatory. Its use of the vernacular tongue established Italian as a rich and expressive language for poetry. Chaucer best known work, *The Canterbury Tales*, is a collection of tales told by pilgrims on a journey to Canterbury. The tales range from funny to serious, satirical to philosophical, and many are insightful and individualistic.

Theatre: In the late Middle Ages, the simple elaborations of the Mass became more substantial; eventually Bible stories, the lives of saints, and didactic allegories were presented. At first, these were given in the Church, using niches around the church for specific scenes. Gradually changes came about, including the incorporation of lay actors (perhaps even females), the emergence of comic scenes, and eventually the move to theaters outside of church.

In France and Italy, drama moved to mansion stages. Differing in configuration and convention from location to location, these stages contained a number of different scenic backgrounds. Perhaps the most elaborate section was the Hellmouth, which featured devils pulling sinners into the mouth of Hell. By the late Middle Ages such scenes, which were originally meant to frighten an audience, became comic. The introduction of humorous and compassionate elements reflected a change of attitude in the late Middle Ages.

In England, parts of France, and the Netherlands, staging was set on a succession of pageant wagons. Each wagon, some of which were quite elaborate, depicted a specific part of the play cycle. Other later developments include a turn to more elaborate and realistic productions, presentations by local guilds outside of the church, and increasing secularization. *Adam*, a typical mystery play of the early 12th century, was performed in the vernacular probably in the square outside of the church. *Le Jeu de Saint Nicholas* by John Bodel of Arras, which deals with the miracle of St. Nicholas, illustrates the expanding subject matter of Christian drama in the 13th century.

Music: Paris was the center of musical activity in the 12th and 13th centuries. Three trends are observed: 1) improvisation gradually gave way to formal composition; 2) standard music notation began to replace oral transmission; and 3) polyphony began to replace monophony as the dominant musical texture even though important examples of monophonic works continued to be composed.

The marked differences in musical style brought about by the 14th century led to the distinction between early music--*ars antiqua*--and new music--*ars nova*. The music of the *ars nova* broke away from the convention of triple groupings of beats, focused more clearly on tonal centers, and began to replace the open-sounding fifths with the sweeter intervals of thirds and sixths.

Several new forms typify the 12th- and 13th-centuries. Organum is a sacred work which eventually developed a style in which the Gregorian Chant was sung slowly in the lowest voice, while newly composed melodic lines sung above. The most important new musical genre was the motet, which also has Gregorian Chant in a low voice and different texts in the upper voices. In its early form, the motet could have sacred or secular texts and be set in Latin, French, or both. By the 14th century, the motet became a sacred work in Latin only.

Secular music also flourished in the late Middle Ages, as the tradition of the poet-composer continued in songs such as Ballades and Rondeaux. Little is known about musical instruments, but we can observe that instrumental ensembles were small in number and that composers did not specify which instrument should play which part.

Dance: The most important type of medieval dancing was group dancing. Particularly intriguing is the danse macabre, during which mass hysteria would cause some people to die from exhaustion. The theatre dance was reborn within the court. Expressive and restrained, theatrical dancing depended upon the guiding hand of a dancing master. Sometimes professional entertainers were employed.

Architecture: Late medieval architecture is dominated by the Gothic style, which is best observed in the cathedral. The beginning of the Gothic style is pinpointed between 1137 and 1144 with the rebuilding of the royal Abbey Church of St. Denis near Paris (Figs. 9.20 and 9.21). The Abbot Suger, an advisor to Louis VI, oversaw the rebuilding, and his philosophies were essential to the development of the Gothic style.

The most prominent characteristic of the Gothic style is the pointed arch, which serves both as a symbol of spirituality and as an engineering practicality that allows an increase in height, thinner walls, and the inclusion of clerestory windows. The structure was supported outside by flying buttresses.

Three examples of French Gothic cathedrals are described in the text. The façade of the Notre Dame of Paris (Fig. 9.20) illustrates the careful, mathematically precise construction of the Gothic style. The Chartres Cathedral (Figs. 9.24-9.27) fascinates us because of the juxtaposition of Romanesque and Gothic features, most dramatically seen in the two spires. The Gothic style also replaced wall paintings and mosaics with colorful stained-glass windows that further mysticized the spiritual experience. Although the Cathedral at Amiens (Fig. 9.28) appears similar to the Notre Dame of Paris, it was created at a later date, and the differences between the two--including a more delicate design and an emphasis on lightness and action instead of stability and and strength--illustrate later developments in the Gothic style.

One of the most beautiful structures of the late Middle Ages is the Salisbury Cathedral (Figs. 9.29-9.30). Built under the supervision of Canon Elias de Dereham, the interior of the Cathedral was completed in 1265. Later additions forced several modifications, and this once again allow us to see characteristics of different stylistic periods. In general, the Salisbury Cathedral differs from French Gothic cathedrals in its horizontal thrust.

The Gothic style also had an impact on secular buildings in 14th-century Venice, as seen in the Doges' Palace (Fig. 9.31). This work offers a sense of openness and tranquility. The treatment of the Gothic style mixed with an eastern style patterning of brickwork illustrates the combination of European and Moorish influences that is characteristic of the city.

Synthesis: Individual national characteristics began to appear in the late medieval world. In England, the pervasive humor of the English peasant found its way into art, as illustrated both by the the *Second Shepherd's Play* and by manuscript illuminations (Fig. 9.32). England also distinguished itself in its unique architecture. The Decorated Style, as seen in Figs. 9.33-9.39, evolved exuberant, complicated forms that anticipated late Gothic developments in Germany and France. Another distinctive late Gothic style in England, the Perpendicular Style, extended window traceries to cover adjacent wall surfaces, such as illustrated by the Gloucester Cathedral (Fig. 9.37).

Important Terms

Gothic style: in architecture, a late medieval style beginning between 1137 and 1144 characterized by pointed arches, rib vaulting, flying buttresses, and light. The term is also applied to other arts of that period. (231-39, 244-57)

Chronicle: a romance of history; not necessarily a factual account. (239)

Mystery plays: medieval drama based on episodes in the life of Christ. (241)

Miracle plays: medieval drama based on episodes in the lives of miracle-working saints. (241)

Morality plays: dramas that gave moral lessons through allegory. (241)

Ars antiqua: literally meaning "old art," this title given to music of the 12th and 13th centuries. (243)

Ars nova: literally meaning "new art," title given to French music of the 14th century. (243)

Motet: polyphonic work with Gregorian Chant in a low voice and newly composed melodies with texts in upper voices. (243)

Madrigal: a 14th-century secular song type in Italy. It is unrelated to the madrigal which flourished in 16th-century Italy. (243)

Danse macabre: literally, dance of death. During the plague, mass hysteria would drive people to dance until some died from exhaustion. (244)

Choreomania: group dancing in England characterized by group psychosis, dementia, and self-flagellation. (244)

Flying buttress: supports that carry the outward thrust of the vaults to the ground. (245)

Decorated Style: architectural style in England between 1280 and 1375, in which exuberant forms were developed. (253-7)

Perpendicular Style: architectural style originating in London in the late Gothic period. (250, 255-57)

Important Names

Jean Pucelle (1300?-1355?): Parisian illuminator and an outstanding miniaturist. (232)

Giotto (1276?-1337?): Florentine painter, architect, and sculptor. Major works include the fresco*The Lamentation*. (233)

Pietro Lorenzetti (c.1280/90-c.1348): Italian painter. *Birth of the Virgin* is considered to be his masterpiece. (233)

Giovanni Cimabue (before 1251-1302): Italian painter. Major works include *Madonna Enthroned*. (233-4)

Nicola Pisano (c.1220-1278/84): Italian sculptor who blended Roman and medieval qualities. (239)

Dante (1265-1321): greatest poet of the Middle Ages. Major work is the *Divine Comedy*, written in Italian. (239)

Petrarch (1304-74): great Italian poet who created the sonnet form. His emphasis on humanism had a strong impact on the Renaissance. (239, 285)

Froissart (c.1333-c.1400): French historian best known for his *Chronicles of England, France, and Spain*. (239)

Geoffrey Chaucer (c.1340-1400): greatest English poet of the Middle Ages. His masterwork is *The Canterbury Tales*. (240)

John Bodel of Arras (c.1167-1210): epic poet and dramatist. His major work is *Le Jeu de Saint Nicholas*, the first miracle play in French. (242)

Abbot Suger (1081-1151): advisor to Louis VI who supervised the rebuilding of St. Denis. His philosophies were instrumental in the development of the Gothic style. (244)

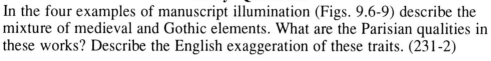

Study Questions

In the four examples of manuscript illumination (Figs. 9.6-9) describe the mixture of medieval and Gothic elements. What are the Parisian qualities in these works? Describe the English exaggeration of these traits. (231-2)

How does Giotto achieve the sense of third-dimensional space in his *Lamentation*? What other new effects do we see in this work? (233)

What are the qualities in Lorenzetti's *Birth of the Virgin* that create a sense of three-dimensional space and realism? (233)

What does Cimabue's *Madonna Enthroned* have in common with Gothic architecture? (233-4)

113

How does Gothic sculpture differ from the works of the early Middle Ages? What stylistic trends can we identify during the Gothic period? (236-9)

What is significant about Dante's *Divine Comedy*? (239)

Describe Chaucer's *The Canterbury Tales*. How do the examples in the text illustrate your generalizations. (240)

What are the principal types of medieval plays? Describe the presentation of these works in the church. (241)

What were productions on the mansion stage like? What other settings outside of the church were used? (241-2)

What were some of the developments in theatre production in the Late Middle Ages? (242-3)

What are the new qualities of music in the 12th and 13th centuries? Of the 14th century? (243)

Describe a motet. How do later models differ from earlier ones? (243)

What was the nature of medieval group dancing? Court dancing? (244)

How does Gothic architecture reflect the philosophies of Abbot Suger? (244)

What effect did the pointed arch have in Gothic architecture? (245)

Describe the Romanesque and Gothic qualities of Chartres. (246-7)

Compare the Notre Dame Cathedral of Paris with the Amiens Cathedral. (245, 248)

What structural defect was found in the Salisbury Cathedral? How did this affect the final shape of the building? (250)

How did English humor find its way into art? (253)

What is the Decorated Style? Perpendicular Style? Describe examples given in your text. (253-7)

PRACTICE TEST

1. The conflict between papacy and laity over ecclesiastical offices was called the   a. schizm b. Investiture Conflict c. Cluny Conflict

2. What does not characterize the life of Bernard of Clairvaux?
   a. he opposed the Crusades   c. he personalized Mary
   b. he was an advisor of King Louis VII d. he expanded the Cistercian order

3. The first Crusade ended
   a. in total failure   c. with the taking of Jerusalem
   b. in a peace treaty   d. before it began

4. What was a significant development of the late Middle Ages?
   a. the Code of Chivarly   c. the establishment of Universities
   b. the rise of the Middle Class d. the emergence of secular arts
   e. all of these

5. What characterizes the Gothic style in two-dimensional art?
   a. immobile figures   c. use of three-dimensional space
   b. crowded frantic scenes d. all of these

6. What does not characterize the example from the Psalter of St. Louis?
   a. drab colors b. elegant figures c. balance d. control

7. What aspect of Parisian painting was exaggerated by the English?
   a. bright colors   c. three-dimensional space
   b. elongated figures   d. all of these

8. What characterizes Giotto's *Lamentation*?
   a. painting is charged with emotion
   b. the horizon is brought to our eye-level
   c. figures are humanized and controlled
   d. all of these

9. What does not characterize Lorenzetti's *Birth of the Virgin*?
   a. fabric shows detail   c. figures are flat and frozen
   b. the spacing is comfortable d. precise attention to detail

10. What characterizes Gothic sculpture?
    a. simple naturalism b. symmetry c. serenity d. all of these

11. What is not a trend in Gothic sculpture?
    a. towards more naturalism
    b. the sacrifice of spiritualism for everyday appeal
    c. increasingly expressed sacred interests
    d. increasing emotionalism

12. Besides its decorative function, the sculpture at Chartres also had an
    important didactic role   a. true   b. false

13. Matching

    Dante   a. *Chronicles of England, France and Spain*

    Chaucer   b. *Decameron*

    Froissart c. sonnets

    Petrarch   d. *The Canterbury Tales*

    Boccaccio e. *Divine Comedy*
    ---

14. A play dealing with the lives of saints is called
    a. mystery b. miracle c. morality d. Santa

15. What does not describe the mansion stage?
    a. there was a uniform size and shape
    b. the audience could completely surround the stage
    c. locations could be depicted realistically
    d. there were elaborate depictions of the Hellmouth

16. What was not a theatrical development in the late Middle Ages?
    a. more realistic depictions   c. elimination of humorous scenes
    b. increasing secularization   d. more elaborate productions

17. What was the principal play of John Bodel of Arras?
    a. *Adam*   b. *Le Jeu de Saint Nicholas*   c. *Anterciste*   d. *Domes Daye*

18. What was not a musical development during the 12th and 13th centuries?
    a. turn away from improvisation   c. dominance of polyphony
    b. standardized musical notation   d. emphasis on tonal centers

19. The music of the 14th century is known as the
    a. ars antiqua b. ars nova c. cantilena music d. organum

20. What is organum?
    a. a musical instrument   c. a type of polyphonic sacred music
    b. a type of secular music   d. a type of monophonic sacred music

21. What is the most important new form of the 13th century?
    a. organum b. ballades c. rondeaux d. motet

22. What was the most important type of medieval dancing?
    a. theatre b. court c. group

23. The danse macabre refers to a mass dance where people literally
    danced themselves to death.   a. true   b. false

24. What is considered to be the first example of Gothic architecture?
    a. Notre Dame, Paris b. Amiens c. Chartres d. St. Denis

25. Who was the advisor to Louis VI whose philosophies helped shape the Gothic style?
    a. Elias de Dereham b. Abbot Suger c. Leonin d. Pisano

26. What does not characterize Gothic architecture?
    a. pointed arches   c. thick ribbing
    b. flying buttresses   d. large clerestory windows

27. Which cathedral stands with two distinct towers built in different time periods?   a. Notre Dame, Paris b. Chartres c. Amiens d. Salisbury

28. How does the Cathedral of Amiens differ from that of Notre Dame?
    a. more delicate b. heavier c. more stable d. all of these

29. How does the Salisbury Cathedral differ from examples of French Gothic architecture?
    a. less decoration   c. an overall horizontal thrust
    b. no windows   d. all of these

30. What characterizes the *Second Shepherd's Play*?
    a. humor b. mystery c. social criticism d. all of these

31. The English architectural style which evolved exuberant forms is called? a. English Gothic b. Decorated Style c. Perpendicular Style

ANSWERS
1. b   2. a   3. c   4. e   5. c   6. a   7. b   8. d 9. c   10. d 11. c 12. a
13. edacb   14. b 15. a 16. c 17. b 18. a 19. b 20. c   21. d 22. c 23. a
24. d 25. b 26. c 27. b 28. a 29. c 30. a   31. b

CHAPTER 10: THE RENAISSANCE

CONTEXTS AND CONCEPTS

Summary
The leading figures of the Renaissance saw their era as a time of rebirth of the social and creative spirit of the individual. There emerged a redefinition of the arts as "liberal arts," making the arts an essential part of the learning and literary culture. Inspired by the accomplishments and ideals of Antiquity, Renaissance artists went on to perfect their technical skills to a level capable not only of emulating, but even of surpassing the works of the Classical world.

The term Renaissance, meaning "rebirth," has many applications. In the most general use, it is applied to the history of Western civilization between 1400 and 1600. During this time, Europe made significant moves towards a modern, industrialized world, with innovations in technology, science, politics, economics, and the arts.

Humanism was a dominant philosophical point of view during the Renaissance. Acknowledging that men and women played an important part in this world, humanism focused on the dignity and intrinsic value of the individual. Dogma was rejected, and the tolerance of all viewpoints was embraced.

The Renaissance viewpoint was inspired by the revived interest in antiquity. Although this did not represent the first revival, it was stronger and more widespread than before. Of special interest was the Roman emphasis on civic responsibility and intellectual competence. Aristotle and the idealized conception of humankind by Periclean Greeks provided inspiration to painting and sculpture. Ideals of nobility, intellect, and physical perfection were stressed, and new conceptions of beauty and proportion were developed. Eventually, a set of rules for proportion and balance was codified.

The emphasis on individual achievement can also be seen in the new economic system of capitalism. The middle class was able to pursue wealth and power as an ultimate goal, with the only restrictions being their own abilities. As a result, there was an explosion of economic activity in the trading of goods and services previously unavailable.

A thirst for discovery--scientific, technological, and geographic--also characterized the Renaissance. Especially important was the invention of the printing press in 1445, which allowed Humanist writings and antique literature to be widely disseminated and brought a higher level of education to the Middle Class. Explorers also increased our knowledge of the world, and the voyage of Magellan around the world in 1522 made a significant impact on the Renaissance world. Another upheaval to the Renaissance world was brought about by Copernicus, who postulated a heliocentric theory of the universe.

During the Renaissance, the Church continued to lose it total authority over all social circumstances. Different systems of government sprang up in different locations: Germany clung to feudalism; Flanders explored democracy; France, England, and Spain were ruled by strong monarchies; and Italy continued to be divided into independent city-states. Particularly important to the arts was Florence, where Lorenzo de' Medici was a strong patron. After the fall of the Medici family, Rome served for a brief time as a leading center of the arts. International struggles dominated Europe in the early 16th century. Italy was invaded by both the French and Spanish, and there was a bitter struggle for the title of Holy Roman Emperor. Among the new powerful monarchs, Francis I became a particularly strong supporter of Humanist ideas.

The major blow to the Christian Church during the Renaissance was the Reformation. Although the movement began as an attempt to reform the Roman Catholic Church, it resulted in several complete breaks from the Church. In Germany, Martin Luther objected to the selling of indulgences in his '95 Theses' (1517). The furor and battle over these views led to the founding of Lutheranism. Elsewhere, John Calvin succeeded in establishing an austere Protestant sect in Switzerland, and Henry VIII, primarily because of political reasons, established the Anglican Church in England. Some of the reform movements became more dogmatic and intolerant than Roman Catholicism, and music and art were viewed by some as inappropriate for religious service. Adding to the political upheavals caused by the Protestant movements, the Catholic Church began the Counter-Reformation, and in 1542 the Roman Catholic Inquisition was established in order to destroy all non-Catholic belief.

Although there is no strong link between Humanism and the Reformation, humanism did help prepare the way for the break. Erasmus, for example, advocated the inwardness of religion and minimized outward images, such as the sacraments. Unlike the Protestant Reformers, the Christian Humanists preferred the contemplative life and believed that reforms could best be carried out within the framework of the traditional church.

Important Terms

Renaissance: general term meaning "rebirth." It is applied to the history of Europe between 1400 and 1600. (260)

Humanism: a cultural and intellectual movement in the Renaissance that focused on man and his capabilities. (260)

Capitalism: an economic system based on private ownership and a free market. (261)

Heliocentric: having the sun as a center of the universe. (262)

Reformation: a movement in 16th-century Europe to reform the Catholic Church resulting in the establishment of Protestant Churches. (263-5)

Counter-Reformation: a reform movement within the Roman Catholic Church that was a response to the Protestant Reformation. (265)

Important Names

Vitruvius (1st century B.C.): Roman architect whose treatise *De Architectura* greatly influenced the Renaissance. (261)

Ferdinand Magellan (1480?-1521): Portugese explorer who commanded the first expedition to circumnavigate the world. (262)

Nicolaus Copernicus (1473-1532): Polish astronomer who formulated the heliocentric theory of the universe. (262)

Michel Eyquem Montaigne (1533-92): French writer of *Essays*, a critical approach to the basic questions of life. (262)

Nicolo Machiavelli (1469-1527): Italian statesman and political theorist. Major work is *The Prince*. (262-3)

Lorenzo de' Medici (1449-92): head of the Medici family that ruled Florence. He was an important patron of the arts. (263)

Martin Luther (1483-1546): German monk. His *'95 Theses'* attacking the selling of indulgences marks the beginning of the Reformation. (263-4)

John Calvin (1509-64): religious reformer who established a new church in Switzerland. (264-5)

Henry VIII (1491-1547): king of England who created the Church of England. (264)

Ulrich Zwingli (1484-1531): Swiss religious reformer who established a new church in Zurich. (264)

Desiderius Erasmus (1466?-1536): Dutch theologian, scholar, and humanist. Major work is *In Praise of Folly*. (265, 290)

Study Questions
What does the term "Renaissance" mean? Why is it a good term for the period between 1400 and 1600? What are the weaknesses of the term? (260)

What is Humanism? What role did it have in the Renaissance viewpoint? (260)

Describe capitalism and its effect on the Renaissance. (261)

What were the major scientific, technological, and geographic discoveries of the Renaissance? (262)

How did the political developments of the Renaissance affect the patronage of art? Who were the leading patrons? (263)

What were the leading centers of the Reformation? Who were the principal leaders? Why did they break away from the Catholic Church? (263-5)

What role did Humanism play in the Reformation? (265)

THE ARTS OF THE RENAISSANCE

Summary

Two-Dimensional Art: A break from the International Gothic style can be seen in Flemish paintings in the early 15th century. Seeking pictorial reality and rational perspective, Flemish artists composed subtle three-dimensional works that differ markedly from the two-dimensional qualities of Gothic art. The new style of Flemish painting was made possible by the development of oil paint, which allowed the artist to vary the surface texture and brilliance, to blend color areas, and to enhance the effect of chiaroscuro.

Three Northern painters are discussed. Jan van Eyck, the originator of the Flemish school, is one of the greatest painters of any age. His *Arnolfini Marriage* (Fig. 10.5) reveals the full range of colors from dark to light. The natural highlights and shadows help to create a sense of reality, but it is a reality that is carefully arranged by the artist. Rogier van der Weyden's *Descent from the Cross* (Fig. 10.6) also illustrates the rational three-dimensionality of the Flemish style. Most striking in this work is the individualization of human emotion. Albrecht Dürer's woodcuts and engravings reflect the emotional tension in northern Europe at the end of the 15th century (Fig. 10.7).

In Italy, the Renaissance found its earliest spark in Florence. Two trends in Florentine painting are described. The first was a lyrical and decorative trend, which is best seen in the works of Botticelli. *Spring* (Fig. 10.8) shows Botticelli's evident concern for undulating curved lines rather than for deep space. Each group of figures carries its own emotion, and we can see Botticelli's simple depiction of human figures, which almost appear like balloons floating in space. The second tradition can be observed in the works of Masaccio, who uses deep space, plasticity, and chiaroscuro to create dramatic contrasts. A new scientific mechanization of single and multiple vanishing-point perspective enhances the sense of realism, as seen in the fresco*The Tribute Money*. Illustrating a continuous narration, this work is remarkable for its realistic figures that seem to stand on the ground, its chiaroscuro, and its use of a single vanishing point at the head of Christ. Similar qualities contribute to the monumentalism of Mantegna's *St. James Led to Execution* (Fig. 10.10). Also noteworthy is Mantegna's accurate portrayal of architecture and costumes and the placement of the horizon line below the painting.

By 1500 the courts of Italian princes had become sources of patronage, and cultural activity centered around them. The arts of the early Renaissance seemed vulgar and naive, and a more aristocratic, elegant, and dignified art was demanded. Responding to these needs were a number of great artists, who created a style known as the High Renaissance. The emergence of Rome as a major patron, especially under Pope Leo X, helped make Rome the center of the High Renaissance until the Spanish invasion of 1527. During this time, a revival of ancient Roman sculptural and architectural style stimulated High Renaissance artists to emulate, not imitate, antique models. As a result, their art idealizes all forms and delights in composition.

One of the leading figures of the High Renaissance was Leonardo da Vinci. In contrast to the linear style of Botticelli (in which forms emerge through outlines, da Vinci blends light and shadow (called sfumato) and creates a fine haze in atmosphere that veils the forms. In the *Last Supper* (Fig. 10.12), the figure of Christ dominates the center, while figures are grouped geometrically around him. Despite the almost mathematical format, the painting captures the drama of Christ's betrayal. A pyramidal, compositional form is the basis for both *Virgin and Child with St. Anne* and *Madonna of the Rocks* (Figs. 10.11 and 10.13). Particularly striking in the latter is the delicate use of chiaroscuro and the meticulous attention to detail. *Mona Lisa* (Fig. 10.14) provided a model for future portraits in its inclusion of the full torso with the hands and arms fully pictured. With his technique of sfumato, Leonardo melts the contour of the face, creating ambiguity of character and mood. The blending of the figure with the landscape contributes further to the mysterious mood, as does the famous smile.

A second and perhaps the most dominant figure of the High Renaissance was Michelangelo Buonarroti. Unlike the skeptic Leonardo, Michelangelo was a man of faith whose fascination with the human form culminated in the monumental example of his genius, the Sistine Chapel ceiling (Figs. 10.15-17). The complex panoply brilliantly blends together nine scenes from Genesis. At the center, Michelangelo creates an unsurpassed image of the most profound of human mysteries--the moment of creation.

Raphael is the third major figure of the High Renaissance. The striking contrast between a strong central triangle within a circle can be seen in his *Alba Madonna* (Fig. 10.18). The figures are superbly modeled, and Raphael's treatment of flesh creates a tactile sensation of real flesh. His mastery of three-dimensional form and deep space is without equal. Many of these elements can also be seen in the *Deliverance of St. Peter* (Fig. 10.19), which is divided into three sections depicting three phases of the miracle.

In the turmoil of the last three-quarters of the 16th century, the most significant trend in painting was Mannerism. The term originates from the mannered or affected appearance of the subjects in the paintings. Coldly formal and inward looking, these works are characterized by distorted proportions and the abandonment of classical balance. An excellent example is Bronzino's *Portrait of a Young Man* (Fig. 10.20), in which the cold colors, stark background, the affected stare of the young man, and the disproportionate relationship between the head and the hands represent the essence of mannerism.

Sculpture: Patronage by the Medici family in Florence produced the most important sculptures of the early Renaissance. Although Greek models were obviously influential, Renaissance sculptors sought the ideal of the glorious individual, even if the image was not quite perfect. As in painting, a systematic and scientific perspective and deep space became important elements of sculptures. Also noteworthy is the return to free-standing, often nude, works not seen since antiquity.

Two major figures of the early Renaissance are described in the text. Ghiberti is best remembered for his *Gates of Paradise* (Figs. 10.23-10.24), in which each of the ten panels conveys a sense of space and perspective. Donatello produced the greatest masterpieces of the 15th century, *David* (Fig. 10.21), the first free-standing nude since classical times. His partial clothing along with his adolescent qualities give him a highly individualized character quite different from Classical sculpture. The *Equestrian Monument of Gattamelata* (Fig. 10.22), perhaps Donatello's most famous work, clearly shows the influence of Rome, but the focus and the triangular composition are Renaissance qualities.

The principal sculptor of the High Renaissance was Michelangelo. Inspired by the neo-platonist ideas of beauty, Michelangelo created the masterwork *David*. Towering 18', the work is both calm and relaxed and charged with energy. Particularly striking are the composition through thrust and counterthrust and the exaggerated detail of its physical features. Michelangelo insisted that measurement was subordinate to judgement, a point of view which is evident in both *David* and *Pietá* (Figs. 10.25-10.26). In the latter, the High Renaissance triangularity of composition contrasts with its late medieval subject matter. The skin and cloth are soft and sensuous. Emotion and energy are captured within the contrasting forces of form, line, and texture.

Few significant manneristic sculptures were produced. One exception is *Mercury* (Fig. 9.27) by Giovanni da Bologna. Mannerist tendencies can be seen in the affected pose, the linear emphasis, and the detachment from earth.

Literature: Early Renaissance literature, largely based on Classical models, was developed in a new way. As a result, it was ordered, integrated, and symmetrical. Boccaccio and Petrarch are the leading figures of the early Renaissance. Boccaccio's *Decameron*, containing 100 stories told by 10 people fleeing from the plague, is an early reflection of the Renaissance spirit. Petrarch, the "Father of Humanism," rejected medieval philosophy and even science. His works exhibit Classical traits, but instilled his works with a new quality of enthusiasm and an emergence of individuality.

In the High Renaissance, writers from other countries made significant literary contributions, including Erasmus' provocative *In Praise of Folly* and Thomas More's *Utopia*. Toward the end of the 16th century, Elizabethan England saw a flowering of Renaissance literature. Lyric poetry enjoyed wide popularity, and courtiers were expected to be able compose a sonnet or to turn a witty phrase. The model Renaissance courtier was Sir Philip Sidney, whose *Defense of Poesie* was a brilliant and forceful polemic. Also prominent at this time were Edmund Spenser and the great William Shakespeare.

Theatre: Prior to the end of the 16th century, theatre retained its medieval characteristics. Mystery plays were produced by the Confrérie de la Passion throughout the 15th century, which included a number of immense cycles. Two new French theatric forms were developed during this time, the sottie-- short theatric entertainment that were often bawdy burlesques of the Catholic Mass--and the farce--an independent, fully-developed play. The most famous French farce was *Maître Pierre Pathélin*. Italian playwrights wrote sentimental pastoral comedies that were witty and polished. Italian drama was primarily intended for the aristocracy.

Three important developments occurred in Italy: a new form of building that enclosed the dramatic action within a "picture frame" or proscenium; the use of painted scenery, such as those by Sebastiano Serlio, which gave a new perspective to stage designs; and the rise of the commedia dell'arte. The commedia is distinguished by improvisation upon a plot outline, stock characters which the audience could easily identify, mime and pantomime, and travelling troupes that brought these comedies all through Europe.

England saw a theatrical flowering in the late 16th century. Shakespeare's plays vary in their settings from England to Italy and from both English and classical history to the fantasy world. In these works, Shakespeare probed deeply into human emotion, and his presentation of life, love, and action were set in magnificent poetry that is unrivaled. Other English playwrights of this time include Christopher Marlowe, whose masterwork *Doctor Faustus* explores the complex character of Faust and employs a powerful poetic language, and Ben Johnson, who wielded a witty and sharp pen.

Music: Music enjoyed a great flowering in the Northern regions during the early and High Renaissance. Sometimes referred to as the Flemish school, the Franco-Flemish school, or the Burgundian school, there came from this area a remarkable line of outstanding composers who dominated European music for over a century. Guillaume Dufay, the first great composer of this school, established a Renaissance style based on true four-part harmony. Josquin des Prez, considered the "father of musicians," excelled in both secular and sacred music. Josquin perfected the High Renaissance style of four-equal voices and pervasive imitation.

In Germany, secular songs (Lieder) began to appear in polyphonic settings by the mid-15th century. The most prominent composer of Lieder was Heinrich Isaac, whose "Innsbruck, I Must Leave Thee" not only became a famous secular work, but also, with a change in text, a well-known chorale hymn. The most important contribution of the Lutheran Church to music was the chorale tune. Intended for performance by the congregation, chorales began to appear in polyphonic settings. The leading composer of such works was Johann Walter.

Dance: The foundations of theatre dance were laid in the courts of Northern Italy, a situation that is not unrelated to the flourish of visual arts in this area. Dancing activities of the Middle Ages became formalized into elaborate entertainments with spectacular displays. A vocabulary of steps and a choreography of patterns were developed, under the guiding hand of dancing masters. Guglielmo Ebreo of Pesaro wrote the first theoretical book describing dance. His observation that memory is the most critical element of dance tradition is still applicable today. Guglielmo attempted to bring dance out of the disrepute into which it had fallen into an acceptable aesthetic artform. In the 15th century, dance moved to the stage, where it was performed by only a skillful few. In the late Renaissance, France established the ballet de cour, which became the beginning of ballet.

Architecture: Early Renaissance architecture centered in Florence, where there were three significant stylistic departures from medieval architecture: 1) a revival of classical models, such as Roman arches, that could serve as a basis for geometric designs; 2) the application of decorative detail to the façade of the building; and 3) the obscuring of support systems on the outside of buildings. Two outstanding architects were dominant in the 15th century. Brunelleschi designed the remarkable dome on the Cathedral of Florence (Fig. 10.33). It is particularly impressive because the support system for this massive structure is completely hidden from view. Brunelleschi's Pazzi Chapel

(Fig. 10.34) illustrates the emphasis on surface decoration. Leon Battista Alberti applied classical forms to non-classical buildings. In the Palazzo Rucellai (Fig. 10.35), classical arches and columns appear almost academic. Alberti's treatise *Concerning Architecture* influenced Western building for centuries.

In the High Renaissance, architects developed a greater concern for space and volume. The more formal, monumental, and serious style is illustrated by Bramante's Tempietto (Fig. 10.36). Manneristic tendencies can be seen in the Lescot wing of the Louvre (Fig. 10.38), where superficial detail, unusual proportions, and the juxtaposition of curvilinear and rectilinear lines create a discomforting design. At this same time, Palladio developed another influential style. His designs for villas and places, such as the Villa Rotonda in Vicenza (Fig. 10.37), show strong classical influences. His works were used as models in America, as can be seen in Thomas Jefferson's Monticello (Fig. 12.31).

Synthesis: The synthesis of Renaissance ideas and reflections can be seen in the splendor of Vatican art and architecture. Pope Julius II commissioned Bramante to construct a new basilica to replace the Old St. Peter's (Fig. 8.15). With his death, a line of prominent architects worked at completing the project, including Raphael, Michelangelo, Della Porta, and Maderno. The colonnades of St. Peter's square are decorated by 140 statues of popes, bishops, and apostles by Bernini. Throughout the complex there are paintings and sculptures representing Renaissance, High Renaissance, Counter-Reformation, and Baroque styles. Included in the complex are Raphael's *Loggia* and Michelangelo's *Last Judgement*.

Important Terms

High Renaissance: term applied to the artistic style at the apex of the Renaissance in the early 16th century. (271-8, 283-5, 298-9)

Mannerism: term applied to the most significant trend following the High Renaissance. The name originates from the mannered or affected appearance of the subjects in the paintings. (279, 285)

Sfumato: ethereal quality achieved by blending light and shade found in the works of Leonardo. (272)

Terrabilita: term describing Michelangelo's supreme confidence. (284)

Confrérie de la Passion: an association of amateur actors in France who produced mystery plays throughout the 15th century. (290)

Sottie : a short satirical play popular in France. (290)

Farce: a theatrical form from France in which improbable characters and plots are used for humorous effect. (290)

Commedia dell'arte: type of Italian comedy characterized by improvisation and stock characters. (292)

Lieder: German word for songs. Secular songs became an important musical genre during the Renaissance. (295)

Chorale: German word for hymn. Chorale melodies were composed for the Lutheran Church to allow the congregation to sing along. (295)

Important Names

Jan van Eyck (c.1385-1441): Flemish painter who brought a new "reality" to painting. Works include *The Arnolfini Marriage*. (266-8)

Rogier van der Weyden (1400-64): Flemish painter. Works include *Descent from the Cross*. (268-9)

Albrecht Dürer (1471-1528): German painter and engraver considered to be the inventor of etching. (269)

Fra Angelico (1387-1455): Florentine painter. (2669

Fra Lippo Lippi (1406?-69): Florentine painter. (269)

Benozzo Gozzoli (1420-97): Florentine painter. (269)

Sandro Botticelli (1444?-1510): Florentine painter whose linear style creates forms that emerge through outline rather than through the use of light and shade. Works include *Spring*. (269-70)

Masaccio (1401-28): Florentine painter who uses deep space, plasticity and chiaroscuro to create dramatic contrasts. His masterwork is *TheTribute Money*. (270-1)

Andrea Mantegna (1431-1506): Italian painter and leader of the Paduan school. (271)

Titian (1477-1576): Italian painter of the High Renaissance. He is considered to be the leader of the Venetian school. (271)

Lodovico Ariosto (1474-1533): Italian poet. Major work is *Orlando Furioso*. (272)

Baldassare Castiglione (1478-1529): Italian writer. Major work is *The Courtier*. (272)

Pope Leo X (1475-1521): son of Lorenzo de' Medici and served as Pope between 1513-21. He was a major patron of the arts. (272)

Leonardo da Vinci (1452-1519): Florentine artist and engineer whose sfumato technique and his emphasis on design and a balanced composition make his paintings among the most admired in the history of Western art. Major works include *The Last Supper* and *Mona Lisa*. (272-5)

Michelangelo Buonarroti (1475-1564): Italian painter, sculptor, architect, and poet whose works reveal a deep understanding of humanity. Major works include the ceiling of the Sistine Chapel, *Pietá*, and *David*. (277-8, 283-5, 299, 303)

Raphael (1483-1520): Italian painter considered, along with Leonardo and Michelangelo, to be the third great figure of the High Renaissance. (278)

Bronzino (1503-72): Florentine mannerist painter. (279).

Donatello (1386-1466): Florentine sculptor who is the unsurpassed master of the early Renaissance. (281)

Lorenzo Ghiberti (1378-1455): Florentine sculptor and painter. His masterwork is the *Gates of Paradise*. (281-3)

Giovanni da Bologna (1529-1608): Italian sculptor of the mannerist period. (285)

Giovanni Boccaccio (1313-75): Italian poet whose *Decameron* is one of the earliest masterworks of the Renaissance spirit. (285-9)

Petrarch (1304-74): Italian poet considered to be the "Father of Humanism." (289)

Thomas More (1478-1535): English statesman and Humanist scholar. His major work is *Utopia*. (290)

Elizabeth I (1558-1603): Queen of England. During her reign, there was a great flourishing of the arts that included the works of Shakespeare.(290)

Sir Philip Sidney (1554-1586): English poet and essayist. (290)

Edmund Spenser (1552-99): English poet. Masterwork is *The Faerie Queen*. (290)

William Shakespeare (1564-1616): English poet and playwright. His understanding of human motivation and characters and his ability to probe deep into emotion result in the Universal Quality of his works and mark him as one of the great literary figures of all time. Major works include *Romeo and Juliet* and *Hamlet*. (290)

Sebastiano Serlio (1475-1554): Italian architect and painter. His theatre designs include painted scenery. (292)

Christopher Marlowe (1564-93): English playwright. His masterwork is *Doctor Faustus*. (293)

Ben Johnson (1573-1637): English playwright. (293-4)

Guillaume Dufay (1400-74): leading composer of the early Renaissance and the first great major representative of the Flemish school. (294)

Josquin des Prez (1450-1521): leading composer during the time of the High Renaissance. His stature is similar to that of Michelangelo. (294)

Heinrich Isaac (1450-1517): composer during the High Renaissance who is best remembered for his Lieder. (294)

Johann Walter (1496-1574): principal composer of polyphonic chorales in the Lutheran Church. (295)

Guglielmo Ebreo: 15th-century author of one of the first compilations of dance description and theory. (296)

Filippo Brunelleschi (1377-1446): foremost architect of the early Renaissance, perhaps best known for his dome on the Florence Cathedral. (296-8)

Leon Battista Alberti (c.1404-72): Florentine scholar, writer, and architect. Works include Palazzo Rucellai and the treatise *Concerning Architecture*. (298)

Bramante (1444-1514): Italian architect of the High Renaissance. Works include The Tempietto in Rome. (299)

Pierre Lescot (c.1510-78): French mannerist architect who designed the Lescot wing of the Louvre. (299-300)

Andrea Palladio (1518-80): Italian architect who designed villas and palaces. (288)

Giacomo della Porta (c.1537-1602): Italian architect who helped complete Michelangelo's design of St. Peter's. (303)

Carlo Fontana ((1634/38-1714): Italian architect who helped complete Michelangelo's design of St. Peter's. (303)

Carlo Maderna (1556-1629): leading Italian architect of the early 17th century. He built addition to Michelangelo's design of St. Peter's. (303)

Gianlorenzo Bernini (1598-1680): Italian sculptor who decorated St. Peter's Square with 140 statues. (303, 319-20)

Study Questions

What was revolutionary about Flemish painting? What new development contributed to the change in Flemish painting? (266)

Who are the leading painters of the North? How are their works similar? Different? (266-9)

What are the two principal trends of Florentine painting in the early Renaissance? Who are the main representatives of these trends? How do their works reflect qualities of the Renaissance? (269-71)

What was the most important center of the High Renaissance? How do works of the High Renaissance differ from those of the early Renaissance? (271-2)

What qualities do the paintings of Leonardo, Michelangelo, and Raphael have in common? What is distinctive about their works? (272-8)

What is Mannerism? What manneristic qualities are seen in Bronzino's *Portrait of a Young Man*? (279)

What is the leading center of sculpture in the early Renaissance? Who are the leading sculptors? Describe their major works. (281-3)

How are Michelangelo's individualistic attitudes and beliefs of neo-Platonic reality and beauty reflected in his sculptures? (283-5)

What does early Renaissance literature owe to Classic models? (285)

How does Boccaccio's *Decameron* reflect the Renaissance spirit? (285)

Who are the leading literary figures of the High Renaissance? Describe their principal works. (289-90)

Who are the leading literary figures in Elizabethan England? (290)

What were the principal types of dramatic productions in France? (290) Italy? (290-2)

What innovations did the Italians bring to the theatre building? (291-2)

What are the four principal characteristics of the commedia dell'arte? (292)

Who are the leading English playwrights of the Elizabethan era? What are the general characteristics of their works? (292-4)

How does Renaissance music differ from that of the late medieval period? In what region does Renaissance music first flourish? (294-5)

Who are the two leading composers of the Flemish school mentioned in your text? What are the qualities of their music? (294-5)

What contribution to music was made by the Lutheran Church? Describe this type of music. (295)

What is the relationship between theatrical dance and the visual arts in the early Italian Renaissance? (296)

What significant contribution to the history of dance was made by Guglielmo Ebreo? (296)

What significant developments in dance took place in the 15th century? (296)

Where did early Renaissance architecture center? What were the three significant stylistic departures from the Middle Ages? How are these changes evident in the works of Brunelleschi? (296-8)

Describe the use of classical detail on Alberti's Palzzo Rucellai. (298)

How does architecture of the High Renaissance differ from that of the early Renaissance? (298-9)

What are the principal architectural movements of the late Renaissance? Who are the main architects? What are their influences? (299-300)

Describe the contributions to the Vatican by Bramante, Michelangelo, Maderno, Bernini, and Raphael. (300-5)

PRACTICE TEST

1. The major movement of the Renaissance that focused on man and his accomplishments is called
   a. capitalism b. humanism c. pragmatism d. reformation

2. The term Renaissance
   a. is applied to the period between 1400-1600   c. means "rebirth"
   b. is applied to specific artistic developments   d. all of these

3. The Renaissance was inspired in part by revived interests in antiquity.
   a. true   b. false

4. Capitalism can eventually be satisfied with the amount of wealth it gains.
   a. True   b. False

5. In what year was the printing press invented?
   a. 1421 b. 1445 c. 1486 d. 1520

6. Who proposed the heliocentric theory of the universe?
   a. Copernicus b. Machiavelli c. Montainge d. Magellan

7. Who was the leading patron of arts in Florence?
   a. Luther b. Francis I c. Lorenzo de' Medici d. the Pope

8. Who did not lead an important reformation movement?
   a. Luther b. Henry VIII c. Zwingli d. Erasmus

9. When did Luther's *95 Theses* appear?
   a. 1517 b. 1524 c. 1542 d. 1588

10. How did Flemish painting differ from Gothic?
    a. pictorial reality   c. rational perspective
    b. sense of completeness   d. all of these

11. What was the major new development in Flemish painting?
    a. canvas   b. oil paint c. new brushes d. all of these

12. The use of light and shade in painting is called
    a. chiaroscuro b. terribilita c. tone d. brilliance

13. What does not characterize Van Eyck's *Arnolfini Marriage*?
  a. full range of colors   c. sense of a candid portrayal
  b. sense of 3-dimensionality   d. symbolism

14. Albrecht Dürer is particularly known for his
  a. sculptures b. paintings c. woodcuts d. frescoes

15. What was the leading center of painting and sculpture in the early
  Renaissance? a. Rome b. Bologna c. Venice d. Florence

16. What characterizes the works of Botticelli?
  a. detailed muscles   c. concern for deep space
  b. a lyric and decorative style d. all of these

17. What characterizes Masaccio's *The Tribute Money*?
  a. a continuous narration   c. figures stand on the ground
  b. a single vanishing point d. all of these

18. Who is not a leading painter of the High Renaissance?
  a. Leonardo b. Raphael c. Titian d. Bronzino

19. What is the principal center of the High Renaissance?
  a. Florence b. Rome c. Venice d. Bologna

20. High Renaissance artists depicted ideal figures, not individuals.
  a. True   b. False

21. What characterizes Leonardo's *Last Supper*?
  a. architecture is the principal focus
  b. geometric proportions are abandoned for dramatic effect
  c. Christ dominates the center of the painting
  d. all of these

22. Leonardo's *Madonna of the Rocks* and *Virgin and Child with St. Anne*
  share what in common?
  a. similar subject b. triangular base c. background d. all of these

23. What characterizes Leonardo's *Mona Lisa*?
  a. detailed background   c. typical bust-like portrait
  b. sfumato   d. all of these

24. What subjects are seen in Michelangelo's Sistine Chapel ceiling?
    a. nudes b. prophets c. sages from antiquity d. all of these

25. According to your text, Raphael was unmatched in his
    a. mastery of 3-dimensional form and space
    b. use of geometric triangle
    c. treatment of flesh
    d. use of chiaroscuro

26. What does not characterize manneristic painting?
    a. distorted proportions   c. classical balance
    b. cold, formal qualities   d. stark backgrounds

27. How do early Renaissance sculptures differ from Classical works?
    a. they are free standing   c. they portray nudes
    b. they show imperfect individuals   d. all of these

28. What characterizes Donatello's *David*?
    a. it shows an adolescent character   c. it is fully nude
    b. it rejects the contrapposto stance   d. all of these

29. Michelangelo's *David* rejects neo-Platonic views of reality and beauty.
    a. true b. false

30. What is the only worked signed by Michelangelo?
    a. Sistine Chapel, ceiling b. *David* c. *Pietá*

31. Matching

        Boccaccio   a. *Utopia*

        Shakespeare   b. Father of Humanism

        Petrarch   c. *Decameron*

        Thomas More   d. *In Praise of Folly*

        Erasmus   e. English sonnet
    ---

32. Who was not active during the Elizabethan age?
   a. Shakespeare b. Sidney c. More d. Spenser

33. What kind of plays were produced by the Confrérie de la Passion?
   a. sottie   b. farces   c. mysteries   d. tragedies

34. What is the most famous farce from the 15th century?
   a. *Les Actes des Apôtres*   c. *Jeu du Prince des Sots*
   b. *Maître Pierre Pathélin*   d. *Doctor Faustus*

35. What does not characterize the commedia dell'arte?
   a. strict adherence to a script   c. use of mime
   b. stock characters   d. traveling troupes

36. What characterizes the plays of Shakespeare?
   a. all plots set in England   c. probing insights
   b. use of ordinary, everyday language   d. all of these

37. What characterizes Marlowe's *Doctor Faustus*?
   a. classical allusions   c. complex characterization
   b. powerful poetic language   d. all of these

38. What was the main music center in the early Renaissance?
   a. Florence   b. Rome   c. Burgundy   d. Paris

39. Who was the first important composer of the Renaissance?
   a. Josquin b. Isaac c. Walther d. Dufay

40. What characterizes the new sound of Renaissance music?
   a. true 4-part harmony   c. consistent imitation
   b. harmonic direction   d. all of these

41. Who is the leading composer of Lieder?
   a. Josquin b. Isaac c. Walther d. Dufay

42. The chorale was used in services by which Church?
   a. Catholic b. Lutheran c. Calvin d. Anglican

43. Where were the foundations of theatre dance laid?
   a. Burgundy b. Northern Italy c. France d. England

44. What was not a change in early Renaissance architecture?
   a. revival of classical models
   b. avoidance of monumental designs
   c. decoration on the façade
   d. hidden external supports

45. Who designed the dome on the Florence Cathedral?
   a. Brunelleschi b. Alberti c. Lescaut d. Bramante

46. What does not apply to Alberti's Palazzo Rucellai?
   a. uses columns
   b. order of columns is consistent
   c. uses arches
   d. design is academic

47. High Renaissance architects show a greater concern for
   a. classical details
   b. space and volume
   c. mathematical symmetry
   d. all of these

48. What does not characterize the Lescot wing of the Louvre?
   a. mathematical proportions
   b. superficial detail
   c. flattened dome
   d. unusual proportions

49. Palladio's Villa Rotonda represents a clear break from classical models.
   a. true b. false

50. Which architect did not work on the Vatican?
   a. Bramante b. Lescot c. Michelangelo d. Maderno

ANSWERS

1. b 2. d 3. a 4. b 5. b 6. a 7. c 8. d 9. a 10. d 11. b 12. a
13. c 14. c 15. d 16. b 17. d 18. d 19. b 20. a 21. c 22. d 23. b 24. d
25. c 26. c 27. b 28. a 29. b 30. c 31. cebad 32. c 33. c 34. b 35. a
36. c 37. d 38. c 39. d 40. d 41. b 42. b 43. b 44. b 45. a 46. b 47. b
48. a 49. b 50. b

CHAPTER 11: THE BAROQUE AGE

CONTEXTS AND CONCEPTS

Summary
The scientific, philosophical, and religious uncertainties of the late 16th century created a nervousness and unease in many leading minds. As the new century dawned artists translated these uncertainties into a new style called baroque, which was the artistic reflection of the new epoch. With its direct appeal to emotions, the opulence, intricacy, and ornateness of baroque art made a grandiose statement which signaled man's final departure from the security, harmony, and clarity of the old world.

The challenge to the Catholic Church posed by the Reformation was answered by the Council of Trent (1543-63). Examining conditions within the Church, the Council provided the main thrust for the Counter Reformation. One decision was to attract more worshippers through art. This change in attitude helped to inspire the new emotional art of the baroque.

Art was also influenced by social and scientific developments. The middle class continued to gather more wealth and power, and they began to become important and enthusiastic patrons of the arts. Following Copernicus, a number of outstanding scientists, mathematicians, and philosophers brought about an understanding of the universe and humanity's place within it. The underlying systematic rationalism was mirrored in the arts by the baroque style, which also sought rational order. One of the most fascinating figures of this period was Francis Bacon, whose talents ranged from scientific to poetic. Bacon established inductive reasoning--that is basing conclusions on verification through experiment and observation--as the basis for scientific inquiry. He also felt that the task of poetry was to conquer nature by freeing the mind.

Monarchies continued to wield absolute power during this epoch. England experienced some turmoil when Cromwell toppled the monarchy, but the Restoration quickly returned the court to elegance and opulence. In France, the Sun King, Louis XIV, was a strong supporter of the arts. But this period is also marked by struggles over secular control of religious events. In both Catholic and Protestant areas, dissidents were often forced underground. The bitter struggle between Catholics and the Huguenots in France also proved to be a struggle over secular or religious control. Particularly powerful in France were two religious figures who were court advisors, Cardinals Richelieu and Mazarin.

Important Terms

Counter-Reformation: a reform movement within the Catholic Church that grew in response to the Reformation. (308)

Council of Trent: an assembly of theologians and officials of the Catholic Church that met from 1545-63 in order to stabilize the Church and keep the Reformation from spreading. (308)

Systematic rationalism: the search for a logical and systematic order in the universe, which was both intricate, moving, and changing and, at the same time, subject to natural and relatively predictable laws. (308)

Absolutism: a type of state where all power resides in the monarch. The absolute monarch received his mandate from God. (309-10)

Jesuits: a Catholic order founded by Saint Ignatius Loyola in 1534 known for their zealous attitude towards Protestants. (310)

Huguenots: French Protestants in the 16th and 17th centuries. They were involved in a bitter conflict with French Catholics. (310)

Important Names

Giordano Bruno (1548-1600): Italian philosopher who speculated upon a universe of infinite size with numerous solar systems and galaxies. (308)

Johannes Kepler (1571-1630): German astronomer and mathematician who postulated the laws of planetary motion. (308)

Galileo Galilei (1564-1642): Italian scientist and philosopher who invented the telescope and anticipated the laws of motion. (308)

René Descartes (1596-1650): French philosopher and mathematician. (308)

Isaac Newton (1642-1727): English mathematician, scientist, and philosopher who discovered the laws of gravity. (308)

Francis Bacon (1561-1642): English scientist, philosopher and writer who established inductive reasoning as the basis for scientific inquiry. (308-9)

Oliver Cromwell (1599-1658): political leader who ran England after toppling the monarchy in 1653. (309)

Louis XIV (1643-1715): king of France known as the Sun King. He was a great patron of the arts. (309-10)

Duc de Richelieu (1585-1642): French Cardinal and statesman. He was the chief advisor to Louis XIII and virtual dictator of France between 1624-42. (310)

Cardinal Mazarin (1602-61): chief advisor to Louis XIV who tightened the grip of royal absolutism on France. (310)

Study Questions

What is the Counter-Reformation? What were their goals? How did it affect the arts? (308)

What affect did the rising middle class have on the arts? systematic rationalism? absolutism? (308-10)

THE ARTS OF THE BAROQUE AGE

Summary

Two-Dimensional Art: The new age that emerged in the 17th century produced a new artistic style, the baroque. This new style was characterized by an appeal to the emotions, opulent ornamentation, systematized and rational composition, emphasis on color and grandeur, and dramatic use of light and shade. Above all, baroque art emphasized feeling rather than form, emotion rather than intellect.

The text defines three types of baroque art: 1) art that pursued the objectives of the Catholic Church--Counter-Reformation baroque; 2) art that reflected the purposes of the aristocracy--aristocratic baroque; and 3) art that reflected the goals of the middle class--bourgeois baroque. Rome was naturally the leading center of the Counter-Reformation baroque, and its foremost painter was Caravaggio. The two works presented in the text (Figs. 11.5-11.6) well-illustrate the dramatic use of light, the realism, and the sacred intent that characterize Counter-Reformation baroque painting. Another example of this style is provided by the Spanish painter El Greco. *St. Jerome* (Fig. 11.7) reveals the strong, inward-looking subjectivity and mysticism of the time. Emotional disturbance is accentuated, as the viewer is allowed to see beyond the surface reality to a special truth within.

Two outstanding painters exemplify the aristocratic baroque: Ruben and Poussin. *The Assumption of the Virgin* (Fig. 11.8) typifies Ruben's style, with its corpulent Cupids, women with soft flesh, warm colors, naturalism, and dramatic swirling composition. Although portraying a religious subject, the work inspires feelings of richness, glamour, and worldly emotion. Poussin often painted scenes from the literature of antiquity, as can be seen in *The Burial of Phocion* (Fig. 11.9) taken from a story by Plutarch. The overpowering landscape, intricate detail, and the strong highlight against shadow are typical of Poussin and of the baroque in general.

In contrast to Rubens, Rembrandt was a middle-class artist who believed that the value of a painting was represented not only in itself but also in its value on the open market. In the two works presented in the text (Figs. 11.10-11.11), Rembrandt's genius for portraying human emotion is vividly depicted. A second painter of the bourgeois baroque, Jacob van Ruisdael, achieved a markedly different effect. Ruisdael focused his works on landscapes. *The Cemetery* (Fig. 11.12) provides an emotional experience full of rich detail, atmosphere, light and shade, and grandiose scale, as humankind is totally subordinate to the universe.

Sculpture: The 17th century was an excellent time for sculpture. Baroque ideas of appealing to emotions, reaching beyond physical confines, and inviting participation by the viewer rather than neutral observation were well-suited to three-dimensional art. These elements are clearly evident in the three works shown in your text (Figs. 11.13-11.5) by Bernini. His ability to capture dramatic action in motion and to combine a wealth of details into an overall composition justifies his reputation as the finest sculptor of the baroque. The realistic portrayal of emotions can also be seen in the works of the French sculptors (Figs. 11.16-11.17).

Literature: Following the Elizabethan age, English poetry turned away from topics of love to an anxious and often anguished inner questioning. John Donne was the leading figure of the Metaphysical poets, whose works are marked by ambiguity and imagery. Another major figure in 17th-century England was John Milton. His masterpiece, *Paradise Lost* can be considered the literary equivalent of the baroque with its rich language and powerful themes.

Satire characterizes the works of a number of English writers at the end of the 17th century, including the poets John Dryden and Alexander Pope, and the Irish satirist Jonathan Swift. In the major works of the latter, *Gulliver's Travels* and *A Modest Proposal*, a biting and bitter edge is evident.

One of the most important events of the period is the development of the novel. *Don Quixote* by Cervantes is the first major work exploiting the potential of a novel. Daniel Defoe established the future direction of the novel with works such as *Robinson Crusoe* and *Moll Flanders*.

Theatre: The baroque equivalent in English theatre was the court masque. Characterized by spectacles, complex scenes, and modest literary merit, the masques provided extravagant entertainment for the nobility during the reign of Charles I. Two important theatrical developments grew out of these productions, a form of staging called forestage-façade, in which actors played on an area in front of the drops, and the elaborate stage designs, for which we recognize Inigo Jones as the leading English designer of the time. After the overthrow of Charles I, theatric entertainments were banned, but the Restoration saw the revival of theatre and the creation of a new type of comedy of manners called English Restoration Comedy.

During the 17th century, France developed a new theatric tradition called French neo-classicism. This movement was prepared by several events: the reign of Catherine de' Medici as queen of France in the late 16th century, the banning of sacred drama, and the rediscovery of ancient Greek playwrights. Rules of drama, which were incorrectly derived from classical drama, insisted that action occur in a single location and within a timespan of 24 hours. The leading French writers of tragedies were Corneille, whose greatest work was *Le Cid*, and Jean Racine. A comic counterpart to these achievements was provided by Molière. His fast-paced action, crisp language, and penetrating human psychology have earned him a prominent place in the history of theatre.

Music: The Counter-Reformation fostered a significant resurgence of music composed for the Catholic Church. One leading composer, Palestrina, returned to a simpler polyphony and is credited for eliminating doubts about music held by the Council of Trent.

The leading secular form of music in the 16th century was the madrigal. Originating in Italy, the madrigal was usually written for four or five solo voices, employed imitative sections, and closely followed the meaning of the text. The madrigal was later adapted in England, where Morley was a leading composer. Similar in style to the madrigal, the chanson flourished in France during the late Renaissance. Jannequin was particularly known for his works that imitated actual sounds such as bird calls. A move towards the baroque style can be seen in the madrigals of Monteverdi, which are more dramatic than earlier works.

In music, the term baroque covers the period 1600-1750. The general characteristics include ornamentation, an appeal to emotion, and a refined system of harmonic progression around tonal centers. The later system was basic to art music of Western civilization up to the 20th century.

One of the most important developments of the baroque was opera. A complex musical drama, opera began as an elaboration of late 16th-century madrigals. The earliest surviving operas were composed by Peri and Caccini. Both operas were entitled *Eurydice*, and the texts for both were written by Rinuccini. The music in opera usually separates into recitative, a type of sung dialogue over slowly changing chords, and arias, a more elaborate and formal solo section. Duets, ensembles, choruses, and dances can also be included. Monteverdi composed the first masterpiece in operatic repertory, *Orfeo*. Opera later spread to France under the patronage of Louis XIV, England during the period of the Commonwealth, and Germany.

Secular song produced the second important development in vocal music. In the early baroque, a type of song developed for solo voice called monody, in which the music was subservient to the text. Later, under the name cantata, it became sectional and began to reflect operatic qualities. The leading composer of secular cantatas was Alessandro Scarlatti. The form was adopted by sacred composers, such as Bach and Buxtehude. Bach was required to compose one sacred cantata a week for several years.

The third new vocal form was a sacred drama called oratorio. Like opera, it contained recitative, arias, and a poetic text. But unlike its secular counterpart, there was no staging or costumes; it was designed for concert performance. The greatest master of the oratorio was Handel. Set in English, his works feature wonderful choral sections in addition to arias and recitative. Handel's most popular work is the oratorio *Messiah.*

Instrumental music began to assume a new importance during the baroque. Significant technical achievements were attained by individual instruments. Particularly noteworthy during the baroque was a series of great violin makers, such as Antonio Stradivari, whose instruments have never been equalled. Also important was the development of a tuning system in which every note of the chromatic scale was equidistant from the one preceding or following. J.S. Bach's two sets of preludes and fugues in all 24 major and minor keys entitled *The Well-Tempered Clavier* illustrated the advantages of the new system. The level of virtuosity achieved by keyboard players (organ and harpsichord) is also evident in the music of Bach. His fugal works for the organ, such as the Fugue in G Minor, are masterpieces, as are his free improvisatory-like compositions such as toccatas and fantasies.

Two other important compositional forms developed in instrumental music. The concerto featured the contrast between a soloist or several soloists and an orchestra. The baroque master of the concerto was Vivaldi, who wrote over 450 concertos. Most of these works are for solo violin and string orchestra, such as his popular programmatic concertos *The Seasons.* Typical for the solo concerto is a three-movement format and a first-movement structure called ritornello, in which an opening melody by the orchestra is heard, in whole or in part, four or five times. During the baroque a special type of concerto appeared called the concerto grosso, which featured two or more soloists. The second new instrumental form was the sonata, a work for a small ensemble of instruments. Essential to the sonata was the basso continuo, a type of accompaniment for a melody bass instrument (like a cello) and an instrument capable of playing chords (like a harpsichord). Especially popular were sonatas with two high melody instruments called trio sonatas. Corelli established a four-movement (slow, fast, slow, fast) format for the sonata.

Dance: Court entertainments of the early and mid-16th century often took the form of dinner ballets called entrées. Here, the dancers could depict mythological characters, recreate battles of the Crusades, or present tales, such as Robin Hood. Theatre dancing at this time was closely connected with social dancing. Gradually, courtly dancing became more professional, and skilled professionals began to perform on a raised platform.

The move towards formal ballet began under the aegis of Catherine de' Medici who became queen of France and ruled for over 30 years. During this time two works were produced that could be considered the first ballets: *Le Ballet de Polonais*, with music by Lasso and a text by Ronsard, and *Ballet Comique de la Reine*, an extravaganza mixing biblical and mythological sources. With only minor dance activity in England, France was established as the leading center of ballet for the next centuries.

During the 17th century, ballet productions in France continued to become more elaborate and more professional, culminating with the reign of Louis XIV, an avid dancer. Important to the blossoming of ballet at this time were Lully, a dancer and outstanding composer, and Beauchamps, who is credited with inventing the five basic dance positions. Ballet productions were characterized by plots from classical mythology, simple noble dancing, and symmetrical gestures. The establishment of the Académie Royale de Danse led to the establishment of rules for positions and movements, the use of professional women dancers, and the placement of dancers on a stage with the audience only on one side.

Architecture: Baroque architecture, like other baroque arts, emphasized intricacy, opulence, and emotion, but it did so on a much grander and dramatic scale. Three outstanding architects representing three different regions are discussed in this section. Giacomo della Porta is the leading Italian architect of this period. His Il Gesù (Fig. 11.26-11.27), which was influential on later church architecture especially in Latin America, can be seen as a transition to the baroque with its elimination of side aisles and its bold double pilasters. In Germany, Balthasar Neumann combined baroque qualities with those of the lighter and more delicate rococo, as seen in Figs. 11.28-11.29. Christopher Wren, England's most notable architect, spent 40 years restoring St. Paul's Cathedral (Figs. 11.31-11.3). This magnificent structure, with its ingenious construction of a superstructure dome, was very influential on architects both in Europe and in the United States. On a smaller scale, the façade of Wren's Hampton Court Palace (Fig. 11.30) shows a similar sophistication and complexity of design.

Synthesis: The Palace of Versailles perhaps best represents the grandeur of the baroque style. Originally a modest hunting lodge of Louis XIII, Versailles evolved over many years and with several architects into a magnificent palace for Louis XIV. Precision and elegance can be seen on both the outside (completed by Jules Hardouin-Mansart) and inside (decorations and furnishings designed by Le Brun). The splendor of this achievement is illustrated in Figs. 11.34-11.40.

Important Terms

Baroque: term used to describe the arts of the 17th and early 18th century. General characteristics include an appeal to emotions and opulent ornamentation. (311)

Counter-Reformation baroque: baroque art that pursued the objectives and visions of the Roman Catholic Church after the Council of Trent. (312, 319-20)

Aristocratic baroque: baroque art that reflected the visions and purposes of the aristocracy. (313-6, 321)

Bourgeois baroque: baroque art that reflected the visions and objectives of the wealthy middle class. (316-9)

Metaphysical poets: 17th-century English poets whose works are characterized by imagery and conceits. (322)

Masque: dramatic entertainment in English court involving spectacle, music, and some dancing. (325)

Forestage-façade: a type of staging in which the actors play on a protruding area in front of drops and wings. (325)

English Restoration Comedy: a sophisticated comedy of manners appearing in England during the late 17th century. (325)

French neo-classicism: a term denoting the revival of drama in 17th-century France inspired by the discovery of Greek drama. (325-6)

Madrigal: secular musical work for a small ensemble of voices. It first appeared in Italy and later in England. It bears no relationship with the medieval madrigal. (327)

Word painting: in music, the depiction of a single word through the sound of the music. (327)

Chanson: French word meaning song. Late Renaissance chansons were similar in style to the Italian madrigal. (327)

Opera: a drama that centers around musical elements. It first appeared in Italy in the early 17th century. (327-8)

Recitative: sung dialogue in opera. (328)

Aria: fully-developed vocal solos in opera. (328)

Monody: term given to the early baroque solo secular songs. (328)

Cantata: a later term for solo song with contrasting sections. (328-9)

Arioso: vocal section in opera that is less organized than an aria, but more rhythmically active than recitative. (329)

Oratorio: a sacred drama that is similar to opera, except that it is not staged. (329)

Equal temperament: new way of tuning developed in the baroque in which every note is equidistant from all other notes. (330)

Fugue: a musical form based on continuous imitation. Bach is a great master. (330)

Concerto: work for a soloist and orchestra in several movements. (330-1)

Concerto grosso: a type of concerto common in the baroque that features more than one soloist. (330)

Ritornello: a musical structure based on a given melody and its recurrence throughout a composition. (331)

Sonata: in the baroque, a work for one or more solo instruments accompanied by the basso continuo. (331)

Trio sonata: a sonata written specifically for two melody instruments accompanied by the basso continuo. (331)

Basso continuo: a type of accompaniment involving a bass melody instrument and an instrument capable of improvising harmonies. (331)

Entrées: danced interludes between courses of a meal. (331)

Le Ballet de Polonais: earliest known dance production in the court of Catherine de' Medici (1572). It marks the beginning of the formal Western ballet tradition. (332)

Ballet Comique de la Reine: extravaganza mixing biblical and mythological sources unified by a single dramatic theme. It has been called the first "true" ballet. (332)

Académie Royale de Danse: founded in 1661 to re-establish the art of dance. The academy set rules for positions and movements and, by the early 18th century, had established ballet as a formal discipline. (333)

Important Names

Michelangelo Caravaggio (1569-1609): Italian painter considered to be the most significant of the Roman baroque painters. (313)

El Greco (1541-1614): Spanish painter born in Crete. Original name was Domenikos Theotokopoulos. He exemplified the inward looking subjectivity and Counter-Reformation mysticism of his time. (313)

Peter Paul Rubens (1577-1640): Flemish painter known for his vast, overwhelming canvases and fleshy female nudes. (313-4)

Nicolas Poussin (1594-1665): French painter of landscapes and scenes from the literature of antiquity. (316)

Rembrandt van Rijn (1606-69): Dutch painter who is considered to be an artist of the new wealthy middle-class. He is known for his depictions of human emotions and characters. (316-8)

Jacob van Ruisdael (1628/9-82): Dutch painter of landscapes. (319)

Gianlorenzo Bernini (1598-1680): foremost sculptor of the baroque whose works exude dynamic power, action, and emotion. (303, 319-20)

Pierre Puget (1620-94): leading French sculptor of the baroque. (320)

John Donne (1573-1631): English poet who was a leading figure of the Metaphysical poets. His mature works explore the meaning of an intelligent man's relationship with his soul and with his God. (322)

George Herbert (1593-1633): English poet of the Metaphysical school. (322)

Andrew Marvell (1621-78): English poet of the Metaphysical school. (322)

John Milton (1608-74): English poet. His masterpiece is *Paradise Lost*. (322)

John Dryden (1631-1700): English poet and critic. (322)

Alexander Pope (1688-1744): English poet. His major works include *Rape of the Lock* and *An Essay on Man*. (322)

Jonathan Swift (1667-1745): Irish satirist. Major works include *Gulliver's Travels* and *A Modest Proposal*. (322-5)

Miguel Cervantes (1547-1616): Spanish writer who first explored the potential of a novel in *Don Quixote*. (325)

Daniel Defoe (1660-1731): English novelist who established the novel tradition with works like *Robinson Crusoe* and *Moll Flanders*. (325)

Inigo Jones (1573-1652): English architect and the most influential stage designer of his time. (325)

Pierre Corneille (1606-84): French playwright. His masterpiece is *Le Cid*. (326)

Jean Racine (1639-99): French playwright who was strongly influenced by Corneille. His major works include *Phèdre*. (326)

Molière (1622-73): French playwright, actor, and manager known for his fast-paced comedies. Major works include *Tartuffe* and *Le Misanthrope*. (326)

Giovanni Palestrina (1524-94): one of the leading composers for the Catholic Church during the Counter-Reformation. (327)

Thomas Morley (1557-1603): English composer of madrigals. (327)

Clement Jannequin (c.1485-1558): French composer best known for his programmatic chanson. (327)

Claudio Monteverdi (1567-1643): Italian composer who is the leading musical figure of the early baroque. Best known for his madrigals and his opera *Orfeo*. (327, 328)

Jacopo Peri (1561-1633): Italian singer credited with composing one of the first surviving operas, *Eurydice*. (328)

Giulio Caccini (c.1546-1618): Italian singer credited with composing one of the first surviving operas, *Eurydice*. He is also remembered for his published monodies. (328)

Ottavio Rinuccini (1562-1621): librettist for the earliest operas, including the two settings of *Eurydice* for Peri and Caccini. (328)

Alessandro Scarlatti (1660-1725): leading Italian composer of opera and cantatas in the late Baroque. (329)

Johann Sebastian Bach (1685-1750): the leading composer of the late baroque. Major works include *The Well-Tempered Clavier*, *The Art of the Fugue*, and numerous sacred cantatas and organ works. (329, 330).

Dietrich Buxtehude (c.1637-1707): important German composer of cantatas and organ works. (329)

George Frederick Handel (1685-1759): major German composer who spent much of his career in London. Best known for his operas and oratorios, including his masterpiece *Messiah*. (329)

Antonio Vivaldi (1669-1741): Italian composer best remembered for his violin concertos. Major works include *The Seasons*. (330-1)

Archangelo Corelli (1653-1713): Italian composer known for his trio sonatas, solo sonatas, and concerto grossos. (331)

Antonio Stradivari (1644-1737): Italian maker of violins, which are considered to be the greatest of all time. (331)

Catherine de' Medici (1519-89): Queen of France who played an important role in bringing ballet into the court. (331-32)

Orlando di Lasso (1532?-94): Belgian composer considered to be one of the major figures of the 17th century. He wrote the music for *Le Ballet de Polonais*. (332)

Pierre Ronsard (1524-85): French poet who wrote the text for *Le Ballet de Polonais*. (332)

Balthasar de Beaujoyeulx (d. 1587): important figure in the history of ballet. He produced the two earliest ballet performances. (332)

Pierre Beauchamps (1636-1705): French dancemaster who is credited with inventing the five basic dance positions. (333)

Jean-Baptiste Lully (1632-87): Italian composer who played a crucial role in the development of French ballet and opera in the 17th century. (333)

Giacomo della Porta (1540-1602): leading Italian architect of the early baroque. Major works include Il Gesù. (333)

Balthasar Neumann (1687-1753): leading German architect of the baroque period. (333-6)

Christopher Wren (1632-1723): leading English architect of the baroque. His masterwork is St. Paul's Cathedral. (336-8)

Jules Hardouin-Mansart (1646-1708): French architect who completed the design of Versailles. (340-3)

Le Brun (1619-90): French painter and designer. He supervised the paintings, sculpture, furnishings, and general decoration for Versailles. (340-3)

Study Questions

What are the general qualities of the baroque style? What distinguishes the Counter-Reformation, aristocratic, and bourgeois baroque styles? (311-9)

Who are the two leading painters of the Counter-Reformation baroque? How do their works differ from those of the High Renaissance? (313)

Compare the works of Rubens and Rembrandt. How do both reflect the trends of the baroque. (313-4, 3316-8)

How do the landscapes of Poussin and van Ruisdael differ? (316, 319)

Compare Bernini's *David* with those of Donatello and Michelangelo. How do each reflect the tendencies of their time period and of their creator? (281, 284, 319-20)

Identify the baroque qualities of the three works by Bernini shown in your text. (319-20)

What role does emotion play in the works by Puget? (321)

Who were the leading Metaphysical Poets? What characterizes their works? (322)

Describe John Milton's masterpiece *Paradise Lost*. (322)

Who were the leading satirists at the end of the 17th century? Describe their works. (322-5)

What role did the baroque play in the development of the novel? Who were the leading novelists and what were their major works? (325)

What is a masque? What was significant about this theatric entertainment? (325)

Define French neo-classicism. What preceded this movement? Who are the leading playwrights? What characterizes their works?   (325-6)

What effect did the Counter-Reformation have on music? Who was the leading composer of Catholic music during this time? (327)

Describe the principal type of secular music in 16th-century Italy. Where did this type of work spread? Who were the principal composers? (327)

How does baroque music reflect the general artistic trends of the period? (327)

What were the three new types of vocal music to emerge during the baroque? Describe each and list the significant composers and works. (327-9)

Describe the variety keyboard works by J.S. Bach mentioned in your text. (330)

What is a concerto? concerto grosso? sonata? Who are the leading composers? How are the works structured? (330-1)

Describe dance entertainments in the early and mid 16th century? (331-2)

Where did formal ballet come of age? Who were the leading figures behind this development? What were the first major productions? (331-3)

Describe the flourishing of ballet in 17th-century France. Who were the leading figures of court of Louis XIV? What role did the Académie Royale de Danse play in the laying of foundations of modern ballet? (333)

Who is the leading architect of Italy in the early baroque? What was his major work? Describe its characteristics. (333)

Describe the construction of St. Paul's Cathedral. How was the dome constructed? What other work by Christopher Wren was discussed? Describe the design of its façade. (338)

What was the original purpose of Versailles? Who were the major artists and architects who worked on the palace? Describe the outside and inside. (327, 340-3)

PRACTICE TEST

1. The Council of Trent decided that
   a. the Church was perfect and needed no changes
   b. polyphonic music should be banned
   c. arts would attract worshippers
   d. all of these

2. Francis Bacon
   a. established inductive reasoning as the basis for science
   b. argued that poetry freed the spirit
   c. is said to have written the plays of Shakespeare
   d. all of these

3. The period in English history after the fall of Cromwell is
   a. Counter-Reformation b. Absolutism c. The Restoration

4. Who was the advisor to Louis XIII who ruled France like a dictator?
   a. Cardinal Richelieu b. Cardinal Mazarin c. Francis Bacon

5. What does not characterize baroque art?
   a. dramatic use of light   c. appeal to emotions
   b. realism replaced by beauty   d. systematized compositions

6. Who was the leading Roman painter in the early baroque?
   a. Caravaggio b. El Greco c. Rubens d. Rembrandt

7. What characterizes the paintings of Caravaggio?
   a. dramatic use of light   c. lack of realism
   b. idealized figures   d. all of these

8. El Greco's *St. Jerome* is characterized by
   a. vivid contrasts of color   c. emotional disturbance
   b. outward-looking objectivity   d. all of these

9. What characterizes the paintings of Rubens?
   a. fleshy female nudes   c. overwhelming canvases
   b. contrasts of light and dark d. all of these

10. What characterizes the paintings of Poussin?
   a. emphasis on man b. religious themes   c. intricate detail d. all of these

11. Who considered himself to be a capitalist artist?
   a. Rubens   b. Caravaggio c. Rembrandt d. van Ruisdael

12. According to your text, Rembrandt was a genius at
   a. depicting human emotions   c. depicting realistic figures
   b. painting landscapes   d. realistic detail

13. What does not characterize the paintings of van Ruisdael?
   a. emphasis on landscapes   c. absence of humans
   b. vision of simple nature   d. emotional experiences

14. What does not characterize baroque sculpture?
   a. energy   c. emphasized observation, not participation
   b. emotions   d. form extended beyond the physical limits

15. Who was the leading sculptor of the baroque?
   a. Bernini b. Michelangelo c. Puget d. Donatello

16. What characterizes the works of Bernini?
   a. detail is elegant and ornamental   c. captures motion
   b. drama and emotion   d. all of these

17. Matching

       John Donne   a. *Gulliver's Travels*

       Alexander Pope b. *Absolom and Architophe*

       John Milton   c. *Rape of the Lock*

       Jonathan Swift   d. *Paradise Lost*

       John Dryden   e. Leading Metaphysical poet
   ---

18. *A Modest Proposal* suggests that the solution to the "Irish problem was to
   a. eat the babies of the poor   c. invade the territory
   b. ban the Catholic Church   d. all of these

167

19. Who wrote *Don Quixote*?
   a. Defoe b. Pope c. Cervantes d. Flanders

20. Who established the future direction of the novel?
   a. Defoe b. Pope c. Cervantes d. Flanders

21. What is forestage-façade?
   a. the front of a stage
   b. staging with actors in front of drops
   c. a pretend stage
   d. front of theatre

22. The masque was prominent in what country?
   a. France b. Spain c. Italy d. England

23. Who was the most influential set designer in 17th-century England?
   a. Palladio   b. Inigo Jones   c. Christopher Wren   d. della Porta

24. What does not characterize the masque?
   a. entertainment for nobility   c. extravagance
   b. strong literary merit   d. complex designs

25. Who was not a leading playwright in 17th-century France?
   a. Corneille b. Molière c. Richelieu d. Racine

26. What important development prepared for the French neo-classic movement?
   a. reign of Catherine de' Medici   c. suppression of religious drama
   b. rediscovery of classic drama   d. all of these

27. Who is the leading composer of the Counter-Reformation?
   a. Lasso b. Morley c. Palestrina d. Monteverdi

28. What does not characterize the Italian madrigal?
   a. word painting b. imitative texture c. sacred text d. frequent 5-part texture

29. Who was a leading composer of chanson?
   a. Jannequin b. Monteverdi c. Morley d. Palestrina

30. What does not describe the baroque style of music?
   a. ornamentation   c. complex forms
   b. emotional appeal   d. unsystematic harmonic system

31. Who was not a composer of early Italian opera?
   a. Caccini b. Monteverdi c. Scarlatti d. Peri

32. In opera, sung dialogue is called
   a. recitative   b. aria   c. arioso d. monody

33. In the late 17th century, Italian secular song was called
   a. opera b. cantata   c. sonata d. concerto

34. How does an oratorio differ from an opera?
   a. it has no arias or recitatives c. it is not staged
   b. it has no plot   d. all of these

35. Who is the best known composer of oratorios?
   a. Bach   b. Handel c. Vivaldi d. Monteverdi

36. A concerto is
   a. a work for solo instruments and basso continuo
   b. a work for solo instruments and orchestra
   c. a work for solo keyboard
   d. a work for orchestra only

37. An instrumental form based on continuous imitation is called
   a. free composition b. fugue c. fantasy d. toccata

38. Matching

Bach	a. *The Seasons*

Handel	b. famous violin maker

Vivaldi	c. *The Art of the Fugue*

Corelli	d. *Messiah*

Stradivari	e. known for his violin sonatas
---	

39. Theatre dancing in the early 16th century was closely connected with
   social dancing.   a. true b. false

40. Formal ballet came of age during the 16th century under the rule of
   a. Catherine de'Medici b. Louis XIII c. Henry IV d. Louis XIV

41. Who is credited with inventing the five basic dance positions?
   a. Caroso b. Negri c. Beaujoyeulx d. Beauchamps

42. What was an important development in ballet brought about by the
   Académie Royale de Danse?
   a. professional women dancers appeared
   b. choreography designed to face an audience on one side
   c. rules for positions and movements were established
   d. all of these

43. What describes Wren's St. Paul's Cathedral?
   a. it took over 40 years work   c. it was widely imitated
   b. dome has timber shell   d. all of these

44. Which architect completed the work on Versailles?
   a. Le Roy b. d'Orbay c. Hardouin-Mansart d. Le Brun

45. For who was the palace of Versailles intended?
   a. Catherine de'Medici b. Henry VI c. Louis XIII d. Louis XIV

ANSWERS
 1. c   2. d 3. c   4. a 5. b   6. a   7. a   8. c   9. d 10. c 11. c 12. a
13. b 14. c 15. a 16. d 17. ecdab   18. a 19. c 20. a 21. b 22. d 23. b
24. b 25. c 26. d 27. c 28. c 29. a 30. d   31. c 32. a 33. b 34. c 35. b
36. b 37. b 38. cdaeb   39. a 40. a 41. d 42. d 43. d 44. c 45. d

CHAPTER 12: THE ENLIGHTENMENT

CONTEXTS AND CONCEPTS

Summary

The 18th century continued to view mankind as consisting of rational beings in a universe governed by natural law, but a new social awareness of individuals within society--an awareness of their needs as well as their rights--marked this century as the Age of Enlightenment. Faith in science, natural human rights, human reason, and progress were touchstones of this era. These ideas produced an age of secularism, in which politics and business were placed outside of religion, and toleration of religious differences increased. A rapid increase in scientific interest created new sciences, such as mineralogy, botany, and zoology.

Great advances in technology paved the way for the Industrial Revolution. Agriculture turned to mechanized seed planting and crop rotation. Improvements in metallurgy, including the replacement of charcoal fuel by coal, led to the widespread use of iron and steel as structural elements. Other advances included more refined optical glass lenses (which led to more sophisticated scientific observations), more precise tooling, and improvements in bridge and road building. Perhaps the most significant invention was Watt's steam engine, which helped to revolutionize the textile industry in England.

Philosophical thought of the 18th century broke with the past. In the 17th century, Descartes' belief that reason was supreme, a philosophy called Cartesianism, was championed by Spinoza and Leibnitz. John Locke challenged this mode of thought, arguing that knowledge is derived from the senses and from experience. This philosophy, known as empiricism, dominated the late 18th century. Two important critics of empiricism appeared. David Hume felt that the mind was incapable of building knowledge upon sensations and that mathematics was the only true science. Immanuel Kant took the major step of separating science from philosophy and attributing different functions and techniques for each.The problems of art and aesthetics intrigued Kant, and his *Critique of Judgment* laid the foundation for modern aesthetic theory.

In addition to concerns with philosophy and invention, the Enlightenment attempted to raise humankind from low social circumstances, a movement called humanitarianism. These ideas were spread largely through the efforts of the philosophes, French writers and critics who were not philosophers in the traditional sense. Their most serious enterprise was the *Encyclopedia*, which was a compendium of all scientific, technical and historical knowledge, with a good deal of social criticism added. The editor of this project was Diderot; Voltaire, Montesquieu, and Rousseau were among the contributors.

Three important figures emerged in the cause of social justice. Locke wrote several treatises asserting that the power of a nation came from its people, and people had the right to withdraw their support. Voltaire took Locke's ideas to France, and untiringly crusaded against social ills. His stinging wit brought about social awareness and helped bring about the French Revolution. Rousseau did not believe in government and felt that man could only be happy in a small, simple community. His views of simplicity, naturalism, and of the noble savage pointed to Romanticism.

Rational attention also turned to economics. The physiocrats criticized mercantilism and government regulation. They favored a laissez-faire approach, in which production and distribution were handled without government interference. These ideas were systematized in Adam Smith's *Wealth of Nations*.

A number of important political leaders appeared during the 18th century, including Frederick the Great of Prussia, Maria Theresa and Joseph II of Austria, and Louis XVI, who would be executed during the French Revolution. Frederick was particularly important as a benevolent despot, a humanitarian ruler who championed thinkers and reformers throughout Europe.

In the 18th century, aesthetic tastes changed from the grandiose of the baroque to the modesty and elegance of the enlightenment. In surroundings, decor, and behavior, charm and finesse set the standards. Classical influences also were pronounced during this time. The discoveries of Pompeii and of Herculaneum created much excitement. The term aesthetics was coined by Gottlieb Baumgarten, and Winckelmann's *History of Ancient Art* brought classical art and its simple and ordered qualities to our attention.

Important Terms

Enlightenment: term applied to the general era of the 18th century, in which rational thought turned towards matters of society. (346)

Industrial Revolution: a period of major social and economic changes brought about by the mechanization of industries in the late 18th century. (346, 380 ff.)

Cartesianism: philosophy expounded by Descartes in which reason was thought to be supreme. (347)

Empiricism: the belief that sensations and experience are the primary sources of knowledge. (348)

Philosophes: French writers of the Enlightenment who championed social justice. (348)

Encyclopedia: the first modern attempt to gather all scientific, technical and historical knowledge into one source. The task was undertaken by the philosophes. (348)

Physiocrats: critics of capitalism who advocated a laissez-faire approach to economics. (349)

Laissez-faire: economic theory that production and distribution was best handled without government interference. (349)

Important Names

James Watt (1736-1819): Scottish engineer who invented a reliable steam engine which paved the way for the Industrial Revolution. (346, 347)

John Locke (1632-1704): English philosopher who stressed sensations and experience as the primary sources of knowledge. (348)

David Hume (1711-76): Scottish philosopher who was skeptical of sciences and sensations. He felt that mathematics was the only true science. (348)

Immanuel Kant (1724-1804): German philosopher, who is considered to be the major philosophic figure in the 18th century. His principal contribution was the separation of science from philosophy. Major works include *Critique of Judgment*. (348)

Denis Diderot (1713-84): French writer and critic who edited the *Encyclopedia*. (348)

Montesquieu (1689-1755): French writer who contributed to the *Encyclopedia*. (348)

Voltaire (1697-1778): French playwright, novelist, essayist, and a leading figure of the philosophes. His stinging wit brought wide awareness to social inequities. Major works include *Merope* and *Candide*. (348, 365)

Jacques Rousseau (1712-72): leading figure of the philosophes who believed that man could only be happy in a small and simple community. His ideas helped pave the way for Romanticism. His major works include *Social Contract*. (348, 362)

Adam Smith (1723-90): Scottish economist who systematized the ideas of the physiocrats in his *Wealth of Nations*. (349)

Frederick the Great (1712-86): powerful ruler of Prussia and supporter of artists and enlightened thinkers. (350)

Gottlieb Baumgarten (1714-62): German philosopher who coined the term "aesthetics." His major work was *Aesthetica*. (350)

Johann Winckelmann (1717-68): German archaeologist and art historian. His *History of Ancient Art* helped to bring popular attention to classical art. (350)

Study Questions

Describe why the term Enlightenment is applied to the 18th century. (346)

What scientific and technological advances were made during this period? (346-7)

How do the philosophies of John Locke differ from those of the 17th century? Describe the criticisms of Locke by Hume and Kant. (347-8)

Who are the leading philosophes? What are the major contributions of each? (348)

What new economic ideas came about during the Enlightenment? (349)

Who were the major political figures of the 18th century? Who was described as a benevolent despot? What does that mean? (349-50)

What were the important developments in aesthetics during the Enlightenment? (350)

THE ARTS OF THE ENLIGHTENMENT

Summary

Two-Dimensional Art: Five distinctive artistic movements are described in the text. The rococo came about as a reaction to the overwhelming scale of the baroque. Emphasizing intimate grace, charm, and delicate superficiality, it was essentially a decorative and non-functional art. Love, sentiment, pleasure, and sincerity were predominant themes. Three major figures represent the rococo movement. Watteau's *Embarkation for Cythera* (Fig. 12.5) illustrates the early rococo, with its soft, fuzzy, and delicate qualities. Intermixed with the affected gaiety is a deep, poetic melancholy. François Boucher continued the rococo tradition with paintings that were decorative, mundane, and slightly erotic. *Venus Consoling Love* (Figs. 12.6) show the exquisitely detailed drapery, nude subjects, and decorative backgrounds that typify his works. Fragonard represents the late rococo. *The Swing* (Fig. 12.1) again illustrates the frivolous sensuality that marks the rococo.

In contrast to the rococo, humanitarian art brought biting satire and social comment to the canvas. William Hogarth portrayed dramatic scenes on moral subjects, such as seen in his *Rake's Progress* and *Harlot's Progress* (Figs. 12.7-8). These works trace a young man and a harlot through their downfalls. The popularity of portraiture and landscape increased in the 18th century. This trend can be seen in the works of Gainsborough, an influential English painter. In the *Market Cart* (Fig. 12.9) human figures are subordinate to the forces of nature, which ebb and flow around and through them.

A fourth trend can be found in the paintings of Chardin. A master of still-life, Chardin chose subjects from the mundane world (Figs. 12.10-11). Richness of texture and color combined with sensitive composition and the use of chiaroscuro ennobles these humble items. The rediscovery of antiquity led to a fifth artistic movement called neo-classicism. Jacques-Louis David was a leading proponent of this movement, and his works (Figs. 12.12-13) reveal an emphasis on compositional unity and historical accuracy.

Sculpture: The 18th century was not a great age for sculpture, but three excellent sculptors are presented in the text. Falconet's *Madame de Pompadour as the Venus of the Doves* (Fig. 12.14), with its partially nude venus and cupid figures, captures the erotic sensuality and delicacy of the rococo. This work exhibits the masterful technique of the rococo sculptors, as does Clodion's *Satyr and Bacchante* (Fig. 12.15). The third sculptor of this period, Houdin, created more serious works, and can perhaps be allied with the neo-classic movement in painting. He is best known for his busts of leading figures of the day, and for his penetrating psychological analysis of his subjects (Figs. 12.16-12.17).

Literature: Trends found in other arts also appear in the literature from the Enlightenment. The focus on the commonplace seen in the paintings of Chardin are evident in the works of the English poet and playwright Goldsmith. Wit and social awareness can be seen in the essays of Samuel Johnson, who used his writings to promote the glory of God.

Several developments in literature foreshadow the emergence of Romanticism. The decline of drama in favor of the novel is evident in the career of Henry Fielding, who left the theatre for the writing of novels such as his outstanding *Tom Jones*. Gothic stories of mystery and the grotesque, as exemplified in the works of Horace Walpole and Ann Radcliffe, and Herder's essays on art and philosophy point to the 19th-century.

Theatre: National theatres in five countries are described in the text. In England, audiences tended more towards the wealthy middle class, and, as a result, sentimental comedies were emphasized. In the works of Cibber, clever plots and witty dialogue persisted. By the end of the century, comedy reached a high point with the works of Goldsmith and Sheridan. Appearing in the early 18th century was ballad opera. John Gay's *Beggar's Opera* was extremely popular, and its satirical portrayal of political figures helped lead to the Licensing Act of 1737, which limited theatric productions to certain theatres and gave the Lord Chamberlain the right of censorship. The physical theatre remained much as it had been, but the art of acting was revolutionized by David Garrick.

In America, theatre had difficulties getting established because of strong Puritan attitudes. The first recorded theatre was built in Williamsburg in 1716, and all of the early plays were given by English troupes. The American Company, consisting of British actors, presented the first American play to receive a professional production in 1767. During the Revolutionary War, few plays were performed, but in the post-War years, the American Company returned to launch a firm tradition of American theatre. Royal Tyler's *The Contrast* was the first American comedy. The first major American playwright was William Dunlap. Another important development was the opening of the Chestnut Street Theatre in Philadelphia in 1794.

After the death of Molière, French theatre underwent a barren period. Two rival companies were established--Comédie-Française and Comedie-Italienne. Especially prominent in their productions were sentimental comedies and tearful tragedies, all of which were conceived to satisfy the growing number of women who wanted to cry at the theatre. An excellent playwright in the early half of the century was Pierre Marivaux, whose plays are charming, sentimental, and meticulously written. Voltaire was the outstanding figure during the mid-century. His plays tend to follow the rules of the French

Academy and adhered to classic principles. The most brilliant French playwright at the end of the century was Beaumarchais. His *Barber of Seville* and *Marriage of Figaro* were entertaining comedies set in neo-classic traditions. Criticism of their social content led to a ban of these works.

Because of the political divisions in Germany, it was difficult to establish a national theatre. In mid-century, Lessing's contributions pointed towards that goal. Especially significant was his placement of scene changes during the break between acts, rather than between scenes, when dramatic action would come to a stop. In 1770, German theatre began a movement towards Romanticism, inspired in part by interest in the plays of Shakespeare. Goethe was a major figure in this movement. His novel *The Sorrows of Werther* is one of the outstanding products of the Sturm und Drang. His masterpiece *Faust* is in two parts; Part I is set as a theatrical play, but Part II is seemingly formless and virtually impossible to stage.

There was no strong tradition of theatre in Italy during the 18th century. But, Italy is important for two developments: its interaction with French theatre which culminated in the sentimental comedies of Carlo Goldoni, and the magnificent scenic designs in 18th-century operatic productions.

Music: Two early 18th century musical styles are discussed in the text. The qualities of rococo art are best seen in the music of François Couperin. His works for harpsichord and organ, his sacred works, and his chamber music illustrate rococo elements of artificial decoration, refinement, and pleasant logic. In contrast, the empfindsamer Stil of Germany emphasized a freedom of expression and a contrast of moods. The principal exponent of this style was C.P.E. Bach, a son of J.S. Bach. His works for clavichord are expressive, delicate, and, at times, unpredictable.

In the late 18th century, the Classical style, emphasizing simplicity and careful attention to form, dominated the international scene. One prominent quality was the division of the melodic line into regularly recurring statements called phrases. This emphasis on melody also entailed an avoidance of complicated polyphonic textures. The most important new form to emerge was sonata form. This structure contains three main sections. The opening section, called the exposition, contains two contrasting keys and generally two or more contrasting melodies. This section, which is often repeated, is followed by the development, in which thematic material from the exposition is manipulated as the harmony moves through several different key areas. The third section, the recapitulation, repeats the material of the exposition in the original key area. The sonata form is used in most first movements of symphonies and other instrumental genres. In the symphony, primary focus was on the string section, but the woodwinds gradually grew more independent.

The career of Haydn spans the beginning of the symphony to its pre-Romantic stage. His early works in the genre reflect typical early Classic traits, but with his middle works of the 1770s, the forms begin to expand and emotions are broadly expressed. Among his late works ,the "Surprise" Symphony illustrates his mastery of form and his delightful sense of humor.

Mozart, a child prodigy, wrote masterworks in instrumental and vocal genres during his brief career. In his Symphony No. 40 in G Minor, the combination of formal perfection, graceful melodies, and intense emotions (some consider this to be the first example of Romanticism) illustrates Mozart's genius. Among his operas, *The Marriage of Figaro*, based on the play by Beaumarchais, has enjoyed immense popularity.

The third great figure of the Classical style, Beethoven, can also be seen as the first great Romantic composer. He wrote nine symphonies that brought about many innovations, such as playing two movements without a break, unleashing a powerful heroic tone, and adding a chorus and solo voices in the last movement of the Symphony No. 9. One of Beethoven's most popular works is the Piano Sonata in C Minor, the "Pathétique." In three movements, this works is based on classical structures, but incorporates the romantic qualities of intense drama and singing melodies.

Dance: Three important changes in ballet are described in the text. One is the rise of the ballerina from a subordinate position to that of an equal to the male dancer. Camargo is considered to be the first woman to "dance like a man." A second change is the move towards a more expressive and emotional style of dancing, as exemplified in the dancing of Marie Sallé. The third was the significant movement towards creating drama through dance. The central figure of this movement was Noverre, who felt that dance should be a play without words. He objected to technical display without purpose and argued for less cumbersome costumes. His philosophies were picked up by several later choreographers. Of these, Didelot was particularly important for introducing tights and suggesting a type of dancing done on the tips of the toes.

Architecture: Three movements in architecture are indentified in the text. The rococo was primarily a style of interior design. Refinement and decorativeness were applied to furniture and decór more than to exterior structures. A second distinctively English style, called Georgian, mixes elements of the rococo--refinement and delicacy--with neo-classicism. Inspired by the discoveries of the past, a debate about the relative merits of Greek and Roman antiquity emerged between Laugier and Piranesi. From this sprang neo-classicism, which was a revolt against the frivolity of the rococo. This style was particularly important for American architects, because it was equated with democracy. These influences are evident in the works of Thomas Jefferson (Figs. 12.30-1).

Synthesis: Perhaps the most important monarch of the Enlightenment was Frederick the Great of Prussia. His skillful handling of administration and his positive reforms kept him from the troubles that beset other European monarchs. Frederick II was an avid patron of music and oversaw the building of the Berlin Opera and the establishment of a tradition of opera performances. Many of his music concerts were held at his Sans Souci Palace, designed by Knobelsdorff. The Palace shows a mixture of Italian baroque, rococo, and classical elements.

Important Terms

Rococo: an early 18th-century French artistic movement that was essentially decorative and non-functional. (351-3, 359-60, 366)

Neo-classicism: artistic movement in the late 18th century inspired by the renewed interest in Greek and Roman antiquity. Works emphasize compositional unity and accurate historical detail. (357-8, 373-4)

Gothic: in the 19th century, the term refers to a literary movement that emphasized the mysterious and grotesque. (362)

Ballad opera: a comic play in England that alternated spoken dialogue with simple, often popular songs. (362)

Licensing Act of 1737: law passed by Parliament limiting legal theatrical production to Drury Lane, Covent Garden, and Haymarket. (362)

American Company: a British acting company that performed the first American play and established a firm tradition of American theatre. (363-4)

Comédie-Française: a company of French actors who performed both comedy and tragedy in 18th-century France. (364)

Comedie-Italienne: a company of Italian actors who performed in France and was a rival to the Comédie-Française. (364 366)

Sturm und Drang: a German romantic literary movement in the late 18th century. Translates as Storm and Stress. (365-6)

Empfindsamer Stil: term used to denote trend in German music in the mid-18th century that emphasized emotions. (366-7)

Classical style: the musical equivalent to the neo-classic movement in the visual arts. The style emphasized simplicity, contrasting emotions, and symmetry. (367)

Sonata form: also known as sonata-allegro, this structure emerged during the Classic period and became the dominant form of Western music for over a century. (367-8)

Minuet: polite aristocratic dance in triple meter. It frequently was used as the third movement in a symphony. (368)

Scherzo: a fast movement in triple meter that replaced the minuet in the symphonies of Beethoven. (370)

Piano sonata: a work for solo piano in several movements. (370)

Ballet d'action: ballet in France that focused on drama. (371-2)

Ballet a entrée: ballet in France that focused on display. (372)

Georgian style: an English style of architecture appearing during the reigns of the Georges who ruled England in the 18th century. (372-3)

Important Names

Antoine Watteau (1683-1721): French painter and leading figure of the rococo style. Best known work is *Embarkation for Cythera*. (351-3)

François Boucher (1703-79): French painter who was a protégé of Madame de Pompadour. He is known for his decorative, mundane, and slightly erotic paintings. (353)

Jean-Honoré Fragonard (1732-1806): French painter of the later Rococo period who was the most eminent pupil of Boucher and Chardin. (353)

William Hogarth (1697-1764): English painter of humanitarian subjects. His major works are *Rake's Progress* and *Harlot's Progress*. (353-4)

Thomas Gainsborough (1727-88): English painter of portraits and landscapes. He was the favorite portratist of British high society. (354)

Jean-Baptiste Chardin (1699-1779): French painter who used everyday events and objects as subjects and found beauty in the commonplace. (354)

Jacques Louis David (1748-1825): French painter who was the leading neo-classic artist of the late 18th century. His works include *The Death of Socrates* and *The Oath of the Horatii*. (357-8)

Étienne-Maurice Falconet (1716-91): French sculptor of the rococo style. (359)

Clodion (1738-1814): also known as Claude Michel, he was a leading sculptor in the French rococo style. (359)

Jean Antoine Houdon (1741-1828): the finest French sculptor of the age who is best known for his busts. (359-60)

Oliver Goldsmith (1730-74): English poet and playwright, whose works often focus on day-to-day occurrences. Works include *She Stoops to Conquer*. (360-1,362)

Samuel Johnson (1709-84): English critic and essayist. The purpose of his works was to promote the glory of God. Major works include the *Rambler* essays and the *Idler* essays. (3361-2)

Henry Fielding (1707-54): English novelist. His most famous works is *Tom Jones*. (362)

Horace Walpole (1717-97): English author of Gothic novels. (362)

Ann Radcliffe (1764-1823): English novelist, considered by some to best represent the Gothic novel. (362)

Johann Gottfried Herder (1744-1803): German essayist who contributed to the pre-Romantic movement. (362)

Colley Cibber (1671-1757): author of witty plays and an essay analyzing English acting. (362)

Richard Brinsley Sheridan (1751-1816): the most famous English playwright of the late 18th century. His works include *School for Scandal*. (362)

John Gay (1685-1732): creator of London's most popular ballad opera, *Beggar's Opera*. (362)

David Garrick (1717-79): great English actor who helped to revolutionize the art of acting. (363)

Royal Tyler (1757-1826): American lawyer and author of the first American comedy, *The Contrast*. (364)

William Dunlap: considered to be the first major American playwright. (364)

Pierre Marivaux (1688-1763): French playwright whose plays can be described as rococo. (365)

Beaumarchais (1732-99): French playwright. Major works are *The Barber of Seville* and *The Marriage of Figaro*. (365)

Gotthold Ephraim Lessing (1729-81): important German playwright. (365)

Johann Wolfgang von Goethe (1749-1832): major German poet, novelist, and playwright. His works are instrumental in establishing Romanticism. Major works include *The Sorrows of Young Werther* and *Faust*. (365-6 410-1)

Friedrich von Klinger (1752-1831): German dramatist and novelist. (365)

Carlo Goldoni (1707-93): Italian playwright and librettist of sophisticated comedies. (366)

François Couperin (1668-1733): foremost French composer of the rococo. (366)

Carl Philipp Emanuel Bach (1714-88): German composer and son of J.S. Bach. He is the principal exponent of empfinsamer Stil. His most important works are his compositions for clavichord and his treatise on keyboard playing. (366-7)

Franz Joseph Haydn (1732-1809): Austrian composer who played a prominent role in the development of the symphony and of the classical style. His major works include the Symphony No. 94 in G Major, "The Surprise." (368-9)

Wolfgang Amadeus Mozart (1756-91): brilliant Austrian composer who penned masterpieces in both instrumental and vocal genres. His major works include the Symphony No. 40 in G Minor and the opera *Marriage of Figaro*. (369-70)

Ludwig van Beethoven (1770-1827): German composer who united Classic and Romantic traits in his powerful compositions. Major works include 9 symphonies and 32 piano sonatas, including the Piano Sonata in C Minor, Opus 13. (370)

Marie Anne Cupis de Camargo (1710-70): considered to be the first ballerina to acquire the technical skills and brilliance of male dancers. (371)

Marie Sallé (1707-56): ballerina who emphasized emotions and expressiveness in her dancing. (371)

John Weaver (1673-1760): London dance master who used movement to communicate a story. (371)

Jean George Noverre (1727-1810): the primary moving force in focusing on drama and expressiveness in drama. His beliefs are presented in *Letters on Dancing and Ballets*. (372)

Salvatore Vigano (1769-1821): major choreographer who stands as a transition figure between classicism and romanticism. (372)

Charles Didelot (1767-1837): French choreographer who had a significant impact on the course of ballet. (372)

Abbé Laugier: author of *Essai sur l'architecture*, a rationalistic approach based on the principles of Greek architecture. (373)

Giambattista Piranesi (1720-78): wrote *Della Magnificenza ed Architettura dei Romani* in order to show the superiority of Roman architecture over Greek. (373-4)

Thomas Jefferson (1743-1826): American president who was also a leading American architect. (374)

Study Questions

Define rococo. Who were the three leading painters of the rococo? Describe their principal works. (351-3)

Who was the leading humanitarian painter? Describe his two major works. (353-4)

What was the typical subject matter of Gainsborough? Chardin? What are the distinctive qualities of both artists? (354- 7)

What inspired neo-classicism? Who was the leading painter? What are the principal characteristics of his works? (357-8)

Compare the works of Falconet and Clodion with those of rococo painters. (351-3, 359-60)

What neo-classic elements are found in the works of Houdon? (359-60)

What general traits found in the visual arts can also be found in the literature from the Enlightenment? (360-2)

What pre-Romantic qualities can be found in 18th-century literature? (362)

What are the five national theatres discussed in the text? Describe each, noting the major playwrights, productions, theatres, and actors involved. (362-6)

What are the two early-Classic musical trends discussed in the text? Who are the leading composers of each style? What qualities do their works display? (366-7)

Describe the principal qualities of the Classical style. Why is this not called the neo-classic style? (367)

Who are the three major figures of the Classic era? What are the distinctive qualities of their music? Cite some of their major works. (368-70)

What role did Camargo have on the emergence of ballet? Marie Sallé? Noverre? Didelot? (371-2)

How does rococo architecture reflect the qualities of rococo art? Compare rococo with Georgian style of architecture. (372-3)

What role did neo-classicism have on architecture? Why was this movement so strong in America? Cite examples. (373-4)

187

PRACTICE TEST

1. What does not characterize the Enlightenment?
   a. belief in natural laws   c. greater prestige for the Church
   b. faith in science   d. concern with social justice

2. Whose invention was described as paving the way for the Industrial Revolution   a. Huntsman b. Tull c. Watt d. Newton

3. The philosophy of Descartes, which linked philosophy to science, is called   a. empiricism b. aesthetics c. physiology d. Cartesianism

4. Who was the leading champion of empiricism?
   a. Leibnitz b. Locke c. Hume d. Kant

5. Who separated philosophy from science?
   a. Leibnitz b. Locke c. Hume d. Kant

6. Who did not participate on the *Encyclopedia* project?
   a. Locke b. Diderot c. Voltaire d. Rousseau

7. Who argued that man was happy only in a small, simple community?
   a. Locke b. Diderot c. Voltaire d. Rousseau

8. Who systematized the ideas of the physiocrats?
   a. Locke b. Voltaire c. Adam Smith d. Baumgarten

9. Who was described as a benevolent despot?
   a. Frederick I b. George III c. Frederick the Great d. Maria Theresa

10. Who first coined the term aesthetics?
    a. Kant b. Baumgarten c. Smith d. Winckelmann

11. Who wrote *History of Ancient Art*?
    a. Kant b. Baumgarten c. Smith d. Winckelmann

12. What does not characterize the rococo?
    a. charm b. delicacy c. grandeur d. superficiality

13. Which of the following is not a rococo painting?
    a. *The Swing*   c. *Venus Consoling Love*
    b. *The Market Cart*   d. *Embarkation for Cythera*

14. What characterizes the works of Boucher?
    a. detailed drapery b. erotic subjects c. detailed background d. all of these

15. Who is the leading figure of humanitarian painting?
    a. Hogarth b. Watteau c. Gainsborough d. Chardin

16. What characterizes the *Market Cart*?
    a. prominent human figures   c. twisted forms of nature
    b. a simple view of nature   d. all of these

17. What are the typical subjects of Chardin?
    a. everyday objects   c. landscapes
    b. historical events   d. the aristocracy

18. What characterizes neo-classic paintings?
    a. copying ancient works   c. medieval subject matter
    b. compositional unity   d. all of these

19. Who is not associated with the rococo?
    a. Houdon b. Clodion c. Falconet d. Watteau

20. What does not describe sculpture from the Enlightenment?
    a. erotic sensuality   c. monumental scale
    b. masterful technique   d. decorative detail

21. What types of subjects did Goldsmith write about?
    a. religious b. commonplace c. fantasy d. historical

22. What was the primary purpose Samuel Johnson's essays?
    a. to satire the government   c. to glorify God
    b. to bring about social justice d. to make money

23. Who is not associated with the Sturm und Drang movement?
    a. Herder b. Lessing c. Goethe d. Klinger

24. Who wrote *Tom Jones*?
    a. Goldsmith b. Walpole c. Radcliffe d. Fielding

25. One of the most significant developments in literature during the 18th century was the rise of the a. novel b. play c. sonnet d. ode

26. Matching

   Sheridan   a. *She Stoops to Conquer*

   John Gay   b. Great English actor

   Garrick   c. *Beggar's Opera*

   Cibber   d. *School for Scandal*

   Goldsmith   e. author of comedies in early 18th century
   ---

27. Who is the first major American playwright?
    a. Hunter b. Tyler c. Godfrey d. Dunlap

28. What was a primary goal of all French plays of the rococo?
    a. to satire the government   c. to bring about social reform
    b. to present revolutionary ideas   d. to bring tears to ladies' eyes

29. Who wrote *The Barber of Seville*?
    a. Marivaux b. Voltaire c. Beaumarchais d. Molière

30. The two parts to Goethe's *Faust* make a masterful theatric production.
    a. true   b. false

31. Which composer is associated with the rococo movement?
    a. Gluck b. Bach c. Couperin d. Haydn

32. The emotional style championed by C.P.E. Bach is called
    a. empfindsamer Stil b. rococo   c. romanticism   d. Sturm und Drang

33. What does not characterize the Classical style?
    a. regularly recurring phrases   c. much use of polyphony
    b. rhythmic variety   d. contrasting emotions

34. The first section of a sonata form is called
    a. ritornello b. rondo c. exposition d. development

35. The primary focus of the classical symphony was on the
    a. strings b. woodwinds c. brass d. percussion

36. How many symphonies did Haydn compose?
    a. 9   b. 22   c. 41   d. over 100

37. The Surprise Symphony gets its name from
    a. the unusual form of the first movement
    b. a loud chord in the slow movement
    c. its presentation at the patron's birthday
    d. the lack of a finale

38. What does not describe Mozart's Symphony in G Minor?
    a. three movements are in sonata form
    b. the first movement has a romantic intensity
    c. the first movement is based on short motives
    d. it was composed in his middle period

39. Who composed the opera *Marriage of Figaro*?
    a. Beethoven b. Mozart c. Haydn d. Gluck

40. How many symphonies did Beethoven compose?
    a. 9   b. 22   c. 41   d. over 100

41. What innovation did Beethoven bring to the symphony?
    a. no breaks between movements
    b. replaced minuet with scherzo
    c. added voices to the orchestra
    d. all of these

42. Who is considered to be the first skilled ballerina?
    a. Camargo b. Sallé c. Martin d. Vigano

43. What new element did Sallé add to her dancing?
    a. leaps b. toe work c. tights d. emotion

44. Who advocated that ballet should be a drama in *Letters on Dancing and Ballets*?   a. Noverre b. Vigano c. Didelot d. Dauberval

45. Who introduced the idea of dancing on tip toes?
    a. Noverre b. Vigano c. Didelot d. Dauberval

46. What does not describe rococo architecture?
   a. exterior ornamental detail   c. decorated furniture
   b. reduced scale   d. lightness and elegance

47. In what country did Georgian style center?
   a. Russia b. France c. England d. Italy

48. What architectural style was particularly strong in America?
   a. rococo b. Georgian c. neo-classic d. baroque

49. Who strongly influenced the works of Thomas Jefferson?
   a. Palladio b. Michelangelo c. Wren d. Della Porta

50. What does not characterize the Sans Souci Palace?
   a. rococo traits   c. no classical implications
   b. rich, delicate interior   d. planned as a retreat

ANSWERS
1. c   2. c   3. d 4. b   5. d   6. a   7. d   8. c   9. c 10. b 11. d 12. c
13. b 14. d 15. a 16. c 17. a 18. b 19. a 20. c   21. b 22. c 23. b 24. d
25. a 26. dcbea   27. d 28. d 29. c 30. b 31. c 32. a   33. c 34. c 35. a
36. d 37. b 38. d 39. b 40. a 41. d 42. a 43. d 44. a   45. c 46. a 47. c
48. c   49. a 50. c

CHAPTER 13: THE AGE OF INDUSTRY

CONTEXTS AND CONCEPTS

Summary

The spirit of the Enlightenment, which had sparked the French Revolution, soon fell victim to this event. With the turn of the century, a new and restless age was born--an age of Napoleon and revolution, of technological advances and industrial might, of middle class power and working class exploitation. It was also an age of a new artistic style. Shunning classical formality, artists turned towards the emotional expression and individualism of romanticism.

The emergence of the middle class and the turn to capitalism, especially in England, were the most significant social and economic developments of the late 18th century. Both encouraged rapid growth in technology. Advances in the production of metals, the development of machine-tool industries, the introduction of precision instruments leading to standardization, and the development of efficient energy systems not only helped to solidify the position of the middle class and of capitalism, but also changed the Western world into a fully mechanized society by the end of the century.

The interests of the middle class were promoted in a political movement called Liberalism. Three goals were advocated: reducing the authority of the church; reducing the power of the aristocracy; and removing economic restrictions. Emphasis was placed on individual freedom. Only the fit (the few rugged individuals) survived, while the unfit (the degraded masses) perished.

The creation of a new class of machine workers, who lived in slums under deplorable conditions, led to a number of reactions. During the course of the century, systems of public education were established in Europe and the United States. Unions began to form, often after violent confrontations. Among the solutions offered to the masses was the socialism of Karl Marx.

Religion faced several crises during this time. The theory of evolution proposed by Darwin prompted an inevitable clash. In addition, some Protestant scholarship acknowledged that the Bible was a compilation of human writings over a period of time. Later, Protestants reconciled these doctrines, but Catholics rejected them and held that the Pope was infallible.

Philosophers of the 19th century reacted against Kant's rationalism and embraced an idealistic appeal to faith called romanticism or idealism. Idealism centered on the emotions and the oneness of God and nature. The movement culminated in the work of Hegel, who felt that art was a step towards reality or "truth." Hegel felt that the objective of art is beauty and that Classical art comprises the perfection of artistic beauty. Romantic art, being subjective, was seen as more spiritual. This idealism was challenged by Schopenhauer, who saw the world as a machine operating under unchanging laws and without a creator. Nietzsche accepted the concept of a mechanical world, but felt that courage, man's highest attribute, would prevail and lead to a race of supermen and women. Outside of Germany, philosophers focused on the sciences. Comte treated matters of worldly existence, not riddles of the unknown universe. His views, called positivism, formed the basis of sociology. Spencer expounded a theory that saw a struggle for existence in society, in which the survival of the fittest was fundamental.

The Western world was brought closer together with new developments in transportation and communications. At the same time, imperialistic competition and advancements in armaments led to a period of turbulence and frustration, as war was ever-present in Western society.

Reflecting the changes in society, the artist was able to support himself without the aid of the aristocracy, and indeed many artists resisted all patronage. Individualism became an important aspect of all art.

Important Terms

Liberalism: a political movement that sought to enhance middle class power through limiting the power of the church and aristocracy and by removing economic restrictions. (384)

Idealism: 19th-century philosophy based on emotion and the oneness of God and nature. (385)

Positivism: a philosophical system forwarded by Comte that sets up a hierarchy of sciences, beginning with mathematics and culminating in sociology. (386)

Important Names

Karl Marx (1818-83): German philosopher who founded the socialist movement that led to Communism. (385)

Charles Darwin (1809-82): British naturalist who expounded the theory of evolution by natural selection. Major work was *Origin of Species*. (385)

Georg Wilhelm Friedrich Hegel (1770-1831): German philosopher who combined German idealism with evolutionary science. He believed that the object of art was beauty. (385)

Arthur Schopenhauer (1788-1860): German philosopher who denied the emotionally centered romantic idealism of Hegel and viewed the world operating under unchangeable laws. (385-6)

Friedrich Wilhelm Nietzsche (1844-1900): German philosopher and poet who found optimism in the mechanical state of the world. He felt that the selective process of courage would produce a super race. (386)

Auguste Comte (1798-1857): French mathematician and philosopher who believed that the task of philosophy was to sort out factual details of man's existence. His approach (positivism) formed the basis of sociology. (386)

Herbert Spencer (1820-1903): British philosopher who believed that principles of evolution could be applied to society. He felt that the survival of the fittest was fundamental to the human condition. (386)

Study Questions

What are the four major areas of technological development discussed in your text? (383) Be able to describe each of these areas.

What are the effects of these advances on the textile industry, agriculture, mining, armaments, and the home and office (382-3)?

Transportation and communication were also greatly affected by technology. What are some of the important changes? (382, 383)

What effect did industrialization have on Western civilization? (383-4)

What were the three goals of liberalism? (384)

Contrast the philosophies and aesthetics of the Enlightenment (Kant and Winkelmann: 348, 350) with those of the 19th century (Hegel, Schopenhauer, Nietzsche: 3885-6).

Describe how some of the basic themes of Romanticism emerged from a war-torn Europe. (387)

Describe the change of the patronage system in the 19th century and show its effects on artists. (387)

Summary

Two-Dimensional Art: The neo-classic traditions of the 18th century continued into the 19th, particularly in France. The *Grande Odalisque* (Fig. 13.5) by Ingres shows a mixture of traits reflecting neo-classicism--simple line, a cool palette, and geometric spatial effects--and romanticism--an exotic subject and individualism.

Romanticism emphasized emotional appeal and tended toward the picturesque, nature, the Gothic, and the macabre. Six romantic painters are examined in the text. The first three works are based on actual events and contain strong elements of social criticism. Géricault was a champion of the downtrodden. His masterwork *The Raft of the "Medussa"* (Fig. 13.6) deals with an event in which government incompetence led to a tragedy. The work, based on two triangles, brilliantly conveys the drama of the moment. The Spanish painter Goya captures the climactic moment of the execution of Madrid citizens in his *The Third of May* (Fig. 13.7). The nightmarish, irrational quality of the event is reinforced by Goya's fragmented composition and portrayal of deindividualized victims, and dehumanized French soldiers. *The Slave Ship* by Turner (Fig. 13.8) is based on an event in which a captain of a slave ship dumped his human cargo into the sea when a disease broke out. In this work, form and content are subordinate to expressive intent, as a turbulent painting technique and a fragmented composition create a sense of prevailing doom.

The remaining three romantic painters show different aspects of romanticism. Delacroix captures a powerful national spirit with *Liberty Leading the People* (Fig. 13.9). The tricolor flag not only provides symbolism for the work, but also serves to unify the colors within the composition. Corot was one of the first to finish his paintings out of doors. His objective of recreating the full luminosity of nature and to capture the perceptual experience is evident in *Volterra* (Fig. 13.10). Bonheur, who can also be considered a realist, portrayed the power and dignity of animals, as can be seen in *Plowing in the Nivernais* (Fig. 13.11).

A new painting style arose in the mid-19th century called realism, a term with a variety of meanings and implications. Courbet is the central figure of this movement. He depicted everyday life; *The Stone Breakers* (Fig. 13.12) presents life-size men as he saw them working beside a road. The emphasis on the tedium of their task and the fact that one man is too old and the other too young are reflections of Courbet's social realism. Another realist, Millet focused on landscapes and peasants. No social realism is seen in *Woman Baking Bread* (Fig. 13.13), just a simple honest figure. Manet followed the realist tradition, although he is often regarded as an impressionist because he sought to paint "only what the eye can see." Manet liberated the canvas from competition with the camera. His *Le Déjeuner sur l'herbe* (Fig. 13.14) shocked the public, as it gave a realistic version of the traditional pastoral scene with nudes common in the rococo. Tanner, the first important black painter, painted realistic images. As can be seen in *The Banjo Lesson* (Fig. 13.15), he contrasts clarity in the central objects with less detail in the surrounding areas. This technique, similar to Corot's experiments, captures the warmth of the atmosphere surrounding the relationship of teacher and pupil.

Manet's observance of lighting and atmospheric effects was assimilated by a small group of painters called impressionists. Their goal was to capture the effect of natural light on objects and atmosphere. Their experiments resulted in a technique in which the juxtaposition of small patches of unmixed primary colors created a new sense of reality. Monet's *On the Seine* (Fig. 13.16) illustrates the optimistic yet fragmentary and fleeting image common to impressionists. These qualities are also captured in the works of Renoir (Fig. 13.17). Renoir specialized in the human figure, and his paintings depict the joy of life, as everyday folk enjoy the given moment. Another member of the impressionist group was Berthe Morisot. As can be seen in her *In the Dining Room* (Fig. 13.18), she often focused on family members with an edge of pathos and sentimentality. In 1877 the American Mary Casatt joined the impressionists. Her favorite subjects, as seen in *The Bath* (Fig. 13.19), were women and children.

In the last two decades of the 19th century, impressionism evolved into a collection of disparate styles called post-impressionism. Although the subject matters were similar to those of the impressionists, individual treatment produced a variety of techniques and interpretations. Four leading figures are discussed in the text. Seurat developed a technique called pointillism, in which paint is applied with the point of a brush one dot at a time. His two works in the text (Figs. 13.20-13.21) show his careful attention to perspective, his willful avoidance of three-dimensionality, and the subordinate role of reality. The return to form and color by many of the post-impressionists can be seen in the works of Cézanne (Fig. 13.22), where shapes are simplified and outlining is used throughout. Cézanne felt that all forms in nature were based on geometric shapes. Gauguin's works show an insistence on form, a resistance to naturalistic effects, and a strong influence of non-Western art, including primitive styles. Gauguin's typically flat, outlined figures, simple forms, and use of symbolism can be seen in *Vision after the Sermon* (Fig. 13.23). A fourth approach to post-impressionism can be seen in the works of Vincent van Gogh (Figs. 13.24-13.25), whose emotionalism in the pursuit of form was unique. Known for his turbulent life and his powerful, energetic paintings, van Gogh produced one of the most personal and subjective viewpoints in the history of Western art.

Sculpture: The principal trends of 19th-century sculpture can be seen in the works of four artists. Neo-classical sculpture, which prevailed during the early years of the nineteenth century, consisted predominantly of reproducing classical works. The ablest neo-classical sculptor was Canova. His *Venus Victrix* (Fig. 13.26) shows a classical pose and classical proportions mixed with influences of the older rococo tradition.

The romantic movement in visual arts did not translate well into sculpture. The term is applied somewhat loosely to the works of Rodin. Idealism and social comment are apparent in *Burghers of Calais* (Fig. 13.27), yet his textures point to the goals of impressionism. The shimmering surfaces seen in Fig. 13.28 not only seem to reflect light, but give the works a dramatic quality as well.

A return to form and emotional content at the turn of the century can be seen in the works of Maillol and Epstein. Maillol's desire to capture emotional qualities has led to comparisons with post-impressionist painters. His belief that a statue should exhibit rest and self-containment is evident in *The Mediterranean* (Fig. 13.29). Post-impressionistic elements, such as energy and subjectivity, can be found in the works of Jacob Epstein. His *Selina* (Fig. 13.30) achieves a tormented effect similar to that in the paintings of van Gogh.

Literature: The early 19th century produced a number of outstanding English writers. William Wordsworth created a world of beauty through his love of nature, which is evident in *Tintern Abbey*. Other romantic themes can be found in the works of Coleridge, Scott, Lord Byron, Percy Byssche Shelley, and John Keats. In the United States, Edgar Allen Poe was a champion of the Romantic spirit.

The 19th-century novel also served as means for expressing romantic subjects. Society came under scrutiny with works by Jane Austen, Balzac, and Dickens. Balzac attempted to survey all aspects in his unfinished cycle of novels called *Comédie Humaine*. Another important movement was naturalism. The works of Flaubert and Zola closely parallel realism in paintings.

Theatre: Romanticism's denial of rules and restraints and the emphasis on free imagination did not transfer well to the theatre. Moreover, the writing of plays by literary men rather than practical theatre men produced a large number of works that were impractical and overindulgent in its emotional appeal. The best romantic theatre were the works of Shakespeare, which were seen as successfully breaking away from neo-classic rules. Victor Hugo, although not entirely successful, opened the way for romantic dramatists such as Dumas, von Kleist, and Buchner. Many of the most significant changes in the 19th-century theatre were in the physical layout of the theatre, the theatre design, the audience, and the acting troupes.

One type of popular theatre production in the 19th century was melodrama. These plays were accompanied by a music which underscored the emotional character of any given moment. In general these works exaggerated emotions and sensationalism. A melodrama based on Harriet Beecher Stowe's *Uncle Tom's Cabin* was particularly popular in the United States.

In the middle of the century, a strong movement towards realism emerged in theatric productions. The realistic translation of contemporary life into a dramatic form was largely accomplished by Scribe. A master of plot, Scribe established a straightforward formula: exposition of the situation; unexpected but logical reversals; build suspense; bring action to a logical resolution. Four major realist dramatists are discussed. Dumas, *fils* achieved worldwide popularity with his portrayal of a courtesan in *Camille*. Norway's Ibsen built powerful realistic dramas that were sometimes controversial. Chekhov, a Russian, drew his subject matter from daily life and gave realistic portrayals of the frustration and depressing qualities of a mundane existence. In England, George Bernard Shaw, dominated the theatre with his wit and brilliance. His plays exhibit originality and the unexpected.

In the late-19th century, a brief anti-realism movement appeared in French literature called symbolism. In the works of the symbolist dramatist Maeterlinck, truth was only suggested through symbols. He believed that great drama contained verbal beauty, contemplation, and a passionate portrayal of nature and of our sentiments.

Two significant developments in theatre occurred at the end of the century. One was the emergence of production unity as a principal aesthetic concern, which gave the director the responsibility for overall unity. The second was the appearance of an independent theatre movement, which allowed private performances. This avoided censorship and nurtured free experimentation.

Music: As in the other arts, romanticism brought about a greater role for emotion and subjectivity in music. Spontaneity was emphasized along with beautiful, expressive melodies. Rhythm varied from simple to complex; conflict was often suggested by juxtaposing conflicting metric patterns. Harmonies became more complex, and traditional harmonic patterns became blurred. Increases in chromaticism and extended use of dissonances led to a search for a new tonal system by the end of the era. Romantic music is also characterized by an interest in color, which led to a great increase in the number and diversity of instruments in the orchestra.

The piano played a prominent role in romantic music, both in an accompanying role for songs and as a solo instrument. The flowering of lyric poetry in Germany led to the rise of German songs called Lieder. The first great composer of Lieder was Schubert. His works present a great variety of forms and complexities. In them, the piano plays an integral role in establishing moods and creating images from the text. One of his major works is the song cycle based on the poems of Müller, *Die Schöne Müllerin*. Schubert was also a masterful composer for solo piano, as were Liszt and Chopin. Liszt is best remembered for his theatric displays of virtuosity, while Chopin often emphasized the more intimate qualities of the instrument. Chopin, who wrote almost exclusively for the piano, composed three types of works: études, which were studies in technique; short intimate pieces, such as preludes, nocturnes, and dances; and larger works, such as ballades and fantasies. Chopin's graceful and lyrical style is exemplified in the Nocturne in E-flat Major.

Composers of orchestral works split into two distinct camps during the 19th century: those who wrote program music (music based on a non-musical idea) and those who wrote traditional symphonies. Two leading composers of program music are described. Berlioz's *Symphony Fantastique* deals with images of a young poet falling in love, being executed for the murder of his beloved, and ultimately witnessing a dance of witches. While Berlioz set the program within the loose design of a symphony, Richard Strauss wrote one movement programmatic works called tone poems or symphonic poems. The leading symphonic composer in the romantic era was Brahms. As is evident in the Symphony No. 3 in F Major, Brahms synthesizes romantic traits with a traditional classic structure.

Nationalism was strong in romantic music. Folk tunes and melodies and folk-like rhythms permeated the works of composers in Russia and throughout Europe. The Russian Tchaikovsky assimilated many of these qualities into classic structures, as heard in his Violin Concerto.

A wide variety of choral music was composed during the romantic era, ranging from small pieces to huge ensemble works using soloists, massive choruses, and full orchestras. The Requiem by Berlioz called for 210 voices, a large orchestra, and four brass bands. One of the finest choral works of the time was Brahms' *German Requiem*, which is based on selected texts from the Lutheran Bible. Brahms' expressive use of tone colors and his lyric melodies support the beauty of the text which offers hope and consolation for the living.

There are three principal centers of opera in the 19th century: France, Italy, and Germany. In France, three important types of opera appeared. Grand opera, which grew out of the efforts by librettist Eugene Scribe and composer Meyerbeer, was characterized by crowd scenes, ballets, and fantastic scenery centering around medieval and contemporary events. A lighter operatic style called opéra comique sometimes led to delightful and witty satires, such as those works by Offenbach. The third form of French romantic opera was called lyric opera. Romantic drama and fantasy were common plots in such works.

Early romantic opera in Italy emphasized the bel canto style, which focused on the beauty of the voice. Rossini's *Barber of Seville* exemplifies this early style. Greater depth and drama were added by Verdi. In his major operas, such as *La Traviata* (based on Dumas' *Camille), Aida*, and *Otello*, Verdi combines his skills for writing beautifully for the voice and for maintaining a tightly woven dramatic structure.

One of the major figures of romantic music was the German opera composer Wagner. Wagner's works not only are dramatically powerful, but are also built upon several revolutionary ideas. Among these are *Gesamtkunstwerk*--a belief that music drama was a comprehensive artwork that combined music, poetry, scenery, acting, and philosophy--and the lietmotif--a method of unifying opera in which a musical idea may represent an object, person, or idea.

Two other trends may be observed in opera. Naturalism presented brute force and immorality, which is perhaps best seen in Bizet's *Carmen*. This spirit was exaggerated at the turn of the century in an Italian movement known as verismo, where adultery, revenge, and murder were common themes.

The anti-romantic movement at the end of the century produced a musical style that is analogous to that of impressionistic painters. The leading figure of this movement is Debussy, who rejected traditional harmony, used brief patches of orchestral color, and reduced melodies to fragmentary motives. Perhaps his most famous work is the symphonic poem *Prelude to the Afternoon of a Faun*, based on a poem by symbolist poet Mallarme.

Dance: Much of what we know about romantic ballet comes from the writings of Gautier and Blasis. Gautier rejected the aesthetics of Noverre and argued that dance should show beautiful forms. His focus on ballerinas helped to establish the female as the principal dancer in ballet. Carlo Blasis systematized the principles of dancing. His fundamental turned-out position still rules ballet today.

Robert the Devil, with music by Meyerbeer, was probably the first truly romantic ballet. Marie Taglioni danced in this production as well as *La Sylphide*, which may be the most famous of romantic ballets. Her lightness, delicacy, and modest grace established the standard for romantic style in dancing. The height of romantic ballet was *Giselle*, in which the highlight was a Pas de Quatre involving four major ballerinas on stage together.

Russia had become increasingly interested in Western artistic developments. The French choreographer Marius Petipa helped establish a serious school of ballet in Russia that became the envy of Europe. In the next generation, productions of *Nutcracker* and *Swan Lake*, with music by Tchaikovsky, secured Russia's role as the leading center of ballet.

In France, ballet declined in quality, though not in popularity, as it took a hedonistic turn. The cancan performed in the Moulin Rouge became a sensation. At this time a young American dancer, Loie Fuller, gained popularity in the Folies Bergère and pointed to the emergence of modern dance.

Architecture: Four architectural movements in the 19th century are described. Classicism can broadly be divided into two periods: before 1815, when Roman architecture was used as models, and after 1815, when Greek architecture was used. A number of substyles can be identified, such as romantic classicism, the federal style, and the English Regency style. Romantic classicism is illustrated by Latrobe's Catholic cathedral in Baltimore (Fig. 13.43), where the classical ionic orders and Roman dome are set against romantic decorations. American houses provide some outstanding examples of classicsm (Figs. 13.44-13.46).

Aspects of Romanticism can be seen in Figs. 13.47-13.49. Exotic influences from the East are reflected in the Royal Pavilion by John Nash. The Houses of Parliament demonstrates the modern tendency in which the exterior walls suggest nothing of the interior design or function. The strong contrast of forms and the asymmetrical balance are also striking. The Crystal Palace exemplifies the 19th-century fascination with new materials and concepts.

A third trend is toward experimentation, which led to the construction of skyscrapers. A leading architect in this style was the American Louis Sullivan, the first truly modern architect.

The final years of the 19th century saw a fourth trend called Art Nouveau. Primarily a decorative style, it is uniquely characterized by lively, serpentine curves and floral forms. (Figs. 13.52-13.53).

Synthesis: The Victorian age was an age of new technology, social stability, and artistic strength. The Victorian spirit held great influence on the continent of Europe and in the United States. Painting during this age shows a diversity of high talent. Romantic themes, such as history, landscape, realism, and fantasy, can be seen in Figs. 13.54-13.57. A particularly important group was the Pre-Raphaelites who, by breaking from the naturalistic school, had a profound influence on a number of 20th-century painters.

Important Terms

Romanticism: a general term applied with a variety of implications. In general, romanticism sought to escape classical suborndination of feeling to formal considerations. Common themes include nature, the macabre, nationalism, exoticism, and images from Medieval times. (388-92, 404-5, 409-11, 413-18, 419-21, 427)

Realism: a general term for the movement in art and literature which sought to create realistic visions, often of everyday life. (392-5, 409, 411-12)

Barbizon School: group of French landscape painters, including Millet, named after a small village near Paris where they worked. Paintings often include peasants doing simple, everyday tasks. (394)

Impressionism: a style of painting originating in France during the 1870s that sought to capture the momentary impression of a scene by treating not only the subject, but also the reflection and absorption of light on and around the subject. The term has also been applied loosely to sculpture and to the musical style of Debussy. (396-9, 405, 418)

Post-Impressionism: a general term used to denote a number of disparate style by French painters in the last two decades of the 19th century. Similar in subject matter to impressionism, post-impressionism contained greater complexity and subjectivity. The term has been loosely applied to sculpture. (400-3, 405-6)

Pointillism: a painting technique characterized by the systematic application of small dots of paint. This technique is associated with the post-Impressionist works of Seurat. (400)

Neo-classicism: a general term (sometimes interchanged with classic) that was first applied to the painting school of the late 18th century emphasizing balance and intellect.This becomes the predominant trend in 19th-century sculpture. (388, 404)

Melodrama: a drama played over music. It is characterized by sensationalism and sentimentality. (411)

Symbolism: a literary movement in the late 19th century that expressed ideas and emotions indirectly through symbols. (412)

Chromaticism: the altering of normal whole- and half-tone relationships in a musical scale. (413)

Lieder: German word for songs (a single song is referred to as a Lied). In the 19th century, the Lied was transformed into an art form by Schubert. These works, based on German lyric poetry, are set for solo voice and are usually accompanied by piano. (413-4)

Étude: a technical study for a musical instrument, such as the piano or violin. (414)

Program music: a piece of instrumental music associated with a narrative or descriptive idea. (414-5)

Tone poem (also referred to as a symphonic poem): a single-movement programmatic work for orchestra. Liszt is the first major composer. Other significant composers include Tchaikovsky and Richard Strauss. (415)

Grand opera: type of French opera appearing around 1830. Featuring spectacular stage effects, ballets, and virtuoso singing, grand opera dazzled middle-class audiences. The principal composer was Meyerbeer. (416-7)

Lyric opera: French operatic form from the 1860s. It is similar to opera comique in its light arias, but the dialogue is sung. Plots tend to be romantic dramas or fantasies. (417)

Opéra comique: French operatic form which originated in the 18th century. Characterized by lighter arias and spoken dialogue, opera comique split into two directions during the 19th century. Some composers, like Offenbach, wrote satirical comedies; others, like Bizet, turned away from comedy and treated serious subjects. (417)

Bel canto: style of singing originating in Italy that emphasizes beauty of sound. (417)

Gesamtkunstwerk: Wagner's term meaning total artwork. Wagner felt that music dramas should be comprehensive artworks combining the best of music, drama, poetry, scenery, and philosophy. (418)

Leitmotif: technique developed by Wagner in which a musical theme represents a person, object, or idea. Whenever one of these appear in the opera, the musical theme is played. (418)

Naturalism: an anti-romantic operatic movement in France. It replaced stylization with brute force and immorality. (418)

Verismo: an Italian operatic movement in the early 20th century. Literally meaning true to life, the term designates those operas, usually in one act, that portray the most passionate and violent aspects of the human condition. Major composers are Mascagni and Leoncavallo. (418)

Federal style: type of architecture produced in the United States that incorporates classical elements. (425)

English Regency style: type of architecture that shares characteristics with that popular during the regency of George, Prince of Wales. (425)

Art Nouveau: a style of architecture from the 1890s based on serpentine curves. (428)

Victorian: style exhibiting qualities associated with England during the reign of Queen Victoria (1837-1901). (429-33)

Pre-Raphaelites: a group formed in 1848 to recapture the spirit and style of painting before Raphael. (431)

Jean-Auguste Dominique Ingres (1780-1867): French painter whose works exhibit neo-classic and romantic elements. Major works include *Grande Odalisque*. (388)

Théodore Géricault (1791-1824): French romantic painter. His best known work is *The Raft of the "Medusa"*. (388-90)

Francisco de Goya (1746-1828): Spanish painter who used his paintings to attack abuses of the Spanish and French governments. Major works include *The Third of May*. (390)

J.M.W. Turner (1775-1851): English painter. In his works, nature is seen as a blind force--the romantic vision of nature. Major works include *The Slave Ship*. (391)

Eugene Delacroix (1798-1863): French painter whose works epitomized the romantic spirit of rebellion. Major works include *Liberty Leading the People*. (391)

Camille Corot (1796-1875): French painter who is best known for his visual realism in paintings of nature. (391-2)

Rosa Bonheur (1822-99): French painter who was both a realist and a romantic in style. Her subjects were mostly animals. (392)

Gustave Courbet (1819-77): French painter who was the central figure of realism. He depicted everyday life, often with a social message. Major works include *The Stone Breakers*. (392-3)

Jean François Millet (1814-75): French painter known for his realistic paintings of landscapes and peasants. (393)

Edouard Manet (1832-83): French painter in the realist tradition who went beyond painting a mere reflection of reality to encompass an artistic reality. He helped lead the way to impressionism. Major works include *Déjeuner sur l'herbe*. (394-5)

Henry O. Tanner (1859-1937): black American realist painter. (395)

Auguste Renoir (1841-1919): French painter associated with impressionism. Especially known for his treatment of people engaged in happy activities. (397-8)

Claude Monet (1840-1926): French painter considered to be the leading figure of impressionism. Major works include *On the Seine at Bennecourt*. (399)

Berthe Morisot (1841-95): a member of the original group of impressionists. Her works tend to focus on family members. (399)

Mary Cassatt (1845-1926): an American impressionist painter. Her favorite subjects were women and children. (399)

Georges Seurat (1859-1919): French painter associated with post-impressionism. He employed a distinctive technique called pointillism. Major works include *Sunday Afternoon on the Island of La Grande*. (400-1)

Paul Cézanne (1839-1906): French painter considered to be the father of modern art. His works are characterized by an emphasis on the fundamental geometric shapes underlying all forms. (401)

Paul Gauguin (1848-1903): post-impressionistic painter who spent the final years of his life in Tahiti. His works, like his life, represent a quest for spiritual meaning. (401-2)

Vincent van Gogh (1853-90): Dutch post-impressionist painter known for his turbulent life and powerful, energetic paintings. Major works include *The Starry Night* and *The Potato Eaters*. (402)

Antonio Canova (1757-1822): French sculptor considered to be the foremost representative of neo-classicism. Major works include *Venus Victrix*. (404)

Auguste Rodin (1840-1917): French sculptor associated with both romanticism and impressionism. Major works include *The Burghers of Calais*, *The Thinker*, and *Balzac*. (405)

Aristide Maillol (1861-1944): French sculptor known for his portrayal of heroic female nudes. Major works include *The Mediterranean*. (405-6)

Jacob Epstein (1880-1959): American-born British sculptor who employs post-impressionistic characteristics. (406)

Edgar Allen Poe (1809-49): American writer remembered for his poetry and horror stories. (407)

William Wordsworth (1770-1850): English poet who is primarily remembered for his works about nature. (407-8)

Samuel Taylor Coleridge (1772-1834): English poet and critic. Best known for his exploration of fantasy and the subconscious. Major works include *The Rime of the Ancient Mariner* and *Kubla Khan*. (408)

Walter Scott (1771-1832): English novelist and poet who wrote novels based on Scottish and English history. Major works include *Ivanhoe*. (408)

Lord Byron (1788-1824): unconventional English poet considered to be the romantic poet *par excellence*. Major works include *Don Juan*. (408)

Percy Bysshe Shelley (1792-1822): English poet who wrote intense lyric poetry. He is considered to be one of the most original intellects of the 19th century. (408)

John Keats (1795-1821): English poet considered to be the greatest of English romantics. Major works include *Ode on a Grecian Urn*. (408)

Jane Austen (1775-1817): English novelist who explored the private lives of the middle class. Major works include *Emma*. (408-9)

Emily Brontë (1818-48): English novelist. Major works include *Wuthering Heights*. (409)

Charlotte Brontë (1816-55): English novelist. Major works include *Jane Eyre*. (409)

Honoré de Balzac (1799-1850): French novelist known for realism. Wrote cycle of novels entitled *Comédie Humaine*. (409)

Charles Dickens (1812-70): English novelist who realistically portrayed inequities of Victorian England. (409)

Gustave Flaubert (1821-80): French realist novelist. His masterpiece is *Madame Bovary*. (405)

Émile Zola (1840-1902): French novelist who depicted characters trapped by environment and heredity. (409)

Charles Baudelaire (1821-67): French poet whose works treat the decadent state of man. Major works include *Les Fleurs du Mal*. (409)

Henry James (1843-1916): American novelist and critic known for his basic theme of innocence against corruption. (409)

Victor Hugo (1802-85): French author of novels, plays, and poetry. Major works include *Hunchback of Notre Dame* and *Les Miserables*. (410-1)

Alexandre Dumas, *pére* (1802-70): French playwright and novelist. Major works include *The Three Muskateers*. (411)

Heinrich von Kleist (1777-1811): German playwright who helped bring German theatre into the 19th century. (411)

Georg Buchner (1813-37): German romantic playwright. (411)

Eugene Scribe (1791-1861): playwright and librettist. Solved problem of dramatic form by a basic plot formula. He played a crucial role in the creation of grand opera. (411, 416)

Alexandre Dumas, *fils* (1824-95): the illegitimate son of Alexandre Dumas, *pére*. His best known work is the novel *Camille*. (411-2)

Henrik Ibsen (1828-1906): Norwegian playwright who was a master of realism. Major works include *A Doll's House* and *Hedda Gabler*. (412)

Anton Chekhov (1860-1904): Russian realist playwright. Major works include *Cherry Orchard*. (412)

George Bernard Shaw (1856-1950): playwright and critic. His works, such as *Man and Superman*, are characterized by wit and originality. (412)

Maurice Maeterlinck (1862-1949): French writer and the principal figure in the symbolist movement. Major works include *Pelléas and Mélisande*. (412)

Franz Schubert (1797-1828): Austrian composer of Lieder, piano works, symphonies, choral music, and chamber music. Considered to be the first great composer of Lieder. Major works include the song cycle *Die Schöne Müllerin*. (413-4)

Franz Liszt (1811-86): Hungarian composer who dazzled Europe with his pianistic virtuosity and his sensational romances. (414)

Frederic Chopin (1810-49): Polish composer of piano music who spent much of his career in Paris. His works, which combine virtuosity and intimacy, are considered to be among the finest ever composed for the instrument. Major works include études, preludes, mazurkas, ballades and other miniatures. (414)

Hector Berlioz (1803-69): French composer who is best known for his brilliant use of orchestral color and for his program symphonies. He also composed operas and choral works. Major works include *Symphonie fantastique, The Trojans*, and the *Requiem Mass*. (414-5, 416, 417)

Richard Strauss (1864-1949): German composer of symphonic poems, operas, and songs. At the turn of the century he was considered to be the foremost progressive composer. Major works include *Don Juan, Till Eulenspiegel*, and *Der Rosenkavalier*. (415)

Johannes Brahms (1833-97): German composer of four symphonies, piano music, songs, chamber music, and choral music. He was the leading composer of traditional Classical forms in the late 19th century. Major works include *Ein Deutsches Requiem*. (415, 416)

Peter Ilyich Tchaikovsky (1840-93): popular Russian composer of symphonies, symphonic poems, concertos, and operas. He is also the foremost ballet composer of the 19th century. Major works include the Violin Concerto and *The Nutcracker*. (412-3, 419)

Giacomo Meyerbeer (1791-1864): German composer who became the foremost composer of French grand opera. Major works include *Robert the Devil* and *The Huguenots*. (416)

Jacques Offenbach (1819-80): French composer of opéra comique. Best known for his smart, witty satires. (417)

Ambroise Thomas (1811-96): French composer of lyric opera. His *Mignon* is one of the most successful operas of all time. (417)

Charles Gounod (1818-93): French composer of lyric opera. His best known opera, *Faust*, is based on Goethe's play. (417)

Gioacchino Rossini (1792-1868): first major composer of Italian opera after Mozart. Today he is best remembered for his overtures, but his success as an opera composer was unparalleled in his time. Major works include *Barber of Seville*. (417)

Giuseppe Verdi (1813-1901): Italian opera composer. His ability to write beautiful melodies and his keen sense of drama made him the greatest Italian opera composer of the 19th century. Major works include *La Traviata, Aida*, and *Otello*. (417)

Richard Wagner (1813-83): German composer of opera. His revolutionary ideas not only changed opera, but also had a significant impact on all music, especially his harmonic innovations. Major works include *Tristan und Isolde* and the *Ring Cycle*. (417-8)

Georges Bizet (1838-75): French opera composer associated with naturalism. His *Carmen* has become one of the most popular operas of all time. (418)

Giacomo Puccini (1858-1924): Italian opera composer known for his intense lyric melodies and realistic plots. He is sometimes associated with verismo. Major works include *La Bohme, Tosca*, and *Manon Lescaut*. (418)

Claude Debussy (1862-1918): French composer most closely associated with impressionism. His music is especially important for its denial of traditional harmonic functions, which paved the way for future harmonic innovations. Major works include *Prelude to the Afternoon of a Faun*. (418)

Théophile Gautier: poet and critic who played a prominent role in the rise of the ballerina in the 19th century. (416)

Carlo Blasis (1803-78): ballet teacher and writer who codified classic ballet technique. (416)

Marie Taglioni (1804-84): ballerina who established the standard for romantic style dancing. (419-20)

Marius Petipa (1819-1910): French choreographer who helped to establish Russian ballet. (421)

Benjamin H. Latrobe (1764-1820): British-born American engineer and architect. He designed the Basilica of the Assumption in Baltimore. (423)

John Nash (1752-1835): British architect who designed the Royal Pavilion. (427)

Sir Joseph Paxton (1801-65): British gardener who turned architect when he designed the Crystal Palace for the Great Exhibition of 1851. (427)

Louis Sullivan (1856-1924): American who is considered to be the first modern architect. He believed that form should flow from function, an idea which became a rubric for modern architecture. (428)

Study Questions

How is the *Odalisque* by Ingres similar to the paintings of David (357-8)? What is new about this work? (388)

What are the goals and common subjects of romanticism (388-91)? How do the paintings reflect these trends?

The Raft of the "Medusa" by Géricault, *The Third of May 1808* by Goya, and *The Slave Ship* by Turner are all based on actual events. How are they similar in content and emotional appeal? How do they differ in color, line, and clarity? (389-91)

What are the goals of realism? of social realism? (392-94) How are they realized in paintings? How do the works of Manet differ from those of Courbet and Millet? (394-5)

In what respects is impressionism related to realism? (396-9)

How do post-impressionistic paintings differ from impressionistic? (400)

Name the four major figures of post-impressionism mentioned in your text. Describe the distinctive qualities of each. (400-3)

How do the works of Canova reflect neo-classic qualities? What are the evident influences of the rococo tradition on his works? (404)

Why does the term romanticism not transfer well from painting to sculpture? (404-5)

How are the goals of impressionism and post-impressionism realized in sculpture? (405-6)

Who are the major figures of English literature discussed in your text? What are their major works? Describe the romantic themes that these works exemplify. (407-9)

Who are the major novelists of the 19th century? Describe their major works. (409)

Why were so many romantic plays unsuccessful? Who were the leading romantic playwrights? Describe their works. (409, 410-11)

What changes in the physical makeup of the theatre, in audiences, and in actors took place in the 19th century? (49-10)

What is melodrama? (411)

Who are the leading realist playwrights? (411-2)

What is symbolism? Who is the leading dramatic symbolist? (412)

What are the principal characteristics of romantic music. (413) How do they differ from those of classic music? (367-8)

What is the role of the piano in Lieder? Why does your text say the Lieder personifies romantic music? (413-4)

What are the three types of piano music composed by Chopin? Name some general titles that he employed. (414)

Why did program music become an important technique for 19th-century composers? Who are the two composers of program music mentioned in your text? How do their works differ from each other? (414-5)

How does nationalism manifest itself in music? How are these traits seen in the music of Tchaikovsky? (416)

What are the three principal types of French opera? Who are the leading composers of each, and how do these types differ from each other? (416-7)

Who are the leading composers of Italian opera? Name their major works. (417)

What is Gesamtkunstwerk? Leitmotif? Who do we associate with these innovations? (417-8)

How are the works of Debussy similar to the paintings of the impressionistic movement? How does Debussy achieve these qualities? (418)

Describe the roles of Théophile Gautier and Carlo Blasis in the creation of the modern concept of ballet. (419)

What are the principal productions of romantic ballet? Describe the dancing style of Marie Taglioni. (419-21)

Discuss the emergence of Russia as the principal center of ballet. Who were the leading figures behind this movement? (421-2)

What are the principal architectural movements described in your text? Cite examples of each. (423-8)

PRACTICE TEST

1. In what country did the Industrial Revolution begin?
   a. France b. Germany c. England d. United States

2. What industry first felt the effect of the industrial revolution?
   a. textile b. mining c. agriculture d. tool manufacturing

3. Who is credited with developing the "American System"?
   a. Elias Howe b. Cyrus McCormick c. Otto von Guericke d. Eli Whitney

4. What would not be a concern of liberalism?
   a. reducing the power of the Church
   b. promoting the power of the aristocracy
   c. removing economic barriers through nationalism

5. According to Hegel, which artistic endeavor is the most spiritual?
   a. painting b. music c. poetry

6. According to Hegel, what is the objective of art?
   a. truth b. beauty c. entertainment d. education

7. Of the following, who was a pessimist?
   a. Schopenhauer b. Hegel c. Nietzsche

8. Who is the founder of what has been called "social Darwinism"?
   a. Schopenhauer   b. Comte c. Spencer d. Darwin

9. What agreement restored to Europe the boundaries and dynasties that
   existed prior to the French Revolution?
   a. Act of Congress of Vienna   b. Treaty of Versaille c. Peace of Amiens

10. What is not a tendency of romanticism?
    a. the picturesque b. nature c. Classic images d. macabre

11. Of the following, who still held ties to neo-classicism?
    a. Ingres b. Corot c. Turner d. Géricault

12. What is a romantic characteristic of Ingres' *Odalisque*?
    a. simple line   c. cool palette
    b. geometric spatial effects   d. exoticism

13. Matching

Monet   a. romanticism

Courbet   b. realism

Géricault   c. impressionism

Millet   d. post-impressionism

Van Gogh

Renoir

Cézanne

---

14. What statement does not characterize Géricault's *Raft of the Medussa*?
   a. it presents a criticism of governmental incompetence
   b. there is a complex three-dimensional design
   c. it projects a sense of drama and climax
   d. it is based on a fictitious event

15. What statement does not characterize Goya's *The Third of May 1808*?
   a. the victims are portrayed as individuals
   b. the soldiers are rigid and appear automated
   c. the background has a murky quality
   d. it is based on an actual event

16. Paintings of Turner, such as *The Slave Ship*, foreshadow
   a. realism b. neo-classicism c. the dissolving image d. simple nature settings

17. What function does the flag serve in Delacroix' *Liberty Leading the People*? a. balance b. unity c. symbolism d. all of these

18. How does Corot achieve a truthfulness of visual effect?
   a. he uses only natural colors
   b. he captures the effect of the perceptual experience
   c. he increases the clarity of details
   d. he chooses only outdoor subjects

19. What are common subjects in the paintings of Bonheur?
   a. peasants b. animals c. landscapes d. portraits

221

20. Who is not a painter associated with realism?
   a. Courbet b. Millet   c. Monet   d. Manet

21. What was a common subject of realism?
   a. heroic visions b. peasants at work c. aristocrats at leisure d. the macabre

22. What statement about Manet is incorrect?
   a. he is a realist, but can be linked with impressionism
   b. he liberated the canvas from competition with the camera
   c. he was faithful to observed atmospheric effects
   d. he portrays only fantasy and mythological themes

23. To what movement does Tanner belong?
   a. romantic b. realism c. impressionism d. neo-classicism

24. Of the following who is not associated with impressionism?
   a. Van Gogh b. Renoir   c. Mary Cassatt d. Monet

25. What does not characterize impressionist paintings?
   a. short, quick brush strokes   c. fragmentary images
   b. a shimmering quality   d. images are camera-like

26. How is post-impressionism similar to impressionism?
   a. both paint similar subjects   b. both are quite complex
           c. both are profoundly personal

27. What does not describe Seurat's *Sunday Afternoon on the Island of La Grande*
   a. it shows an influence from Japanese art
   b. it uses the technique of applying small specks of paint
   c. it shows no concern for an accurate depiction of light
   d. it avoids three-dimensionality

28. Cézanne believed that
   a. all forms in nature were based on geometric shapes
   b. art should abandon formal design
   c. geometric shapes should be complicated   d. all of these

29. What does not characterize Gauguin's *The Vision after the Sermon*?
   a. flat figures b. lack of symbolism c. simple forms d. unnatural colors

30. Which statement does not describe Van Gogh?
  a. he led a turbulent life
  b. his paintings are filled with energy
  c. his paintings are impersonal and objective
  d. his use of flattened forms suggest a Japanese influence

31. Who is the model for Canova's *Venus Victrix*?
  a. Marie Antoinette b. Napoleon's sister c. Canova's wife d. unknown

32. What work is not by Rodin?
  a. Balzac b. The Burghers of Calais c. The Mediterranean d. The Thinker

33. What does not characterize the works of Rodin?
  a. social commentary
  b his surfaces appear to shimmer
  c. he employs irregular features
  d. they lack dramatic qualities

34. What does Maillol share in common with post-impressionistic painters?
  a. his works capture emotional qualities
  b. his emphasis on rigid, simple forms
  c. his concern for formal composition

35. The works of Epstein are similar to those of which painter?
  a. Seurat b. Gauguin c. Van Gogh d. Monet

36. When can we date the beginning of Romantic literature?
  a. 1790 b. 1800 c. 1810 d. 1820

37. Matching
  Lord Byron   a. *The Rime of the Ancient Mariner*

  Coleridge   b. *Ode to a Grecian Urn*

  John Keats   c. quiet, meditative style

  Percy Bysshe Shelly   d. believed in harmony between man and nature
  ---
  Wordsworth   e. *Don Juan*
  ---

38. Matching
   Charles Dickens   a. *Les Fleurs du Mal*

   Emily Brontë   b. *Comédie Humaine*

   Balzac   c. *Wuthering Heights*

   Jane Austen   d. *Jane Eyre*

   Charlotte Brontë   e. *Emma*

   Charles Baudelaire   f. *Bleak House*
   ---

39. Who was the best author of romantic theatre?
  a. Hugo b. Kean c. Buchner d. Shakespeare

40. What does not describe the theatre of the 19th century?
   a. the lower class was admitted to performances
   b. historical accuracy gave way to exaggeration
   c. actors spoke lines within the confines of the scenery
   d. travelling touring companies were common

41. What does not characterize melodrama?
   a. sensationalism   c. accompaniment of music
   b. sentimentality   d. moderation

42. Who solved the problem of translating contemporary life into dramatic
   form? a. Dumas, *fils* b. Scribe c. Ibsen d. Shaw

43. Henrik Ibsen is from which country?
   a. England b. Belgium c. Norway d. Russia

44. Who is the principal dramatic symbolist?
  a. Shaw b. Maeterlinck c. Chekhov d. Ibsen

45. What does not characterize Romantic music?
   a. an emphasis on subjective emotions   c. simple harmonies
   b. expressive melodies   d. varied colors

46. Music of the 19th century becomes less dissonant. a. true   b. false

47. Who was the first important composer of Lieder?
   a. Brahms b. Schubert   c. Schumann d. Wagner

48. What type of piano work did Chopin not compose?
   a. étude b. mazurka c. ballade d. piano trio

49. What does not characterize the piano works of Chopin?
   a. virtuosity b. Polish folk rhythms c. classical forms d. intimate character

50. Who was not a composer of program music?
   a. Berlioz b. Brahms c. R. Strauss

51. Who is the leading composer of traditional symphonies?
   a. Liszt b. Brahms c. Strauss d. Berlioz

52. For whom is Brahms' *Ein Deutsches Requiem* composed?
   a. the dearly departed   c. Robert Schumann's wife
   b. the consolation of the living   d. the victims of war

53. Of the following, what is not a characteristic of French grand opera?
   a. ballets b. choruses c. simple scenery d. spectacle

54. Which opera is not by Verdi?
   a. *Barber of Seville*   b. *Aida*   c. *Rigoletto*   d. *La Traviata*

55. A musical idea in Wagner's operas that represents a person, object or idea
   is called a. Gesamtkunstwerk b. Leitmotif c. bel canto

56. Which opera does your text cite as the best example of naturalism?
   a. *La Traviata*   b. *Otello*   c. *Aida*   d. *Carmen*

57. The Italian operatic movement in the early 20th century that emphasizes
   passion and violence is called
   a. verismo b. impressionism c. realism d. bel canto

58. Which composer is associated with impressionism?
   a. R. Strauss b. Puccini c. Debussy d. Bizet

59. What does not characterize musical impressionism?
   a. long flowing melodies   c. delicate use of color
   b. irregular rhythm   d. denial of traditional harmony

60. What characterizes the beliefs of Théopile Gautier?
   a. truth is beauty   c. focus should be on females
   b. dance has no deep meaning   d. all of these

61. Who systematized the training and positions of dancers?
   a. Noverre b. Gaultier c. Blase d. Taglioni

62. Which work is described as the first truly romantic ballet?
   a. *Giselle*   b. *Le Papillon*   c. *Robert the Devil*

63. Matching
   Meyerbeer   a. Gesamtkunstwerk

   Wagner   b. Lyric opera

   Rossini   c. Grand opera

   Verdi   d. verismo

   Offenbach   e. early composer of Italian opera

   Leoncavallo   f. greatest composer of Italian opera

   Gounod   g. opéra comique
   ---

64. Who is the choreographer who played a major role in establishing Russian
   ballet?   a. Petipa   b. Coralli   c. Ivanov   d. Grisi

65. Which architectural style was prevalent in the United States?
   a. romanticism b. classicism c. art nouveau d. baroque

66. What describes the Houses of Parliament?
   a. exemplifies neo-classicism   c. symmetrically balance
   b. no relationship between exterior and interior d. all of these

67. The skyscraper is a result of which movement?
   a. classicism   c. romanticism
   b. experimentation   d. art nouveau

68. What characterizes Art Nouveau?
   a. geometric shapes c. perpendicular lines
   b. serpentine curves d. classic imitations

69. What does not characterize the Victorian age?
   a. new technology   c. international influences
   b. social stability   d. disregard for the arts

70. What does not characterize the The Pre-Raphaelite movement?
   a. it embraced naturalism   c. it influence later painters
   b. it was formed in 1848   d. it return to direct symbols

ANSWERS
1. c   2. a   3. d   4. b   5. c   6. b   7. a   8. c   9. a 10. c   11. a 12. d
13. cbabdcd 14. d 15. a 16. c 17. d 18. b 19. b 20. c 21. b 22. d 23. b
24. a   25. d 26. a 27. c 28. a 29. b 30. c 31. b 32. c 33. d 34. a   35. c
36. a 37. eabcd   38. fcbeda   39. d 40. b   41. d 42. b 43. c 44. b   45. c
46. b 47. b 48. d 49. c 50. b 51. b 52. b   53. c 54. a 55. b 56. d 57. a
58. c 59. a 60. d   61. c 62. c 63. caefgdb   64. a 65. b 66. b 67. b 68. b
69. d 70. a

CHAPTER 14: THE EARLY TWENTIETH CENTURY

CONTEXTS AND CONCEPTS

Summary

The 20th century has been both a period of great achievements and a time of turmoil and upheaval. Many of the most remarkable achievements have been in science. New ideas, such as the Quantum Theory, the Theory of Relativity, and Atomic theory, have reshaped fundamental concepts. Reflecting the 20th-century orientation, a new philosophy emerged called pragmatism. Abandoning the search for answers to questions of God and existence, pragmatism sought more modest goals, such as morals and aesthetic values in an industrialized society. A leading spokesman of pragmatism, John Dewey, argued that experience was fundamental in all areas, particularly in aesthetics. For Dewey, aesthetics was the "crown of philosophy."

After the stunning explorations of the inner mind by Sigmund Freud, a new area of research was opened. John Watson and B.F. Skinner studied behaviorism. Carl Jung expanded upon the concept of intuition, which he felt was separate from thinking. He felt that within every individual lay primordial images and that the creative process was the unconscious expression of these images. In addition to these developments, important strides were taken towards improving society. The government took a larger role in controlling excesses of capitalism, women earned the right to vote, and labor laws protected workers.

Yet, for the most part, this century has been dominated by political conflict. The optimistic belief that we were headed toward the best that progress in science could offer was shattered by World War I. A series of shocking events continued throughout the century, including: the Russian Revolution, which established an adversarial role between the East and West; the economic collapse of 1929; the rise of Hitler and the global conflict involving Japan in the 1940s; and the destruction of Hiroshima by a nuclear explosion in 1945.

Important Terms

Pragmatism: philosophical view that bases its meaning on observable actions and consequences. (436)

Treaty of Versailles (1919): treaty that concluded World War I. It failed in its goal to limit the power of Germany. (439)

Important Names

John Dewey (1859-1952): American author and philosopher. He was an advocate of pragmatism. (436)

Carl Jung (1875-1961): Swiss psychologist who separated intuition from thinking. (436-7)

Albert Einstein (1879-1955): scientist whose Theory of Relativity overturned the physics of Newton. (438, 442)

Sigmund Freud (1856-1939): Austrian physician who founded psychoanalysis. (438, 448)

Study Questions

Define pragmatism. Why is this an appropriate philosophy for the 20th century? What new views about intuition appeared in this century? (436-7)

What have been the benefits in scientific progress during this century? What have been the drawbacks? (437-40)

THE ARTS OF THE EARLY TWENTIETH CENTURY

Summary

Two-Dimensional Art: Six major artistic movements of the early 20th century are described in the text. Expressionism focused on a joint artist/respondent reaction to composition elements. Subject matter was less important than evoking a response from the viewer that was similar to the artist's. The distorted figures in Beckmann's *Christ and the Woman Taken in Adultery* (Fig. 14.6) transmits the artist's revulsion against physical cruelty.

Fauvism is a movement that emphasizes violent distortion and outrageous coloring. These elements can be seen in *The Blue Nude* (Fig. 14.7) by the leading figure of this movement, Henri Matisse. This work does not portray a nude as the artist saw it in life, but expresses his feelings about the nude as an object of aesthetic interest, and in this way fauvism is tied with Expressionism.

Rejecting all concepts of two- or three-dimensional space, cubism sought to make the area around an object part of that object. The style grew out of experiments by Picasso and Braque. Picasso, the most influential artist of this century, went through two well-known phases called the Blue Period and the Rose Period before he began to explore cubism. In his masterwork *Les Demoiselles D'Avignon* (Fig. 14.8), the influence of African art can be seen in the flat forms and the exaggeration of certain features. Classic proportions are denied, as the subjects are broken into angular wedges. A new reality has been created. A similar effect is created in Léger's *Three Women* (Fig. 14.9), which uses perspective, but without normal logic.

Abstraction or non-representational art contains minimal reference to objects of the natural world. It explores the expressive qualities of formal design elements in their own right. Numerous painters and approaches can be linked to this movement. Piet Mondrian created a fascinating series of paintings consisting of straight lines and right angles (Fig. 14.10), and Kasimir Malevich created the puzzling work *White on White* (Fig. 14.11).

Dadaism was essentially a protest movement against Western society. Irrationality, meaningless malevolence, and mechanical effects are typical, as evident in the examples by Max Ernst and Marcel Duchamp (Figs. 14.12-14.14). Fascination with the subconscious led to surrealism, a movement that tied the subconscious mind to painting. The irrational qualities seen in the works of Chirico and Dali (Figs. 14.15-14.16) provide entrancing visions of the world of dreams.

The 20th century saw the emergence of a strong and vigorous production of paintings in the United States. An early group, called the Eight, portrayed a warm, sentimental view of American city life, without social criticism. The modern movement was launched after an international exhibit of art in 1913. Three major American figures are discussed in the text. Georgia O'Keeffe was an original artist who abstracted objects in unique ways. In *Dark Abstraction* (Fig. 14.17), she creates a sense of reality that takes us beyond the surface of our perceptions. Stuart Davis took natural objects and arranged them into abstract groupings, as evident in *Lucky Strike* (Fig. 14.19). Grant Wood continued realist traditions. His *American Gothic* (Fig. 14.18) celebrates America's heartland with its portrayal of simple, hard-working people.

A remarkable and vital production of art occurred in both Harlem and in Central America. Harlem became the capital of black culture between 1919 and 1925, and black painters, sculptors, musicians, poets, and novelists took up three primary themes: the African heritage, the tradition of black folklore, and the daily life of black people. Aaron Douglas (Figs. 14.20-14.21) was perhaps the foremost painter of the Harlem Renaissance. In Central America, Diego Rivera revived the fresco mural as an art form. Works, such as Fig. 14.22, blends European and native traditions and makes a strong social comment.

Sculpture: Sculpture revived significantly in the 20th century, partly due to interests in other cultures where sculpture played a prominent role. Classicism continued to exert influence on sculptors such as Maillol and MacNeil, who focused on simplicity of form, clear line, and structure (Figs. 14.23-14.24). In strong contrast are the works of futurist sculptor Boccioni. Futurists sought qualities that represented our mechanized society; the sculpture of Fig. 14.1 portrays mercury as a machine in motion.

African influences are noted in the works of three sculptors. Brancusi captured the primitive essence of African art in Figs. 14.25-14.26. Despite their apparent simplicity, these works are animated and possess great psychological complexities. Henry Moore explored numerous ways of depicting the human figure (Fig. 14.27), and his works show varying influences of Mexican figures, the monoliths of Stonehenge, and of classicism. Perhaps his most famous feature is the use of negative space. Lipchitz experimented with elements of negative space, cubism, and primitive art (Fig. 14. 28).

Literature: Between 1914 and 1939 the novel came to the fore as a literary medium, as it dealt with the complex ideas and experiences served up to 20th-century man. Subject matter was enriched and traditional methods of writing were attacked. James Joyce explored the unconscious mind in his brilliant *Ulysses*, which details the thoughts and actions of one individual in a single day. More traditional were the novels of D.H. Lawrence, which are linked with the romantic tradition of the previous century. Among other important novelists are Virginia Woolf and Thomas Mann. The American William

Faulkner utilized stream of consciousness in his masterwork *The Sound and the Fury*. He wrote more than 20 novels centering on characters in an imaginary county in the South.

The traditions of poetry were also challenged, as can be seen in the works of T.S. Eliot and Ezra Pound. W.H. Auden shunned complexity and wrote epigrammatic and satirical poetry. The African-American poet Langston Hughes focused on the humor, pathos, irony, and humiliation of being black in America.

Theatre: The 20th century brought about revolutionary ideas of theatre production. Two important theorists emerged. Adolphe Appia felt that depictive reality was unnecessary, and that the audience's attention should be on the character, not on scenic details. Gordon Craig believed in a spiritual relationship between setting and action. He advocated moving figures, light and shadow, and dramatic color. Appia and Craig were proponents of eclecticism (sometimes called artistic realism), which held that the stage environment must be appropriate to the given play. These principles were carried out in the works of Max Reinhardt.

A number of important theatric movements developed during the first half of this century, five of which are described in the text. Expressionism was reflected both in the visual form of scenic design and in the realism and naturalism of the play itself. Strindberg used the theatre to express his reaction to the universe and turned inward to the subconscious. Disillusionment can be seen in the expressionist works of the German Ernst Toller and the American Elmer Rice.

A second important movement was social action, which sought not only to entertain but also to teach and to motivate the audience into action outside of the theatre. The plays of Meyerhold were a product of the Russian Revolution. His central viewpoint was that the audience should never confuse theatre with life. Hence, curtains were removed so that backstage areas were fully visible. He also introduced constructivism, which consisted of various levels and playing areas of a non-objective nature. Social action also found a home in American theatre. Clifford Odets' *Waiting for Lefty*, written during the Depression, made the audience a part of the play itself.

The Independent Art Theatre Movement, which is discussed in the previous chapter, continued to be a force in 20th-century theatre. Particularly significant was the Provincetown Players who played a crucial role in the early career of Eugene O'Neill, one of America's most prolific and best known playwrights.

Epic theatre is a term coined by Bertolt Brecht for his own works. In his efforts to move the audience out of its role of passive spectator, he postulated three circumstances: historification, which removed events from the present to the past; alienation, which alienated the audience from the play's events so that it could see the play as a comment on life; and epic, which referred to the epic poem qualities of the play.

Absurdism was strongly tied to the philosophy of existentialism. Both focused on the disillusionment of the individual in an uncaring and often hostile world. Leading figures were the Italian Pirandello, who questions reality, the French existentialists Sartre and Camus, Samuel Beckett, author of *Waiting for Godot*, and Ionesco, who used nonsense syllables, meaningless repetition, and plots with no development.

Film: The last decade of the 19th and the early years of the 20th centuries brought about a number of exciting developments to a new artform, film. The first public projection of movies on a large screen was provided by the Lumière brothers in France in 1895. The following year, the Vitascope, an improved projection machine invented by Armat, was premiered in New York. Within the next 15 year, a large number of films were produced, over 1,000 by George Melies alone.The most popular film of this time was the 12-minute *Great Train Robbery* by Edwin S. Porter.

During the 1910s the film industry was still international in nature. In the U.S., Charles   , the screen's first mogul, made hundreds of films. At this time, there began a move by American film makers to a sleepy Western town, Hollywood. D.W. Griffith produced the most significant film of the decade, the three-hour *Birth of a Nation*. Also during the time came the Keystone Kops comedies directed by Mack Sennet, the earliest cowboy heros, and the brilliant comedian Charlie Chaplin. In Europe, expressionist films were made in Germany and other important films were made in England, France, and Russia.

The 1920s were the heyday of Hollywood, as the studios' star system produced a legion of popular figures, including Rudolph Valentino, Greta Garbo, and Laurel and Hardy. One of the greatest achievements of this period was *Ten Commandments* by Cecil B. DeMille. But the most important development was the use of sound in the 1927 film *Jazz Singer*. In the 1930s films of crime and violence with Edward G. Robinson were popular. Also noteworthy were the movies with sexually explicit dialogue by Mae West, the musicals of Fred Astaire and Ginger Rogers, the animated features of Walt Disney, the debut of Shirley Temple, John Ford's classic Western *Stage Coach* featuring the young John Wayne, and the comedies of the Marx Brothers and W.C. Fields. Among the best individual films are Judy Garland's *Wizard of Oz*, Chaplin's brilliant *City Lights*, and the great epic *Gone with the Wind*. In Europe, the vigorous German film industry suffered at the hands of the Nazis, but the British produced a young director named Alfred Hitchcock.

Music: Music broke away from the past in three principal ways: a move towards greater rhythmic complexity, an emphasis on dissonant harmony, and a rejection of traditional harmony. The direction towards these developments were largely pointed by the works of Wagner and Debussy. Not all composers severed ties with the past completely. Ravel, in works such as the Piano Concerto in G, sustained a neo-classic tradition. Similar effects can be seen in the works of William Schuman and Prokofiev. Paul Hindemith, an important theorist and composer, abandoned harshly dissonant works later in his career and produced music that was understandable to the public.

A number of outstanding figures dominated the music of the early century. The Hungarian Bartók combined nationalistic and neo-classic features. Particularly important are his string quartets, which illustrate his dissonant harmonies and energetic rhythms. Stravinsky created a near riot with his ballet *The Rite of Spring*, written for Diaghilev. In this work, his unconventional treatment of rhythm set a standard for the century. Later, he turned towards neo-classicism, and, after World War II, serialism. Schoenberg turned away from the late romantic style and explored atonality, a system where there was no prominent key center. His works from this time, such as *Pierrot Lunaire*, have been called expressionistic. In the 1920s, he developed a new compositional technique in which the composer ordered the 12 pitches of the chromatic scale and then manipulated that order in a variety of ways. Schoenberg had two important pupils, Webern and Berg.

America produced a number of outstanding composers. The first was Charles Ives, a highly original composer who worked in obscurity. Many of his experiments predate important compositional techniques of the century. Copland integrated American idioms, such as jazz, dissonance, and hymns, into his compositions. One of his finest works is the ballet *Appalachian Spring*. Perhaps the most important contribution of America to music is jazz. Based on the syncopated style of Scott Joplin and improvisation, jazz grew out of New Orleans in the 1920s.

Dance: Dance in the 20th century can be divided into two broad categories: ballet and modern dance. The most important figure in ballet at the beginning of the century was Diaghilev, whose *Ballets russes* successfully brought together some of the world's greatest artistic talents. Composing for the company were leading figures including Stravinsky (*Firebird* and *Rite of Spring*), Debussy, Ravel, and Prokofiev. Costume designers included Leon Bakst and Picasso. Among the choreographers who staged works for Diaghilev were Fokine, who reintroduced the male dancer as the premier performer, Nijinsky, who is perhaps the greatest dancer of the century, Massine, who turned towards cubism and surrealism, and Balanchine. The latter was particularly important for establishing ballet in the

United States. The 1930s saw a number of ballet companies appear in this country, and perhaps because of the excitement created by a tour of the *Ballets russes de Monte Carlo*, the American public began to accept this art form.

A number of important figures laid the foundations for modern dance. Isadora Duncan helped to inspire the movement with her deeply emotional dancing and her use of barefeet and Greek tunics and draperies. Concrete foundations for the movement were laid by Ruth St. Denis. Along with her husband Ted Shawn, she founded the Denishawn school and company which took an eclectic approach to dance--any and all traditions were included. Breaking away from Denishawn was Martha Graham, who would be the most influential figure in modern dance. For her, there were no rules; each work creates its own code. In general, the modern dance style would be angular and asymmetrical, and the dancers would hug the floor and dance with barefeet. Above all, dance was to express emotion. One of her most renown works was *Appalachian Spring*, composed by Aaron Copland. Among other early pioneers was Doris Humphrey.

Architecture: Art Nouveau continued in the early 20th century in works such as Gaudi's Casa Batlló (Fig. 14.34), but for the most part this time period saw much experimentation. Six individual approaches are discussed in the text. Auguste Perret developed formulas for building with ferro-concrete, and his personal style, as shown in Fig. 14.35, was quite influential. Unlike Perret's single-minded approach, Frank Lloyd Wright pursued experimentation and the exploration of various interrelationships of spaces and forms. One result was the prairie style, which was inspired by the flat landscape of the Midwest (Fig. 14.36). Wright tried to relate the exterior of the building to its context or natural environment, as is brilliantly evident in the Kaufmann House (Fig. 14.37). Wright also designed furniture for his houses with the goals of comfort, function, and design. Peter Behrens applied new techniques of poured concrete and exposed steel and the use of glass side walls in the A.E.G. turbine factory (Fig. 14.38). Le Corbusier believed that a structure should function as efficiently as a machine, and he developed a domino system of design for houses, using a series of slabs supported on slender columns (Fig. 14.39). Also noteworthy are Cass Gilbert's "Gothic" Woolworth Building (Fig. 14.40), and the important Bauhaus School founded by Walter Gropius.

Synthesis: The Bauhaus School of Art, Applied Arts, and Architecture was founded in 1919 by Walter Gropius and Adolph Meyer. Its purpose was to approach aesthetics from a spirit of engineering and to unify art and technology. For this purpose Gropius brought together not only architects, but painters as well. In this way, the Bauhaus became an important synthesis of the arts of the 20th century.

Important Terms

Expressionism: a term given to a general artistic movement in the late 19th and early 20th centuries that emphasized the expression of inner experience, generally the dark side of human experience. Distortion is often employed. (441, 461-2, 465, 469)

Fauvism: a brief artistic movement characterized by violent distortion and outrageous color. Matisse is a leading figure in the movement. (441-2)

Cubism: an artistic movement in the early 20th century that reduced natural forms to geometric units and then reordered to extend the object outside of itself. (442-4)

Abstraction: major artistic movement which contains minimal reference to natural objects. A more precise term is non-representational art. (444-7)

Dadaism: an artistic movement in the early 20th century that is characterized by irrationality, mechanical effects, and a whimsical subject. (447)

Surrealism: an artistic movement that depicts the irrational world of dreams and of the subconscious. (448)

The Eight: a group of American painters that emerged in 1908. Their works contained warm, sentimental views of American city life. (448)

The Harlem Renaissance: an artistic movement centering in Harlem that included black painters, sculptors, musicians, poets, and novelists. Their focus was on the African heritage, black folklore, and the daily life of black people. (451-2)

Futurism: an artistic movement originating in Italy that denounced contemporary culture and attempted to reflect the mechanistic quality of modern life. (453)

Negative space: holes or spaces built into a sculpture. (455)

Stream of consciousness: technique used in novels in which a first-person narration follows a character's thought process, which often involves moving from present to past and juxtaposing seemingly unrelated events or ideas. (457)

Eclecticism: also called artistic realism or organic unity, this term designates the belief that a stage environment should be appropriate to a given play. (461)

New Stagecraft: name given to the organic approach to theatre when it reached the United States. (461)

Social action: trend in theatre which sought to teach and motivate the audience. (462)

Biomechanics: system of actor training devised by Meyerhold. (462)

Constructivism: the use of various levels and playing areas in the theatre without scenery or traditional settings. (462)

Provincetown Players: group of young actors and writers who spent summers together on Cape Cod. Important to the development of Eugene O'Neill. (462)

Epic theatre: term associated with the plays of Brecht, in which the audience was brought into a dynamic relationship with the play. (463)

Absurdism: movement in theatre which portrayed man's meaningless existence in a chaotic universe. It is based on existentialism. (463-4)

Existentialism: a predominant philosophy in the 19th and 20th centuries that emphasizes the isolation of the individual in an indifferent or even hostile environment. (463-4)

Vitascope: an early type of motion-picture projector. (464)

Serialism: a technique of musical composition in the 20th century in which musical elements, such as pitch, rhythm, or dynamics, are assigned a specific order that is retained throughout a composition. (467, 505)

Twelve-tone technique: a type of serialism in which the 12 pitches of the chromatic scale are ordered and then used in a number of prescribed ways. (467, 469)

Atonality: term referring to the lack of a central tonal center in music. Schoenberg preferred the term pantonality. (469)

Jazz: a popular style of musical performance based on improvisation and syncopation. (470)

Ballets russes: dance company founded by Diagilev that gave brilliant and sometimes controversial productions in the early 20th century. Among those who contributed to performances were Nijinsky, Fokine, Balanchine, Stravinsky, and Picasso. (470-1)

Modern dance: although much variety exists, general qualities of angularity, asymmetry, use of the floor, and barefoot dancers distinguish it from ballet. (471-2)

Denishawn school: important school of modern dance founded by Ruth St. Denis and her husband Ted Shawn. (472)

Ferro-concrete: poured concrete containing steel bars or metal netting to increase its strength. (473)

Prairie style: architectural style development by Wright that drew upon the flat landscape of the Midwest for its tone. (474)

Bauhaus: an institute founded in 1919 for the study of art and architecture by Walter Gropius. (444, 477-9)

Important Names

Max Beckmann (1884-1950): German painter who was a principal figure in the Expressionist movement. (441)

Henri Matisse (1869-1954): French painter who was a leader of Fauvism. Major works include *Blue Nude*. (441-2)

Pablo Picasso (1881-1973): Spanish painter who greatly influenced 20th-century art. He was the leading figure of cubism. Major works include *Les Demoiselles d'Avignon*. (442-3)

Georges Braque (1882-1963): French painter who is one of the leading figures of cubism. (442)

Fernand Léger (1881-1955): French painter who continued cubism throughout the first half of the century. (444)

Piet Mondrian (1872-1944): Dutch painter who was a leading figure in abstract art. (444-5)

Kasimir Malevich (1878-1935): Russian painter who was a member of a non-representational movement called suprematism. His best known work is *Suprematist Composition: White on White*. (445)

Marcel Duchamp (1887-1968): French painter who used mechanistic themes in *Nude Descending a Staircase* and *The Bride*. (447)

Max Ernst (1891-1976): German-born American painter who is associated with dadaism and surrealism. (447)

Giorgio de Chirico (1888-1978): Greek-born artist associated with surrealism. Major works include *The Nostalgia of the Infinite*. (448)

Salvador Dali (1904-89): Spanish painter who was a leader in the surrealist movement. Major works include *The Persistence of Memory*. (448)

Georgia O'Keeffe (1887-1986): American painter who developed an original abstract style. (449)

Stuart Davis (1894-1964): American painter who took natural objects and arranged them into abstract groupings. Major works include *Lucky Strike*. (449-51)

Grant Wood (1892-1942): American painter who continued the realist tradition. His most famous work is *American Gothic*. (451)

Langston Hughes (1902-67): American novelist and poet. (451, 460-1)

Aaron Douglas (1899-1979): American painter who was arguably the foremost painter of the Harlem Renaissance. Best known for his illustrations and cover designs for books by black authors. (451-2)

Diego Rivera (1886-1957): Mexican painter who revived the fresco mural as an art form. (452)

Aristide Maillol (1861-1944): French sculptor who specialized in female nudes. (405-6, 453)

Hermon MacNeil: sculptor who sustained classicism in the 20th century. (453)

Umberto Boccioni (1882-1916): Italian sculptor who was a futurist. One of his best known works is *Unique Forms of Continuity in Space*. (453)

Constantin Brancusi (1876-1957): sculptor who was influenced by African art. His best known work is *Bird in Space*. (454)

Henry Moore (1898-1986): English sculptor who explored numerous ways of depicting the human figure. He is noted for using negative space. (455)

Jacques Lipchitz (1891-1973): Lithuanian sculptor whose works share many features in common with the paintings of Picasso. His best known work is *Man with a Guitar*. (456)

James Joyce (1882-1941): Irish novelist who explored the unconscious mind. Major works included *Ulysses*. (456-7)

D.H. Lawrence (1885-1930): English novelist who is linked with the romantics of the 19th century. Major works include *Women in Love* and *Lady Chatterley's Lover*. (457)

Virginia Woolf (1882-1941): English writer who explored inner feelings and emotion. (457)

Thomas Mann (1875-1955): German author who delved into psychological portraits. Major works include *Death in Venice* and his masterpiece *The Magic Mountain*. (457)

T.S. Eliot (1888-1965): American-born English poet who cast aside traditional meters and rhyme. His most famous work is *The Waste Land*. (457)

W.H. Auden (1907-73): English-born American poet who wrote epigrammatic and satirical poems. (457)

William Faulkner (1897-1962): American novelist and writer of short stories. Known for his stream of consciousness and his settings in the South. Major work is *The Sound and the Fury*. (457-60)

Adolphe Appia (1862-1928): Swiss theorist of the theatre who argued that the audience should focus on the actor, not scenery. (461)

Gordon Craig (1872-1966): English theorist of the theatre who advocated a spiritual relationship between setting and action. (461)

Max Reinhardt (1873-1943): major theatre director who was a strong advocate of eclecticism. (461)

August Strindberg (1849-1912): Swedish playwright who was a leading figure in expressionism. (461)

Ernst Toller (1893-1939): playwright who expressed the disillusionment of German expressionism. (461-2)

Elmer Rice (1892-1967): American expressionist playwright. (462)

Vsevolod Meyerhold (1874-1942): Russian playwright who was central to the social action and constructivism movements. (462)

Clifford Odets (1906-63): American playwright of social action and protest. (462)

Eugene O'Neill (1888-1953): prolific American playwright who was influenced by expressionism. (462-3)

Bertolt Brecht (1898-1956): German playwright who was influenced by social action. He developed a type of play which he called epic theatre. (463)

Luigi Pirandello (1867-1936): disillusioned Italian playwright whose non-realistic works can be linked to absurdism. (463)

Jean Paul Sartre (1905-80): philosopher and playwright who is a leading figure in existentialism and absurdism. (463-4)

Albert Camus (1913-60): French novelist and playwright whose works represent existentialism and absurdism. (464)

Thomas Armat: the inventor of the Vitascope. (464)

D.W. Griffith (1875-1948): American producer and director. His most important work is *Birth of a Nation*. (464)

Mack Sennet (1884-1960): Canadian-born American producer and director who is famous for his comedies. (464)

Charlie Chaplin (1889-1977): British actor who is best remembered for his brilliant comedies. (464-5)

Cecil B. DeMille (1881-1959): American producer and director. Major works include *Ten Commandments*. (465)

Maurice Ravel (1875-1937): French composer who began in an impressionistic style, but soon turned to neo-classicism. Major works include *Bolero* and the Piano Concerto in G. (467-8)

William Schuman (b.1910): American composer who continued to employ traditional musical features. (468)

Sergei Prokofiev (1891-1953): Russian composer who sometimes employed traditional elements. (468)

Paul Hindemith (1895-1963): German composer and theorist. Major works include *Kleine Kammermusik* and the theory book *The Craft of Musical Composition*. (468)

Bela Bartók (1881-1945): Hungarian composer known for his use of folk-like qualities, classical structures, harsh dissonances, and energetic rhythms. (468)

Igor Stravinsky (1882-1971): Russian composer who revolutionized the treatment of rhythm in *Rite of Spring*. (468-9)

Arnold Schoenberg (1875-1951): an early explorer of atonality and musical expressionism. Later he developed the 12-tone system. Major works include *Pierrot Lunaire*. (469)

Alban Berg (1885-1935): pupil of Schoenberg. Major works include *Lyric Suite*. (469)

Anton Webern (1883-1945): pupil of Schoenberg whose works were influential after World War II. (469)

Charles Ives (1874-1954): experimental American composer. Major works include *Unanswered Question*. (469)

Aaron Copland (b.1900): American nationalist composer who was a leading figure in developing an American sound. Major works include the ballet *Appalachian Spring*. (469-70)

Scott Joplin (1868-1917): black pianist known as the King of Ragtime. His method of syncopation was influential on American popular music. (470)

Sergei Diaghilev (1872-1929): founder and director of the *Ballets russes*. (470-1)

Vaslav Nijinsky (1890-1950): Russian dancer and choreographer who is considered by many to be the greatest dancer of our age. (470-1)

Mikhail Fokine (1880-1942): Russian choreographer whose original approach helped to turn the *Ballets russes* into a resounding success. (470-1)

Léonide Massine (1896-1975): Russian choreographer who turned the *Ballets russes* towards cubism and surrealism. (471)

George Balanchine (b.1904): Russian choreographer who was to become the most influential figure in American ballet in this century. He worked for the *Ballets russes* and later founded the New York City Ballet. (471, 472)

Isadora Duncan (1878-1927): American dancer whose unorthodox and controversial dancing style provided the inspiration for modern ballet. (471)

Ruth St. Denis (1877-1968): American dancer who helped lay the foundations of modern dance. (472)

Martha Graham (b.1893): American dancer and choreographer who is the most influential figure in modern dance. (472)

Doris Humphrey (1895-1958): American dancer and pioneer of modern dance. (472)

Antoni Gaudi (1852-1926): Italian architect who continued the traditions of Art Nouveau into this century. (473)

Auguste Perret (1874-1954): influential architect who developed formulas for building with ferro-concrete. (473)

Frank Lloyd Wright (1867-1959): great American architect who was one of the most influential and innovative architects in this century. Major works include the Kaufmann House. (473-5)

Peter Behrens (1868-1940): German architect who was a pioneer in industrial design. (474)

Le Corbusier (1887-1965): Swiss architect who felt that a structure should function as efficiently as a machine. (474-76)

Cass Gilbert (1859-1934): American architect. Major works include the Woolworth Building. (476)

Walter Gropius (1883-1969): major German architect who was the founder of the Bauhaus. (477-9)

Study Questions

What is expressionism? How is it applied in painting? (441) theatre? (461-2) film? (465) music? (469)

How is fauvism related to expressionism? What is distinctive about it? (441-2)

What is cubism? Who are its leading figures? (442-4) Describe abstraction (444-7), dadaism (447) and surrealism. (448)

What characterized the works of the Eight? Who are the other three American composers discussed in the text? Describe their techniques and works (448-50)

Who are the principal figures of the Harlem Renaissance? What were their common themes? What is distinctive about the works of Diego Rivera? (451-2)

Which sculptors still retain classical characteristics? (453)

What is futurism and how do its goals manifest themselves in sculpture? (453)

Who are the leading sculptors who were influenced by sculptures from other cultures? Describe their works. (453-6)

How did novelists and poets challenge their respective traditions? Who are the leading literary figures of this century? (456-61)

Describe some of the new approaches to theatre production. Who are the principal figures behind these changes? (461)

What is social action? Who are the leading figures? How do Brecht's plays resemble social action? What are the three circumstances of the Epic as described by Brecht? (462)

What is absurdism? What philosophical movement is it tied to? Who are the leading figures? works? (463-4)

Describe the principal events, key figures, and major works in film prior to the 1920s (464-5), during the 1920s (465-6), during the 1930s (466-7).

What are the three new directions of music in the 20th century discussed in the text? Explain each. (467)

Which composers continued to employ traditional elements in this century? (468)

Who are the major musical figures of the early 20th century? Describe their general style and name their important works. (468-69)

Who are the leading American composers? Describe their works. (469-70)

Describe jazz. Who were the leading performers? (470)

What is the *Ballets russes*? Who are the leading figures that participated in this artistic endeavor? (470-1)

What role did Isadora Duncan have in the establishment of modern dance? Ruth St. Denis? Martha Graham? Name other leading figures of the movement. (486-7)

Who are the principal architects of the early 20th century? Describe their style and contributions to architecture. (473-6)

What is the Bauhaus? What architectural style did they advocate? Why does your text consider this a synthesis of 20th-century art? (477-9)

PRACTICE TEST

1. Double matching

Expressionism -- --	A. portrayed dream-like states	a. Picasso
Fauvism -- --	B. non-representational art	b. Beckmann
Cubism -- --	C. distortions and outrageous colors	c. Dali
Abstraction -- --	D. elicits specific emotional emotional response	d. Matisse
Dada -- --	E. area around object becomes part of the object	e. Mondrian
Surrealism -- --	F. irrational, meaningless, uses mechanical effects	f. Duchamp

2. What does not characterize Beckmann's *Christ and the Woman Taken in Adultery*? a. distorted figures c. classical perspective
   b. shallow space d. Gothic spiritualism

3. Who was not a cubist? a. Matisse b. Picasso c. Braque d. Léger

4. Kasimir Malevich's abstract works can be tied with what movement?
   a. Stijl b. suprematist c. constuctivist d. Bauhaus

5. The early 20th-century group of American painters were called
   a. fauves b. realists c. the Eight d. futurists

6. Of the following, who was an American realist?
   a. O'Keeffe b. Stuart Davis c. Mark Rothko d. Grant Wood

7. What movement is Maillol associated with?
   a. futurism b. classical c. abstraction d. minimalism

8. In what country did futurism begin?
   a. United States b. Germany c. France d. Italy

9. Which sculptor is known for his use of negative space?
   a. Maillol b. Oldenburg c. Moore d. Christo

10. The works of Lipchitz have been linked to the paintings of
   a. Matisse b. Beckmann c. Pollock d. Picasso

11. What does not characterize *Ulysses* by James Joyce?
   a. it was a serial publication   c. it takes place in a single day
   b. it was popular in the U.S.   d. it explored the unconscious mind

12. Who can still be linked with the romantic novel of the past?
   a. Joyce b. Lawrence c. Woolf d. Mann

13. What characterizes Faulkner's *The Sound and the Fury*?
   a. stream of consciousness   c. it is based on actual events
   b. plot set in New York   d. all of these

14. What does not characterize the ideas of Appia, Craig, and Reinhardt?
   a. production should be guided by a superdirector
   b. each play should dictate its own stage environment
   c. reality in scenic design was essential
   d. the physical environment is vital to communication

15. Who was not associated with expressionist theatre?
   a. Strindberg b. Beckett c. Toller d. Rice

16. What was not an innovation by Meyerhold?
   a. constructivism b. social action c. eclecticism d. biomechanics

17. The Provincetown Players helped the career of which playwright?
   a. Brecht b. Beckett c. O'Neill d. Miller

18. Who is associated with epic theatre?
   a. Brecht b. Beckett c. O'Neill d. Miller

19. Who is not associated with absurdism?
   a. Pirandello b. O'Neill c. Sartre d. Camus

20. The Vitascope was invented by
   a. Lumière b. Armat c. Porter d. Melies

21. Who produced *Birth of a Nation*?
   a. Porter b. Melies c.   d. Griffith

22. What comic genius began his career in the silent films of the 1910s?
   a. Chaplin b. Fields c. West d. Laurel and Hardy

23. What was the first talking film?
   a. *Birth of a Nation* b. *Jazz Singer* c. *Intolerance* d. *Little Caesar*

24. What does not represent a major difference between the music of the 19th and 20th centuries?
   a. dissonant harmonies c. colorful orchestration
   b. complex rhythms   d. rejection of traditional tonality

25. Which composer is not linked with traditional elements?
   a. Ravel b. Prokofiev c. Schuman d. Schoenberg

26. What does not characterize the music of Bartók?
   a. folk elements   c. traditional harmonies
   b. neo-classic structures d. rhythmic energy

27. What does not describe Stravinsky's *Rite of Spring*?
   a. an enthusiastic reception   c. revolutionary orchestration
   b. written as a ballet   d. revolutionary rhythm

28. Who developed the dodecaphonic technique?
   a. Hindemith b. Bartók c. Stravinsky d. Schoenberg

29. Which composer is the highly original American who was ahead of his time in the early 20th century? a. Ives b. Copland c. Babbitt c. Cage

30. Jazz is based on the syncopated style of
   a. Bess Smith b. Ives c. Scott Joplin d. Cage

31. Who was the founder of the *Ballets russes*?
   a. Nijinsky b. Diagilev c. Bakst d. Nouvel

32. Who was not a choreographer for the *Ballets russes*?
   a. Fokine b. Balanchine c. Bakst d. Nijinsky

33. The *Ballet russes* centered in what city
   a. St. Petersburg b. Paris c. Berlin d. London

34. Who was the brilliant dancer who choreographed *The Rite of Spring*?
a. Fokine b. Nijinsky c. Massine d. Balanchine

35. Who was the woman who revolutionized dance with her emotions and barefeet? a. Duncan   b. St. Denis c. Graham d. Humphrey

36. Who is considered the most influential figure in modern dance?
a. Duncan   b. St. Denis c. Graham d. Humphrey

37. Which architect continued the traditions of Art Nouveau?
a. Wright b. Gaudi c. Perret d. Le Corbusier

38. Which architect explored ferro-concrete?
a. Wright b. Gaudi c. Perret d. Le Corbusier

39. What does not characterize the work of Frank Lloyd Wright?
a. he relates building to environment
b. he designed furniture for some of his houses
c. each work is an individual creation not following a mold
d. he bent to the wishes of his patron

40. Who was a principal figure in founding the Bauhaus?
a. Fuller b. Wright c. Gropius d. Le Corbusier

41. What characterizes the Bauhaus?
a. intended for architects only
b. advocates external ornamentation
c. sought to unify art and technology
d. all of these

ANSWERS

1. Db Cd Ea Be Ff Ac 2. c 3. a 4. b   5. c   6. d   7. b   8. d   9. c 10. d
11. b   12. b   13. a 14. c 15. b 16. b 17. c 18. a 19. b 20. b 21. d 22. a
23. b   24. c   25. d 26. c 27. a 28. d 29. a 30. c 31. b 32. c 33. b 34. b
35. a   36. c 37. b 38. c 39. d 40. c 41. c

CHAPTER 15: THE LATE TWENTIETH CENTURY

CONTEXTS AND CONCEPTS

Summary

Art of the late 20th century continues to be characterized by an inexhaustible quest for originality and freshness. This period has witnessed the worst and best that humanity has to offer. The turbulence and contradictions of our time have created a troublesome vision of ourselves. The threats and worry that we encounter in our daily lives--from pollution to nuclear weapons--cast an ominous shadow over our attempts to understand what it means to be human. It is to renew our spirit that we turn to the arts and ideas of the past as well as of the present in order to cope with our finitude--not only of individual human lives but of our whole world as well.

Following World War II, the world faced two major crises: the decolonization of the third world and the Cold War between the major superpowers. The withdrawal of European colonial support, often only after violent uprisings, left many third-world countries open to oppressive military dictatorships and without the ability to feed themselves. Even while much of the world today is celebrating a new peace, ethnic violence and famine remain prevalent. These problems developed while the major economic powers were polarized in the Cold War. The United States and the Soviet Union became antagonists, and by 1949, China, under Mao Zedong, turned to communism, further complicating world relations. Between 1946 and 1973 major conflicts developed in Korea and Vietnam, and the world was brought to the brink of nuclear holocaust with the Cuban missile crisis.

Much of this tension has been released in recent years, as Mikhail Gorbachev has led his country towards democracy, the two Germanies have united, and Eastern Europe has moved away from communism. Now the major powers can focus on common problems, as was evidenced in the unified action against Saddam Hussein in 1991. Still major problems face us, particularly relating to the function and role of science in today's society and our weakened economy. Our future in the third millennium is uncertain.

Important Terms

Decolonization: the process by which former European colonies gained their independence following World War II. (482)

Cold War: the state of political tension that existed between the Soviet Union and the United States after World War II which stopped just short of full-scale war. (482-3)

Important Names

Mao Zedong (1893-1976): principal Marxist theorist who the Communist revolution in China. He served as Chairman of the state for 10 years. (483)

Mikhail Gorbachev (1931): Premier of the Soviet Union who led the country towards democracy. (483)

Saddam Hussein (1937): political leader of Iraq, who challenged the Western world that prompted a United Nations action. (484)

Study Questions

What is decolonization? What were the consequences of this development? (482)

What were the major crises of the Cold War? What recent developments signaled the end of the Cold War? What major problems now face the United States and the world in general? (483-4)

Summary

Two-Dimensional Art: The dominant artistic trend immediately following World War II was abstract expressionism. Although a large number of variations exist, two qualities are consistent: freedom from the traditional use of brushwork and avoidance of representational subject matter. By the early 1960s, the movement had all but ceased to exist. Four artists associated with this style are discussed. The most heralded artist of this style was Jackson Pollock. His works, as evident in Fig. 15.4, exemplify action painting, in which paint was dripped, spilled or thrown on canvases placed on the floor. The works of Willem de Kooning (Fig. 15.5) reveal sophisticated textures and focal areas, and give the impression of spontaneity and free action. Another highly individual style is that of Mark Rothko, who followed a process of reduction and simplification. His works (Fig. 15.6) are deeply personal and reflect great sensitivity. The abstract expressionist tradition continues in the works of Helen Frankenthaler, whose "staining" technique consists of pouring paint across unprimed canvases (Fig. 15.7).

A number of other art movements arose after the War, many as a reaction to abstract expressionism. Six are discussed in the text. Pop art, which chose subjects and treatments from mass culture, sprang up in the 1950s. Lichtenstein, often depicting cartoon characters, is the most familiar figure in the movement (Fig. 15.8). Andy Warhol (Fig. 15.9) often focused on popular culture and contemporary consumerism in his ultra-representaitional art. Op art, as evident in the works of Vasarély (Fig. 15.10), is based on perceptual tricks that mislead the eye. Hard edge explores design for its own sake and employs flat color areas separated from each other by hard edges. Frank Stella often abandoned the rectangular shape of the canvas and used iridescent metal powder (Fig. 15.11). Photo-realism is a movement that uses photographic images as a basis. Conceptual art is an anti-art movement that insists that only the imagination is art (Fig. 15.12). The final trend is neo-expressionism, as illustrated by the works of Francesco Clemente. These works attempt to record desires and images "that the rest of us repress." Fig. 15.13 is repulsive and yet fascinates us with its vibrant colors and balanced form.

Sculpture: Since World War II, much sculpture resembles abstract expressionist painting, especially in the rejection of traditional materials. Still, a great variety of artists and techniques can be found. Primary Structures was a movement that sought extreme simplicity of shapes and a kinship with architecture. Unlike other sculpture, these works invite the viewer to experience the three-dimensional space by walking around or through the work. David Smith's *Cubi XIX* (Fig. 15.15) is based on simple rectangles, squares, and a cylinder that appear to be in perfect balance. *Black Wall* by Nevelson (Fig. 16.16), a relief-like wall unit painted black, provides an intense appeal to the imagination. Four examples of abstract sculpture (Figs. 15.17-115.20) are described in the text: Noguchi's *Kouros*, which contains an abstract relationship with archaic Greek sculpture; Hepworth's *Sphere with Internal Form*; a mobile by Calder; and Giacometti's tormented stick figure *Man Pointing*.

A variety of other approaches to sculpture are mentioned. Found sculpture presents objects from life as art, and junk culture assembles natural objects into a single artwork. Pop sculpture focuses on pop objects, such as seen in Oldenburg's *Dual Hamburgers* (Fig. 15.21). George Segal depicted scenes from everyday life with unpainted plaster images (Fig. 15.22). Using life-like figures to expose middle class tastelessness is Duane Hanson. Minimalism sought to reduce design complexity to a minimum by concentrating on impersonal geometric structures. Light art uses light as an element in sculpture. Chryssa's neon designs often assume simple shapes and serve as symbolic comments on modern life. Ephemeral art is art, like Christo's *Running Fence* (Fig. 15.26), that makes a statement then ceases to exist. Environmental art interacts with its surroundings, as seen in *Fardin d'Email* by Dubuffet (Fig. 15.24) and Robert Smithson's *Spiral Jetty* (Fig. 15.25). "Environments" which have been expanded into roomsize settings are called "installations." *Dragons* by Judy Pfaff (Fig. 15.27) has been likened to "exotic indoor landscapes," comparable to the action paintings of Jackson Pollock. Television has become a medium for artistic expression. Nam June Paik (15.28) is perhaps the most prominent figure in video art.

Literature: Literature since World War II has been beset by a bewildering variety of schools and approaches, including a "deconstruction" criticism movement that attempted to remove meaning from the literary work. Four writers are described in the text. Elie Wiesel, a European Jew who survived a concentrations camp, penned the moving autobiographical novel *Night*. American Joseph Heller, who also dealt with the impact of war in his novel *Catch* 22, employs black humor, satire and surrealism. Alice Walker battles for the rights of blacks and women in her novels, poetry and critical writings. R.K. Naryan, India's foremost novelist, writes in English for an international audience. His fictional works center on the middle-class life in southern India.

Theatre: Two principal movements appeared after World War II: Realism and Absurdism. Realism expanded its 19th-century definition to include fragmentary settings, symbolism, and other new theatrical effects. Leading playwrights include Tennessee Williams (*Glass Menagerie*) and Arthur Miller

(*Death of a Salesman*). This movement also encompasses a number of black playwrights, most notably Lorraine Hansberry, whose *A Raisin in the Sun* deals with a black family in Chicago. Absurdism was strongly tied to the philosophy of existentialism. Both focused on the disillusionment of the individual in an uncaring and often hostile world. Leading figures were the Italian Pirandello, who questions reality, the French existentialists Sartre and Camus, Samuel Beckett, author of *Waiting for Godot*, and Ionesco, who used nonsense syllables, meaningless repetition, and plots with no development.

The theatrical black liberation movement began in the 1960s and provided a vehicle for expressing the ideas of angry, militant blacks. Among these playwrights are LeRoi Jones and Charles Gordonne. New black theatre companies also emerged, such as the Negro Ensemble Company founded by Douglas Turner Ward. August Wilson, the founder of the Playwrights Center in Minneapolis, focused on the complexity of being an Afro-American.

The past 25 years have seen a great diversity in theatre. Revolutionary ideas included happenings, group gropes, and performances in garages and streets. The reaction against traditional commercial theatre spanned a movement called New Theatre that stressed creativity and non-traditional productions. Also important for bringing new plays to production has been the Actor's Theatre of Louisville, which is responsible for producing such works as *Gin Game* and *Agnes of God*.

Two major European directors are described in the text. The Polish director Jerzy Grotowski asked his actors to use every technique available to them to fuse movement and meaning. In his *Towards a Poor Theatre*, he advocates stripping all nonessentials in order for the performer to be left alone with the audience. The British director Peter Brook attacked traditional theatre and was leader of the Avant garde.

In the United States, a limited movement called the "New Theatre" sprang up in coffee-houses and off-Broadway theatres. The "Living Theatre," one of the most visible parts of New Theatre, attempted to break down the barrier between actors and audience. A similar goal was achieved by the Performance Group in New York. Among other recent trends, we find an appeal to the visual rather than formal scripts, an emphasis on improvisations, and stunning advances in the field of design, which now project the essence of the play, not just its environment.

Film:: In the 1940s, a number of films stunned the film world with their artistic social criticism, including John Ford's *Grapes of Wrath* and Orson Welles' *Citizen Kane*. After the war, MacCarthyism had a tremendous impact on the industry, as hundreds of careers were destroyed. Some of the greatest films at this time were made on the international scene by the hands of directors such as Italy's Fellini (*La Dolce Vita*), Japan's Kurosawa (*Seven Samurai*), and Sweden's Bergman (*Wild Strawberries*). In recent years many have come to regard film as an art form, and a number of films, such as *Star Wars*, have achieved both popular and artistic success.

Music: A number of diverse compositional styles emerged after World War II. Complicated serial techniques as explored by Webern inspired a decade of complex works by composers such as Milton Babbitt and Pierre Boulez. By contrast, aleatory music allowed elements of the music composition to be determined by random chance. John Cage was the leading figure in this movement, but it also attracted Boulez and Stockhausen. Of special significance is the growth of electronic music. Beginning with the simple reproduction of sounds via a tape machine (a technique called musique concrète), electronic music grew to a point where there were newly generated sounds and a synthesizer capable of creating and imitating a wide variety of sounds. Experiments in these areas continued through the 1960s and 70s in works by Berio, Elliot Carter, and Steve Reich. One of the most colorful composers of this generation is the Polish Krzysztof Penderecki, who has been able to generate exciting new sounds out of traditional instruments.

Dance: After World War II, Martha Graham's troupe produced a radical and controversial choreographer, Merce Cunningham. He incorporated elements of aleatory or chance, much like the composer with whom he was associated, John Cage. He also employed everyday activities along with dance movements. With these qualities, the same dance could be entirely different each time it was performed. Other recent figures in modern dance include Paul Taylor, Alwin Nikolai, and Alvin Ailey. An important new dance form, which has some roots in modern dance, but is mostly drawn from black culture, is jazz dance.

Architecture: After the World War II, architecture can be broadly divided into modernism and post-modernism. Modernism has been dominated by the international style, which produced a plethora of rectangular skyscrapers with sides of glass. A leading figure in this movement was Mies van der Rohe, whose beliefs in the simple straight line and in the function of a building were very influential. Others, as evident in Figs. 15.37-15.40 have reacted against straight lines and designed buildings that often suggest their function. Post-modern architecture takes different themes from the past without directly copying them, as can be seen in the works of Bofill and Graves (Figs. 15.41-15.44). Particularly striking is the Pompidou Center in Paris, which externalizes its network of ducts, pipes, and elevators.

Important Terms

Abstract expressionism: the most dominant trend in art during the first fifteen years after World War II. A great variety of artists and techniques are blanketed by this term, but generally it involves freedom from the traditional use of brushwork, and it avoids representational subject matter. (485-6)

Action painting: a technique associated with abstract expressionism in which paint is applied by dripping, splattering, or other action-oriented activities. (485)

Pop art: a movement in painting that came about in the 1950s, in which the subjects and treatments come from mass culture and commercial design. (487-8)

Op art: a movement in painting that emerged from the 1950s, in which perceptual tricks and misleading images were utilized. (488-9)

Hard edge: a movement in art that explored design for its own sake. (489)

Photo-realism: an art movement that created photo-realist images. (490)

Conceptual art: an art movement that insists that only imagination, not the artwork, is art. (490)

Neo-expressionism: a recent and controversial movement in art that records desires and images that "the rest of us suppress." (490)

Primary Structures: a movement in sculpture that pursued the goals of extreme simplicity of shapes and a kinship with architecture. (492)

Mobiles: a type of sculpture in which parts move, generally in response to air currents. (493)

Found sculpture: objects taken from life and presented as art. (494)

Junk culture: sculpture created by assembling natural objects. (494)

Minimalism: a style in painting and sculpture that reduced design complexity and focused on impersonal geometric structures. (495)

Light Art: art that encorporates light as an element. (495)

Ephemeral art: art or sculpture that is designed to be transitory. (497)

Environmental art: works conceived as an integral part of their natural surroundings. (497)

Installations: Environments that have been expanded into room-size settings. (497-8)

Video art: art that employs television as an idiom. (498)

Deconstruction: an approach to literary criticism that attempted to remove meaning from the work. (499)

Absurdism: movement in theatre which portrayed man's meaningless existence in a chaotic universe. It is based on existentialism. (499)

Black liberation movement: theatrical movement beginning in 1960s that promoted black consciousness. (500)

New Theatre: a limited theatrical movement that stressed creativity and non-traditional productions. (501-2)

Living Theatre: founded by Judith Malina and Julian Beck, it freely mixed actors and audience. (502)

The Performance Group: New York company that worked on removing all barriers between audience and actor. (502)

McCarthyism: the publication of accusations of disloyalty or subversion with insufficient regard to evidence. It destroyed hundreds of careers in the movie industry. (504)

Aleatory music: musical compositions in which a number of parameters of the work are left to the whims of the performer or of the environment. It is similar in effect to the mobile. Also called indeterminacy. (505)

Synthesizer: a machine with a simple keyboard that can duplicate sounds of other instruments. (506)

Musique concrète: the use of recorded acoustically produced sounds in musical compositions. (506)

Jazz dance: no set of generalities can yet be derived for this, but it draws its roots from modern ballet and the black musical heritage. (508)

International style: style of architecture that features rectangular high rises made of glass. (493-4)

Post-modern style: architectural style that puts new manifestations on past styles. (496-8)

Important Names

Jackson Pollock (1912-56): the most heralded artist of abstract expressionism known for his use of action painting. One of his best known works is *Number 1*. (485)

Willem de Kooning (b.1904): Dutch-born American painter who is associated with abstract expressionism. (485-6)

Mark Rothko (1903-70): Russian-born American painter who is associated with abstract expressionism. (486)

Helen Frankenthaler (b.1928): the daughter of a New York Supreme Court Justice, she is associated with abstract expressionism. (486)

Roy Lichtenstein (b.1923): the most familiar figure in pop art. (487)

Andy Warhol (1928-87): leading figure in pop art (488).

Victor Vasarély (b.1908): painter associated with op art. (488-9)

Frank Stella (b.1936): American artist who often abandoned the rectangular format of the canvas. He is associated with hard edge. (489)

Joseph Kosuth (b.1945): artist whose *One and Three Chairs* exemplifies conceptualism. (490)

Francesco Clemente (b.1952): Italian painter of neo-expressionist art. (490)

Anselm Kiefer (b. 1945): German artist in the neo-exrpessionist movement. (490)

David Smith (b.1906): sculptor who created a series of works based on cubes. (492)

Louise Nevelson (1900-88): American sculptor who is associated with the Primary Structures movement. (492)

Isamu Noguchi (b.1904): Japanese-American sculptor who experimented with abstract sculptural design. (493)

Barbara Hepworth (1903-75): sculptor in the abstract movement. (493)

Alexander Calder (1898-1976): sculptor known for his mobiles. (493)

Alberto Giacometti (1901-66): Swiss-born sculptor, once a surrealist, produced a number of works portraying people as stick figures, as in *Man Pointing*. (493)

Claes Oldenburg (b.1929): sculptor of pop objects. (494)

George Segal (b.1924): sculptor known for his unpainted life-like figures. (494)

Duane Hanson (b.1925): sculptor whose photo-realistic depictions of human figures allows him to expose middle-class tastelessness. (494-5)

Chryssa (b. 1933): a leading artist in the Light art movement. (495)

Christo (b.1935): Bulgarian sculptor who is known for his ephemeral artworks. (497)

Jean Dubuffet (b.1901): sculptor of environmental art. (497)

Robert Smithson (1928-73): created *Spiral Jetty* in Utah, an example of environmental art. (465-6)

Judy Pfaff (b. 1946): a leading figure in the Installation movement. (497-8)

Nam June Paik (b. 1932): a leading figure in video art. (498)

Elie Wiesel (b. 1928): European Jewish author who wrote about his experiences in a concentration camp in the novel *Night*. (466)

Joseph Heller (b. 1923): attacks war through black humor, satire, and surrealism. Major work is *Catch 22*. (499)

Alice Walker (b. 1944): American writer of novels, poems, and critical writings who fought for black and women rights. (499)

R.K. Narayan (b. 1906): Indian writer who centered his fiction around middle-class life in southern India. (499)

Tennessee Williams (1912-83): American realist playwright. Major works include *Glass Menagerie*. (499)

Arthur Miller (b.1915): American playwright and novelist. Major works include *Death of a Salesman*. (499)

Samual Becket (b. 1906): Irish playwright. His *Waiting for Godot* is one of the most popular examples of absurdism. (499)

Lorraine Hansberry (1930-65): Black playwright whose *Raisin in the Sun* dealt with black life in Chicago. (500)

August Wilson (b. 1945): black founder of the Playwrights Center in Minneapolis. His plays deal with the complexities of being an Afro-American. (500)

Jerzy Grotowski (b. 1933): Polish director who advocated stripping away all nonessentials in order for the performer to be left alone with the audience. (501)

Peter Brook (b. 1925): British director who is a leading figure in the avant garde. (501)

Robert Wilson (b. 1941): leading figure in experimental theatre who placed visual appeal above the written script. (501)

Milton Babbitt (b.1916): American composer who explored the complexities of serialism and electronic music. (505)

Pierre Boulez (b.1925): French composer who explored the complexities of serialism, aleatory music, and electronic music. (505)

John Cage (b.1912): American composer and a leading force in aleatory music. Also wrote electronic works. (505, 506)

Miles Davis (b.1926): black American jazz trumpeter who established a number of important trends. (483, 484)

Karl Stockhausen (b.1928): German composer of aleatory and electronic music. (506)

Elliot Carter (b.1908): American composer who developed a unique and highly organized technique of composition. (506)

Luciano Berio (b. 1925): the leading Italian composer in the postwar period. (506)

Krzysztof Penderecki (b.1933): Polish composer known for his ability to produce striking new sounds. (507)

Merce Cunningham (b.1919): American dancer who incorporated aleatory elements into to his choreography. (507)

Paul Taylor (b.1930): American dancer known for his highly ebullient and unrestrained dances. (507)

Alwin Nikolais (b.1912): American dancer who is known for his mixed-media extravaganzas. (508)

Alvin Ailey (1931-1989): American dancer whose troupe is known for its energetic free movements. (508)

Mies van der Rohe (1886-1969): German-born American architect whose works epitomize the International style. (509-10)

Pier Luigi Nervi (1891-1979): Italian architect. Works include Small Sports Palace. (511)

R. Buckminster Fuller (1895-1983): American architect. Major works include Climatron. (511)

Ricardo Bofill (b.1939): Spanish post-modern architect. (512)

Michael Graves (b.1934): American post-modern architect. (512)

Study Questions

Describe abstract expressionism and the four artists discussed in this section. (485-6)

What are the other artistic styles after World War II detailed in the text. Mention major figures and works. (487-91)

What are the major styles of contemporary sculpture described in your text? Mention important figures and works. (492-98)

Who are the leading figures of realism? (499)

What is absurdism? What philosophical movement is it tied to? Who are the leading figures? works? (499)

How has theatre provided a forum for black issues? (500)

Describe developments within the theatre during the past 25 years. (500-1)

Name the principal directors and theatre companies since World War II. What has been their goals? (501-2)

Name the principal trends in music after the second world war. Who are the leading composers? What role does electronics play? (505-7)

What are the principal developments in American dance after the War? (507-8)

Describe the international style. Who is the leading architect associated with it? What are some of the reactions? (508-11)

What is post-modernism? Cite examples in your text. (512)

PRACTICE TEST

1. What technique of painting is associated with Jackson Pollock?
   a. action painting b. pointillism c. hard edge d. scraping

2. Of the following, who is not an abstract expressionist?
   a. Pollock b. Frankenthaler c. de Kooning d. Vasarély

3. Who is known for his Pop art?
   a. Rothko b. Lichtenstein c. Stella d. Clemente

4. Matching

   Abstract expressionism   a. based on perceptual tricks

   Pop art   b. only imagination is art, not an artwork

   Op art   c. freedom from traditional brush-strokes

   Hard edge   d. records repressed desires and images

   Neo-expressionism   e. takes subjects from pop culture

   Conceptual art   f. explores design for its own sake
   ---

5. What characterizes Primary Structures?
   a. simple shapes   c. kinship with architecture
   b. space-time relationship   d. all of these

6. What does not characterizes the works of David Smith?
   a. precarious balance   c. use of geometric shapes
   b. miniature size   d. shimmering surface quality

7. Who is not associated with abstract sculpture?
   a. Noguchi b. Segal c. Hepworth d. Calder

8. Who worked with mobiles? a. Noguchi b. Segal c. Hepworth d. Calder

9. Who is not associated with Pop sculpture?
   a. Giacometti b. Oldenburg c. Segal d. Hanson

10. What artistic style makes a statement and then ceases to exist?
  a. minimalism b. ephemeral art c. environmental art d. junk

11. Who is not associated with absurdism?
  a. Pirandello b. Miller c. Sartre d. Beckett

12. What play was not presented by Actor's Theatre of Louisville?
  a. *Gin Game*   c. *Bald Soprano*
  b. *Crimes of the Heart*   d. *Agnes of God*

13. Who is the leading figure of aleatory music?
  a. Ives b. Copland c. Babbitt d. Cage

14. Matching
   Penderecki   a. American composer of complex serial music

   Boulez   b. Jazz trumpeter who established a number of trends
   ---
   Miles Davis   c. Polish composer of original sounds

   Carter   d. French composer of serial, aleatory and electronic music
   ---
   Babbitt   e. American composer of an individual highly organized
   ---   technique

15. Of the following, who is noted for his mixed-media extravaganzas?
  a. Paul Taylor   c. Alwin Nikolais
  b. Alvin Ailey   d. José Limon

16. What does not characterize the works of Merce Cunningham?
  a. use of aleatory elements
  b. use of everyday activity
  c. focus is on center stage
  d. no beat-for-beat relationship between dance and music

17. What does not characterize the international style?
  a. rectangular shape   c. glass sides
  b. skyrise buildings   d. limited influence

18. Mies van der Rohe is associated with
  a. international style b. prairie style c. post-modernism d. all of these

19. The black liberation theatre movement sought to disassociated itself from the angry militant blacks. a. true   b. false

20. Matching
Jerzy Grotowski   a. director who favoured visual appeal over script
-----
Peter Brook   b. founder of Polish Laboratory Theatre

Robert Wilson   c. co-founder of Living Theatre

Richard Schechner d. British director who attacked traditional drama
-----
Judith Malina   e. founder of the Performance Group

ANSWERS

1. a   2. d   3. b   4. ceafdb   5. d   6. b   7. b   8. d   9. a   10. b   11. b   12. c   13. d   14. cdbea   15. c   16. c   17. d   18. a   19. b   20. bdaec